SharePoint® 2010 Development®

FOR

DUMMIES®

SharePoint® 2010 Development®

FOR

DUMMIES®

by Ken Withee

WILEY

Wiley Publishing, Inc.

SharePoint® 2010 Development For Dummies®

Published by
Wiley Publishing, Inc.
111 River Street
Hoboken, NJ 07030-5774
www.wiley.com

WILEY

About the Author

Ken Withee is President of Portal Integrators LLC (www.portalintegrators. com), a professional services firm specializing in Microsoft SharePoint, SharePoint Online, and Microsoft Office 365. He lives with his wife Rosemarie in Seattle, Washington. He is author of *Microsoft Business Intelligence For Dummies* and coauthor of *Professional Microsoft SQL Server 2008 Reporting Services* (WROX).

Ken earned a Master of Science degree in Computer Science studying under Dr. Edward Lank at San Francisco State University.

Ken has more than 12 years of professional computer and management experience working with a vast range of technologies. He is a Microsoft Certified Technology Specialist and is certified in SharePoint, SQL Server, and .NET.

Dedication

I dedicate this book to my wife and best friend, Rosemarie Withee, who encouraged me daily throughout this time-intensive process. I owe her another year's worth of late nights and weekends and hope to make it up to her during our long future together. I love you!

Author's Acknowledgments

I would like to acknowledge my grandma Tiny Withee who turns 98 this year and is still going strong. I would also like to acknowledge my wife Rosemarie Withee, mother Maggie Blair, father Ken Withee, sister Kate Henneinke, and parents-in-law Alfonso and Lourdes Supetran and family.

Thanks to Katie Feltman, Rebecca Huehls, Barry Childs-Helton, Mike Talley, and the rest of the *For Dummies* team for providing more support than I ever thought possible. It is truly amazing how much work goes into a single book.

Here is another book for you. Notha

love Dad
Xmas 2013

Publisher's Acknowledgments

We're proud of this book; please send us your comments at http://dummies.custhelp.com. For other comments, please contact our Customer Care Department within the U.S. at 877-762-2974, outside the U.S. at 317-572-3993, or fax 317-572-4002.

Some of the people who helped bring this book to market include the following:

Acquisitions, Editorial, and Media Development

Project Editor: Rebecca Huehls

Senior Acquisitions Editor: Katie Feltman

Senior Copy Editor: Barry Childs-Helton

Technical Editor: Mike Talley

Editorial Manager: Leah P. Cameron

Media Development Assistant Project Manager: Jenny Swisher

Editorial Assistant: Amanda Graham

Sr. Editorial Assistant: Cherie Case

Cartoons: Rich Tennant (www.the5thwave.com)

Composition Services

Project Coordinator: Katherine Crocker

Layout and Graphics: Samantha K. Cherolis

Proofreaders: Jessica Kramer, The Well-Chosen Word

Indexer: Broccoli Information Mgt.

Publishing and Editorial for Technology Dummies

    Richard Swadley, Vice President and Executive Group Publisher

    Andy Cummings, Vice President and Publisher

    Mary Bednarek, Executive Acquisitions Director

    Mary C. Corder, Editorial Director

Publishing for Consumer Dummies

    Diane Graves Steele, Vice President and Publisher

Composition Services

    Debbie Stailey, Director of Composition Services

Contents at a Glance

Table of Contents

Introduction

Any fool can make things bigger and more complex. It takes a touch of genius – and a lot of courage – to move in the opposite direction.

— Albert Einstein

*I*n the last few years SharePoint has taken the world by storm. In fact, the product is one of the fastest growing products in the history of Microsoft. Companies of all sizes are rapidly implementing SharePoint and moving it to the center of their organization. The interesting thing about SharePoint, however, is that if you ask ten different people what it is, they will probably give you ten different answers. The reason is because SharePoint has become a platform with many different capabilities. Sure, it has document management — but it also includes features that span everything from business intelligence to electronic form management. With so much functionality, used in so many different ways, no wonder people think of so many different things when they think of SharePoint.

Having been a consultant for more than a decade, I can attest to the fact that every organization is different. The differences in organizations span everything from culture nuances to product-development cycles and everything in between. As a result, every organization implements and uses SharePoint in a way that makes sense within its own walls. Implementing SharePoint would be much easier if every organization could be shoehorned into the same little box. But every organization different — so too is the way every organization adopts SharePoint. To make matters worse SharePoint is dynamic. The needs of an organization are constantly shifting; the way SharePoint is used shifts as well. At first, you might want to use SharePoint as a portal to the company intranet (or, for that matter, to the Internet) and to manage your electronic content. As the portal is adopted, however, you might decide that you need to adopt a business-intelligence strategy. After you put your BI strategy is in place, integrating your backend Enterprise Resource Planning (ERP) system with SharePoint might become a priority as well.

If working with SharePoint were as simple as installing the product and watching it solve problems, then consultants like me would be out of a job. SharePoint is an extensive platform and requires development at nearly every junction. The good news is that SharePoint redefines the term "developer." A SharePoint developer is no longer only the computer science guru who spends time sorting through bits and bytes, looking at line after line of computer code in hopes of enlightenment (or "optimizing a complex algorithm," if you will). The SharePoint platform is designed with the end user in mind — and provides tools that anyone can use to develop a SharePoint solution.

About This Book

This book is about understanding how to develop solutions on the SharePoint platform, and have the result come out rich with features and functionality. Using all that SharePoint has to offer is vital, Grasshopper, if you would bend the platform to your particular needs. By no means, however, do you need a degree in computer science (or even an understanding of computer code) to develop for SharePoint. Everyday users, rejoice: If you've worked with Microsoft Office or Excel, then you can develop a SharePoint solution.

The tools vary but they all have one thing in common: You use them to extend SharePoint capabilities in ways that give you a solution that fits your needs. This book looks at the tools that are required — and how to use them.

How to Use This Book

Okay, this book won't replace your favorite beach reading (unless, of course, the SharePoint bug bites really hard). No need to read the whole book through from front to back — although, if you do, you'll emerge with a holistic knowledge of SharePoint development. If you need to come up to speed on a particular tool (like, *yesterday*), then you can jump to that chapter prior to reading every chapter that precedes it. Get what you need first.

That said, this book does assume at least minimal SharePoint knowledge. If you are brand new to SharePoint, I'd recommend *SharePoint 2010 For Dummies* by Vanessa L. Williams as a quick way to get up to speed on basic SharePoint features and concepts.

How This Book Is Organized

This book is divvied up into five parts, beginning with an introduction to the different versions of SharePoint — and what kind of impact the version you have has on your development work. Other parts introduce you to the basics of SharePoint development, as well as best practices for using the primary development tools built in to SharePoint 2010. Read on for details.

Part I: Understanding the SharePoint Development Platform

This part gives a high-level overview of what SharePoint is all about — and the main features and components you can use to add value for business users. Chapter 1 provides a brief introduction to SharePoint. Chapter 2 discusses SharePoint Online, Microsoft's hosted-solution offering that hangs out in the Internet "cloud". Chapter 3 then walks you through an overview of SharePoint development and previews the topics covered throughout the book.

Part II: Developing with Your Web Browser and Microsoft Office

It's amazing how much SharePoint development you can do without ever leaving your Web browser. SharePoint is a Web application — meant to be used with a Web browser such as Internet Explorer or Firefox. So the chapters in this part show you how that works: Chapter 4 discusses using your browser to develop SharePoint solutions. Chapter 5 discusses Excel in SharePoint, in its superpowered guise as Excel Services. Chapter 6 walks you through forms development with InfoPath Form Services. Finally, Chapter 7 discusses developing solutions that use Microsoft Word and Visio.

Part III: Exploring Standalone SharePoint Development Tools

Part III of the book discusses standalone tools that you use to develop SharePoint solutions. Chapter 8 discusses using SharePoint Designer to develop everything from sites and pages to content types and workflows. Chapter 9 covers Report Builder, which you can use to create reports that take advantage of SQL Server Reporting Services (SSRS). Finally, PerformancePoint development is the order of the day in Chapter 10, where you see how to use Dashboard Designer to build dashboards and other content friendly to business intelligence.

Part IV: Unleashing the Programmer Within

This part dives into programming code by exploring Visual Studio as it relates to SharePoint (Chapter 11) and the SharePoint object model (Chapter 12). Chapter 13 walks you through developing Web Parts — a fundamental idea behind SharePoint. Finally, Chapter 14 explores developing PowerShell scripts for SharePoint, grappling with code fearlessly at the command line.

Part V: The Part of Tens

The Part of Tens provides a quick reference to three topics to keep in mind as you start developing SharePoint solutions. Chapter 15 provides a top-ten list of SharePoint development tools. Chapter 16 lists ten places to learn more about SharePoint development. And Chapter 17 walks you through some of the best ways to reduce your business costs by using a solution that you (the mighty SharePoint user) develop.

Icons Used In This Book

The familiar *For Dummies* icons offer visual clues about the material contained within this book. Look for the following icons throughout the chapters:

Whenever you see a Tip icon, take note. I use it whenever I want you to pay particular attention to a point gleaned from my years of developing SharePoint solutions; the idea here is to shed some focused light on your SharePoint development efforts.

Whenever you see a Remember icon, get out your notebook and (ahem) take note — because chances are good that you'll see these topics crop up again in your development efforts.

Okay, a consulting career has its roadblocks, no less than any other. It often takes hours to figure something out the first time — and then (fortunately) only minutes the next time you encounter the same problem. Often the root cause of your problem is a bug or some quirky behavior. I have tried to ferret out those little pitfalls so they won't trip you up. Take note and beware.

When a particular development task or technique crosses paths with some heavy-duty technical knowledge (okay, some do), I call it out using the Technical Stuff icon. But relax. You don't have to slave over every technical detail. The information is here if you decide you want to dig farther.

Part I

Understanding the SharePoint Development Platform

The 5th Wave   By Rich Tennant

"Just how accurately should my Web site reflect my place of business?"

In this part . . .

In this part you get a bird's-eye-view introduction to SharePoint as a development platform — that is, a look at what SharePoint is and how it works as a fundamental part of developing business solutions (custom-tailored deployments of SharePoint capabilities). Traditionally, SharePoint is implemented on-site in an organization's data center — but as software moves to "the cloud' (that is, becomes one of many services delivered over the Web), new opportunities open up. Here you explore how Microsoft has turned SharePoint into a collection of services that live in the cloud. Not to worry; shifting some of the management and infrastructure-maintenance headaches to Microsoft can free you to focus your efforts on what matters most — your business. The part wraps up with a high-level overview of SharePoint development to show how some of the tools you'll be using use fit together in the bigger picture.

Chapter 1

Understanding the SharePoint Hype

I had one simple idea about telling friends about arts and technology events. People in the community suggested everything else to us, and that's our theme. We're really run by the people who use the site. We just run the infrastructure, and help out with problems.

— Craig Newmark (founder, Craigslist.org)

*E*ven though SharePoint implementations are way more common now than they used to be, I'm constantly amazed at how many nontechnical folks have heard about or used SharePoint. As a consultant and author, I'm constantly meeting new people from different walks of life. When the conversation gets around to what it is we do for a living — and I mention that I am a SharePoint consultant — the typical response is usually along the lines of, "Oh SharePoint! We use that at my work." Or "Oh yes, I use SharePoint at work. Can you help me with this thing it's been doing?" Or "I have heard of SharePoint. A friend of mine uses it." On the one hand, it's reassuring to know that SharePoint is so pervasive that even people who are as far as possible from a techie mindset still use it in some fashion. On the other hand, I'm always amazed about what people think SharePoint *is.* I've heard it described as a Web site, a way to send documents, and almost everything else high-tech (except maybe a death ray).

In this chapter, I give a brief history of SharePoint and explain exactly what all the hype is about. Because SharePoint is as much a development platform as it is a software product with many different pieces, I stitch those pieces together for you so you're armed with a big-picture view of what to expect as you begin developing SharePoint solutions. Finally, I introduce SharePoint development to you and fill you in on a secret that SharePoint developers would rather not discuss: You don't have to be a programmer to develop solutions on the SharePoint platform. If you can use a Web browser, then you can develop a SharePoint solution. If you're ready to add "SharePoint Developer" to your résumé, all you have to do to get started is read on.

Everyone Can Be a SharePoint Developer

When most people think of a "developer," they think of a computer-science geek sitting in a basement with a can of Mountain Dew banging out complex computer code. In the past, this was often not far wrong; getting a computer to do something specific to solve your problem required writing a computer application using special programming languages that would then be compiled down into the 1s and 0s that a computer could understand. These languages were, and still are, complex and mysterious and require an extraordinary amount of dedication and knowledge.

If you're a hard-core programmer, no sweat — your skills will always be useful. Until computers take on thoughts of their own, we need programmers just as we need surgeons for our (very human) bodies. The good news, however, is that software applications are evolving in a very real and exciting way. Tools are becoming available that give users and analysts outside the IT department more effective ways to command their computers to create solutions to real-world business problems. That's where SharePoint comes in.

SharePoint 2010 provides a number of tools and features designed to shift more of the development power away from programmers and into the hands of the people who understand their particular business problems best. By and large, these are businesspeople who could care less about technology and are just trying to do their jobs. The SharePoint development tools allow users to create no-code solutions in a self-serve manner; no need to interact with IT. This takes some of the time burden off of the IT department so it can focus on (say) creating stable, redundant, always-available, and secure computing environments. Everybody wins — at least that's the idea.

As a technology consultant, I'm constantly filling the role of intermediary between the business users and the technology people. I'm very excited to see this quiet change in development responsibilities. Because the SharePoint 2010 platform and tools for developing business solutions are designed with the end users in mind, a new level of business efficiency and productivity becomes available.

Tracing the Origins of SharePoint

Computers created an information revolution that fully blossomed as they started to get connected together into large networks. The biggest network of all, the Internet — and the fact that computers became cheap enough to sit on nearly every desk at home and work — created a recipe for sharing information. To fulfill this need, technology such as e-mail and the World Wide Web cropped up in the 1990s. Soon Web sites flourished, nearly everyone had an e-mail address, and information flowed freely. Throughout the 2000s organizations rapidly adopted corporate e-mail systems in order to facilitate communication.

In addition to e-mail, organizations also adopted large enterprise computer systems that handled everything from inventory to human resources. These systems are known as Enterprise Resource Planning (ERP) — with some of the biggest players being SAP, Oracle, Microsoft, and Sage. As companies adopted ERP systems in the '90s, others followed suit to stay competitive. As we head into the 2010s, the next wave of efficiency and productivity for knowledge-based workers will come from communication, collaboration, and centralized information sharing.

As SharePoint has come of age, it's put more tentacles into the Microsoft Office applications — resulting in a centralized, integrated portal platform that's controllable from familiar applications — so the race to implement SharePoint continues. Various companies offer software products for creating and using a company portal space — but so far the clear winner is SharePoint.

So What Exactly Is SharePoint, Anyway?

Microsoft highlights these defining characteristics of SharePoint:

- ✔ SharePoint Server is a suite of integrated server capabilities. In essence, if you install SharePoint on your server, you give it a new range of information-wrangling powers that work together.

- ✔ SharePoint manages content (your business information) and provides enterprise-wide search capabilities. Wherever the needed information is in your organization, SharePoint can find it, make it usable, and keep it secure.

- ✔ SharePoint, when used to full advantage, accelerates business processes that require collaboration by making communication easier (and information easier to share) across departmental boundaries.

✔ SharePoint can help improve the administration of your company server, extend existing software applications with server-based capabilities, and help a wide range of software and hardware play well (and work well) together.

These points are great and tell you what SharePoint can do, but they don't really tell you what it is. If you're like me, you're looking for an explanation that has some roots. Something concrete. Is SharePoint a software program or a standalone supercomputer? Is SharePoint something that runs on my local computer like Microsoft Office or does it live somewhere in a data center?

To get a handle on SharePoint, start from the bottom and work up through its components — which you can see in Figure 1-1. The following sections explain each part of Figure 1-1 in more detail.

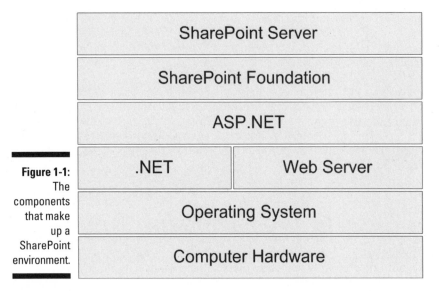

Figure 1-1:
The components that make up a SharePoint environment.

Starting with the roots — computer hardware

Every computer system starts with physical components — central processing unit (CPU), memory, a hard drive, power supply, and motherboard. Typically a computer comes into your workplace in one of two ways: You can buy all the individual pieces and put them together yourself or you can purchase an already-assembled computer from a vendor that specializes in building them, such as HP, Dell, or IBM. What this means is that a range of components from various makers and vendors have to work together without compatibility hassles. In order for all these hardware components to work together, you need a specialized piece of software designed to make everything hum. This software — the operating system (OS) — is what Microsoft began its corporate life creating.

A new trend that you may have heard about involves virtual computers. A *virtual computer* (also called a *guest computer*) is essentially a self-contained operating system running within a host computer; it behaves just like a separate computer — except it interacts only with its host computer. The host computer handles all interactions with actual system hardware. You can have multiple guest computers — all performing different server functions — running on the same host computer; that, in essence, is *virtualization*. Running an entire operating system (such as Windows 7 or Windows Server) as an application within the host computer's operating system allows you to separate the various server duties to different guest computers without having to run separate physical hardware.

As you can imagine, the host computer becomes crucially important. You don't want the host to crash and take its guests with it, so virtualization companies such as VMware have created very clever software to manage host and guest computers. Because the guest computers are really just applications, they can be moved quickly between host computers (the physical computers) without even needing to be shut down. And nobody has to go get the forklift to move all those "computers."

The reason it's critical to understand how the hardware and operating system work is that SharePoint only runs on Microsoft operating systems. Although you can have a Microsoft operating system installed on a multitude of different hardware types — HP or Dell, for instance — SharePoint can only be installed on a computer running the Microsoft operating system. You might already have a server running a different OS (such as UNIX or Linux), but unfortunately you can't install SharePoint on it. There is one limited workaround: If your server computers are running virtualization software such as VMware, then the guest computers can be installed as virtual Windows machines — even though the host system is running (say) Linux. In this scenario, you're back in business and can run SharePoint on the virtualized Windows operating system. If all this is giving you a headache, — don't worry about it. Call in your trusty IT team; it's their bailiwick, and you pay them the big bucks to worry about it.

Software that talks to the hardware — the operating system

The software that makes all the hardware components actually do something — the *operating system* (OS) — usually comes in two major versions — one for end users (client) and one for the organization's heavy computing requirements (server). In the Microsoft world, both OSs are called *Windows.* Windows 7 is the latest client OS; Windows Server 2008 R2 is the latest server OS. Note that the R2 means Release 2. The previous version of the Windows Server OS was called Windows Server 2008, without the R2. (Okay, I could make a cheap *Star Wars* joke here, but I won't.)

If you're going to run server software such as SQL Server and SharePoint, you need to have the appropriate version of Windows Server OS installed on your server computer(s). Normally end users throughout the organization have the client OS running on their desktop or laptop computers. All those personal computers have to connect to the server computers (running somewhere in a data center) in order to interact with the server software.

Software frameworks and servers — .NET and IIS

The .NET software framework runs on the Windows OS (both client and server versions) and keeps the various hardware components on speaking terms with each other. (I discuss the .NET framework — and its role in maintaining compatibility — in more detail in Chapter 11.)

Also running on the Windows Server OS is the Microsoft Web server called *Internet Information Services* (IIS).

In nearly any discussion of corporate networking, you hear the term *server* used to describe both hardware (the server computer) and software (the server operating system that tells the hardware what to do). True, a computer running a server operating system *is* a server, but so is the operating system itself (a computer can't function as a server without a server OS) — *and* (are you ready for this?) so is the software designed to work with a server OS. They're all called "server." (It's like saying, "This is my sister Kate, this is my *other* sister Kate, and this is *her* sister Kate." Only worse.) But all sanity is not lost; get a grip and hang on for this example:

- ✔ Windows Server 2008 R2 is an operating system designed to run specialized software optimally — on a server computer.

- ✔ The networked computer on which you install the Windows Server OS is your server computer. Usually server computers are high-capacity and high-performance machines designed and built for that job.

- ✔ Server software applications act like short-order cooks and waiters: They serve up information to client computers in the form of Web pages, FTP sites, or e-mail communications. SQL Server and SharePoint Server are such applications.

Put those three aspects together, and you have a functioning server; just be careful which aspect of it you're talking about. And here's where the function of a server can help dispel the confusion of the term: What a server *does* is provide a consistent place where the network's users can access data. Because data can play many roles, servers can specialize accordingly — as (say) a database server, file server, or content-management server.

The *.NET Framework* is a bundle of computer languages, programs, and standards designed to make software programmers more efficient — so long as they're programming for Microsoft operating systems. The Microsoft Web server is called Internet Information Services (IIS) and it is responsible for serving up Web pages. Since SharePoint is all about Web pages IIS is a critical component. The portion of the .NET framework that is specifically designed to work with IIS and thus the tools Microsoft used to develop SharePoint is called ASP.NET. For more about ASP.NET read on.

The .NET framework has nothing to do with the `.net` that you often find at the end of a Web address such as `www.iis.net`. They are completely separate things that have nothing to do with each other.

A computer language for the Web — ASP.NET

ASP.NET is a specialized extension of the .NET software Framework for building Web applications (including custom Web pages) to run on — and be served up by — the IIS Web server (Microsoft's Web server). Typically you find ASP.NET used to build custom Web pages, often in programming languages such as C#.NET or VB.NET. (For more information about .NET and programming languages, check out Chapter 11.)

The ASP stands for Active Server Pages; the .NET declares it as part of the .NET Framework. So, even though ASP.NET sounds like a Web address, it isn't — although (stay with me, now) you *can* go to a Web address that incorporates the name — www.asp.net — for more information about ASP.NET the Microsoft product. ASP.NET itself is a framework for building Web applications on the Microsoft platform using the IIS Web server; the Web address offers information about the ASP.NET framework. (As if life isn't confusing enough, right?)

The first step into the SharePoint world — SharePoint Foundation

ASP.NET commands are what run SharePoint Foundation, previously known as Windows SharePoint Services (WSS), a basic set of software features that demonstrate some vital SharePoint capabilities. SharePoint Foundation is essentially a "lite," or limited, version of SharePoint: It provides some collaboration and communications features (such as lists and document libraries) that developers can build into custom applications and Web sites. Because SharePoint Foundation is built on the ASP.NET framework (which is, keep in mind, an extension of .NET), it provides endless opportunities for customizing applications. SharePoint Foundation, however, isn't quite powerful enough to pinch-hit for industrial-strength SharePoint if an organization is large and complex. (But then, that's what the Enterprise edition of SharePoint is for, as detailed in the next section.)

A finished product — SharePoint Server

Microsoft used SharePoint Foundation as a solid footing on which to build SharePoint Server. The goal was to create a software product that could solve business problems with its built-in features, cutting down on the time-intensive (and expensive) customization of software.

As a full-featured version of SharePoint, SharePoint Server is designed as a large-scale, enterprise-level portal platform: Your organization can use it for content management, communication, collaboration, information portals, doing enterprise-wide searches for specific information, and the documentation of business processes (even including the design of forms).

Untangling the versions and editions of SharePoint

Like other software, SharePoint has a history of versions and editions. A *version* is a dated (or numbered) release of a software product that usually incorporates significant updates. For example, the previous version of SharePoint was released in 2007 and the latest version of SharePoint was released in 2010. Each version has two primary editions. The first is a "free" edition of SharePoint that comes along with the Windows Server operating system. The second is a deluxe edition, purchased separately.

The previous version of SharePoint consisted of Windows SharePoint Services (WSS) 3.0 — the free edition — and Microsoft Office SharePoint Server (MOSS) 2007 — the deluxe edition. The current version of SharePoint consists of SharePoint Foundation 2010 (the successor to WSS) and SharePoint Server 2010 (the successor to MOSS 2007). One great aspect of this shift in marketing terminology is that Microsoft actually simplified the product names (what a concept!). Now instead of the two major editions of SharePoint being called WSS and MOSS — do you remember what they mean (no fair peeking)? — the two SharePoint editions are simply called SharePoint Foundation and SharePoint Server. Easy enough to remember.

You may wonder why there isn't just *one* SharePoint edition. Here's the short answer: Because no two businesses are exactly the same in terms of size, complexity, or mission — and Microsoft wants to offer editions of SharePoint that all will find appealing. Thus the Foundation version of SharePoint and the deluxe Server version. If you're considering the Foundation version, note that "free" is relative — and (in this case) proprietary: SharePoint only runs on the Windows operating system. In order to get the "free" Foundation version of SharePoint, you have to purchase the operating system. The Foundation version, essentially SharePoint lite, contains features and functionality that are critical to organizations of all sizes but doesn't include heavy-duty enterprise-level features such as Excel Services, InfoPath Services, PerformancePoint Services, Visio Services, and Access Services.

The specific features of each edition of SharePoint can be found online here:

    sharepoint.microsoft.com/en-us/buy/Pages/Editions-Comparison.aspx

To segment SharePoint Server even further, Microsoft breaks the licensing of the product into two primary categories. The first is geared to sites that face the wilds of the Internet; the second is geared to sites that face the (internal) corporate intranet. Each of these site categories, *external-facing* and *internal-facing* respectively, comes in a Standard edition and an Enterprise edition.

Climbing the SharePoint development ladder

The easiest way to think about ASP.NET, SharePoint Foundation, and SharePoint Server is to picture them as rungs on a ladder of software sophistication: Each adds capabilities and value as you move up in complexity and scale.

Starting (relatively) simple, if you need a specific solution that provides features such as communication, collaboration, and document management, then you could pay developers to build all those capabilities from scratch. Just be prepared to make a time investment. Trust me on this one: Back in grad school, a team of us did just that, using the Java programming language. Our Web application was a content-management system that tracked electronic content and allowed people to check content in and out, as well as purchase content from an online store. This took us more than 6 months to put together; it involved team members from Germany, China, Colombia, and at least one other exotic locale (San Francisco).

So suppose you've given your Microsoft-savvy developers a similar task: "Build nearly everything from scratch and come up with a solution that provides communication, collaboration, and document management." They might assume they'll have to work the whole thing up in ASP.NET. But if they start with the SharePoint Foundation framework, they can use the ready-made document-management and collaboration components of SharePoint — and then just build and customize the rest of the solution to your specifications. Definitely faster.

But suppose your company has finally graduated from, "Where did I put my Word document?" to "How can we integrate our portal with our business in order to increase efficiency and productivity?" For that you need heavy-duty bang for your buck.

That's why Microsoft used ASP.NET and SharePoint Foundation to build into SharePoint Server nearly all the features you'd want in that custom-made solution. SharePoint Server is customizable, of course, but Microsoft has already done most of the heavy lifting by building the product. All you have to do is pay for it, install it, and begin developing solutions on the platform.

Chapter 2

SharePoint Online

We have technology, finally, that for the first time in human history allows people to really maintain rich connections with much larger numbers of people.

— Pierre Omidyar

One of the biggest investments in both time and money when implementing SharePoint involves setting up the infrastructure. A SharePoint platform requires a number of server computers that in turn require a data center. The server computers require operating systems and software that must be installed and constantly updated. The environment also needs a disaster recovery plan, backup plan, and security plan. Wouldn't it be nice if you could just tell Microsoft to handle all these things while you focus your energy on building business solutions that *just happen to* take advantage of the SharePoint platform?

Such a scenario would allow you to focus on your SharePoint development and solving your business problems instead of worrying about keeping the platform afloat. Well, I'm happy to say that Microsoft has just such a solution. It's called SharePoint Online and it's the focus of this chapter.

This chapter offers a bird's-eye view of what SharePoint Online is all about and how it works. At this heady altitude, it's easier to discover why SharePoint Online is also called a "cloud solution" — and why cloud solutions have gained popularity so quickly. Finally, you explore the benefits — and some pitfalls — of using SharePoint Online, and figure out why Microsoft expects nearly everyone to be using the cloud in the future.

Introducing SharePoint Online

When you first hear about SharePoint Online, you might ask yourself the same question that I did, "I work with SharePoint all the time and I'm online when I work with it — so what's this 'SharePoint Online' business all about?" The thing to keep in mind with SharePoint is that it's a platform that you can use however you deem necessary for your business. Chapter 1 walks you through the components that make up the SharePoint platform — everything from physical computers to the software that SharePoint requires in order to function. This entire *stack* of requirements exists merely to present the SharePoint platform to users. With the platform in place, you're free to develop business solutions to solve real problems (what a concept). The sticky part is that the platform on which you build those dazzling solutions isn't a trivial matter.

What Microsoft means by SharePoint *Online* is that they're selling their SharePoint platform as a *service* dished up by the actual servers and software running in their data centers and managed and maintained by their employees. You don't even install it on your machine. As a customer of Microsoft, you connect to this managed version of SharePoint over a secure channel of the Internet — and use it to develop business solutions on the SharePoint platform. Figure 2-1 illustrates how this works.

The alternative would be running the whole SharePoint environment locally, in your own data center — managing and maintaining it with your own people. In this scenario, SharePoint runs *On Premise* instead of Online; you'd only buy the licensing from Microsoft and tech support when you need it. Maybe a better name for SharePoint Online would have been "SharePoint Hosted and Managed by Microsoft" — much more descriptive, although the inevitable acronym, SHMM, would sound like some new style of yoga. I guess SharePoint Online isn't such a bad name after all.

What's this cloud business all about?

Network diagrams often show a network as a cloud because a diagram developer cannot be bothered to detail the complexities of all the components that make up the network (such as routers, switches, cables, and hubs). It's become traditional just to show a cloud in place of that mess, as shown in the following figure.

The cloud drawing is simply an abstraction of a computer network, put there because *all* the fiddly bits would never fit on the page. The biggest network (and cloud) of all is the Internet. When a diagram shows communication over the Internet and you see a big cloud, here's what it signifies: "At this point, the information goes through a mass of complex network hardware between two points that use the Internet — let's just assume that communication can occur between those points." Result: Tidier diagram, smaller headache.

If a company sells access to software that lives in their data centers — and customers connect to the data center over the Internet to get the access they bought — then that solution lives "in the cloud" from the perspective of the customers using the software service. They might not have zero idea where the actual servers are that serve up the software; they've just accessed the software using an Internet domain name. So whenever you surf the Web, you're using a service in the cloud. Each Web site you browse is in the cloud. Who really knows where the actual server is that's serving up the Web site? I'm betting you don't know and don't really care. You just know that when you type in the Web address, the site appears in your browser. As this concept continues to catch on with business applications, you'll hear more about cloud solutions.

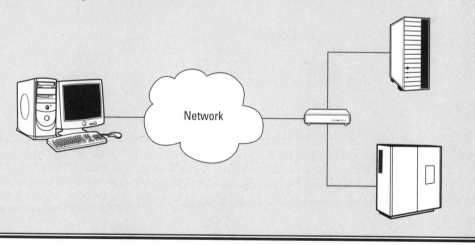

Network

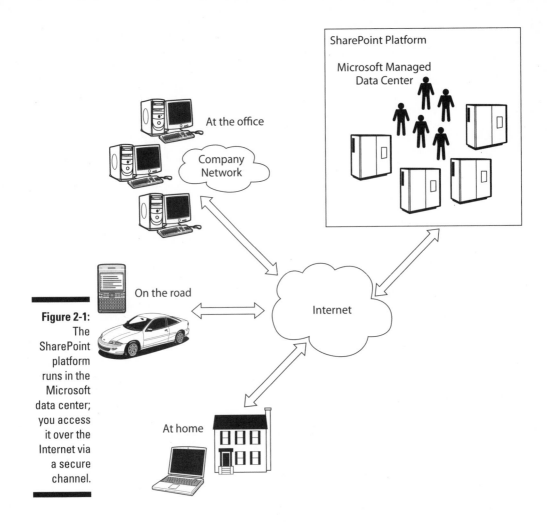

Figure 2-1:
The SharePoint platform runs in the Microsoft data center; you access it over the Internet via a secure channel.

Why SharePoint Online Is Becoming So Popular

Putting a complex computer platform in place is, frankly, difficult. Organizations learned this when they implemented Enterprise Resource Planning (ERP) software in the 1990s and 2000s; it still holds true today. Putting the SharePoint platform in place is no walk in the park — especially because larger organizations usually require a more complex implementation. As that complexity increases, so do the costs, time, and risk.

The current best practice is to use an experienced consulting firm with expertise in implementing a SharePoint platform. As in dealing with any services company, sometimes you pick a winner, and sometimes it's a complete disaster. But read on. . . .

If you need a recommendation for a services firm that specializes in SharePoint, the best place to inquire is Microsoft. After all, those folks have a vested interest in making sure you're pleased with their products so you'll buy more licenses. (For that matter, you can always contact me directly at www. portalintegrators.com as well. Having worked in the field for more than a decade, I can tell you who the best companies are to match the size and complexity of implementation you're considering.)

SharePoint Online takes the implementation of the infrastructure out of the equation with a known variable in cost and resources. Having a known variable in place for the infrastructure frees up resources to focus on the actual business problems. Which, by the way, are your main reasons for implementing SharePoint in the first place. A perfect analogy would be worrying about building a car instead of getting to your appointments. Life is difficult enough trying to juggle appointments, or business problems, without having to worry about the car, or (in this case) the computing platform. That's why SharePoint Online and other cloud solutions are becoming so popular: They reduce complexity, provide a fixed and certain cost, and offer a platform that's guaranteed to follow documented best practices.

Microsoft has introduced the SharePoint Online offering to cater to everyone from small businesses to large multinationals and everything in between. In fact, you can even purchase as few as five licenses for the Online Suite. Because Microsoft has already built the service and put it in place, offering the same reliability and security to small and large companies alike is pretty straightforward. Everybody's after the same product, and gets to it via the same route. The only difference is the scale.

Exploring the Benefits of SharePoint Online

There are a number of benefits to using SharePoint Online instead of trying to build and manage the platform yourself. In particular Microsoft takes care of the data center and hardware, the stack of software that makes up the SharePoint platform, and also the backup, redundancy, and security that are expected in order to ensure integrity for the environment.

Data center and hardware

If you've ever had the privilege of touring a modern data center, then you have a handle on the sheer amount of effort and resources it takes to keep everything running. There are rows and rows of computers with flashing lights, humming fans, and snakes of coils of cables running from ceiling to floor. Monitoring all these servers are control rooms that resemble something NASA would use to run space missions. The computers and monitors report on everything in the data center — from temperature and humidity to individual fans in particular servers, and everything in between. Often you'll hear such a control room called a Network Operation Center (NOC); it's the nerve center of a modern data center.

Most organizations that need servers (and these days, who doesn't?) find a modern data center to host their gear instead of building a facility of their own. Hosting your computers in a dedicated data center can cost a fortune but paying to host your own gear in an inferior environment (say, somebody's retrofitted old warehouse) can cost even more in the long run.

Microsoft invested a tremendous amount of money in building their own state of the art data centers that they use to house the servers that make up their SharePoint Online offerings. The nice thing about the SharePoint Online offering is that you don't have to worry about the various costs of hosting and managing your own gear. The price you pay for SharePoint Online covers everything including the data center.

The servers that run SharePoint Online are state of the art and come from the leading industry manufacturers. In fact, Microsoft has modularized the setup; the computers come in massive containers that look like those you see on cargo ships. These container pods are sealed by the manufacturer and never opened once at the data center. This is a security mechanism to keep humans from fiddling with the computers. When a single piece of hardware fails, the workload of that server simply shifts automatically to other servers (possibly in other pods). When enough servers fail, the pod is taken offline and the workload of the failed pod is shifted to another pod — without service interruption. A new pod with the latest hardware is then shipped to replace the old pod, which is then decommissioned — a process that wipes the data to meet security standards and sends it back to the manufacturer.

Microsoft has developed this system of data centers and pods throughout the country with built-in redundancy. If a data center goes down, the workload is shifted to another data center. If a pod goes down the workload of that pod is shifted to another pod. If a server within a pod goes down the workload of that server is shifted to another server. This system of redundancy is included into the price of SharePoint Online. You might care about how it works or you might just care that Microsoft has guaranteed uptime of 99.9 percent without caring how they've done it. In the end, you're free to focus on your business and solving business problems using the SharePoint platform without having to worry what it takes to make that platform consistently available.

Software platform

The physical computers required to run the SharePoint platform are really just the beginning; you also have to take into account the operating systems and associated software that run on the server computers — such as the Web servers, databases, and SharePoint itself. The Microsoft platform uses the Windows Server operating system, the Internet Information Service (IIS) Web server, and the SQL Server database (as described in Chapter 1). All these software systems are just the supporting actors for the SharePoint software itself. The amount of time and resources needed to get all these software components installed, updated, and configured can be daunting. Network administrators' time is a valuable resource — often better spent dealing with the desktop computers of users — so many organizations welcome the opportunity to (shall we say) "outsource" the maintenance of software components.

When you sign up for SharePoint Online, you don't have to worry about installing and managing the software components that make up the SharePoint platform. Microsoft takes care of all that for you — and it's all included in the price. In addition, when new versions of the software stack are released, Microsoft upgrades everything automatically — without additional cost for the service. In addition, Microsoft monitors the servers (and the system logs) 24 hours a day to make sure nothing goes awry. The monitoring takes place in those space-age-looking Network Operation Centers described in the previous section.

Backup, redundancy, and security

You might think that with the hardware and software in place, the rest would be easy — but you'd be mistaken. After all, Murphy's Law never sleeps. The SharePoint platform itself needs a plan for backup and disaster recovery — in addition to being available, redundant, and secure. With SharePoint Online, the Microsoft teams take care of all that for you (and include a guarantee in the contract).

With the hardware, software, and plans in place, you as a customer are free to focus on developing business solutions on the platform instead of working through the process of setting up everything yourself.

Figuring Out Where SharePoint Online Is Going

Okay, no technology is perfect (you knew that). One of the downsides of using SharePoint Online is that the version available Online usually lags behind the version available On Premise. For example, when SharePoint 2010 was released, the Online version continued to be 2007 for some time.

The reason for this lag is that the Online team is working through all the same quirks that go along with upgrading from the previous version to the new version. It's much the same scenario as what companies around the world have to work through when they upgrade their own platforms. Only after the Online team has created a stable and secure platform can they start moving Online customers to the new platform.

Keep in mind, as well, that Online upgrades happen automatically. If you're an Online customer and want to stay with the old version of SharePoint, you're out of luck. The platform mitigates this by allowing for upgrades that don't affect the look and feel of the sites that use the platform, even when the underlying SharePoint version is upgraded. If you have a SharePoint 2007 team site and you upgrade to the 2010 version, your site can continue to look like nothing's changed (which is often reassuring to the users) but what's under the hood is now SharePoint 2010. When your administrators decide to take advantage of the new features, they can introduce the features to the user base gradually.

Speaking of features, one fairly big downside to using SharePoint Online is that not all the On Premise features and functionality are available in the Online version. Microsoft is working hard to make On Premise features available in SharePoint Online, but there's always a lag. If your organization needs a critical feature that's only available when SharePoint is deployed On Premise, then using a combination of SharePoint On Premise and SharePoint Online is always an option. Deciding which approach is best for you — Online, On Premise, or some combination — can be difficult. The best option is to take advantage of some dedicated SharePoint smarts called in from outside — whether from Microsoft itself or a trusted services firm with proven expertise in the area.

Chapter 3

SharePoint Development Overview

Productivity is being able to do things that you were never able to do before.

— Franz Kafka

*W*hen you're facing a mountain of technology, attaining a perspective on how all the pieces fit together is a difficult task. You might ask someone what SharePoint development means — and get an answer that veers off topic and launches right into Visual Studio or the SharePoint Object Model (OM). You might ask someone else and get an answer that equates SharePoint development with using Report Builder and Dashboard Designer to build business intelligence (BI) solutions. Both of these answers are correct — and not enough by themselves.

When you're trying to decide how best to develop a SharePoint solution to solve a problem, a holistic view of the available development tools gives you a leg up. Having a broad understanding of what is available provides you with perspective and allows you to pick the best path before diving into the details. Think of this chapter as a SharePoint Development map. It provides you with the big picture and gives you a high-level perspective on the paths and obstacles you'll encounter on your journey. When you have a handle on what's available — and on the tools and methods you need to develop your solution — you can dive into the details of particular tools.

This chapter introduces SharePoint development by hitting the highlights of the chapters throughout the rest of the book — stitching them together into a big-picture view. We start with the definition of a developer — and how you need not be a programmer to develop solutions in SharePoint. Next you explore different types of SharePoint development and the tools you use in your development efforts.

After reading this chapter, you might want to jump around to other parts of the book to find the type of development that piques your fancy.

Redefining What It Means to Be a Developer

I always cringe when I hear people talking about trying to find "SharePoint devs" to build a SharePoint solution. Many people still think a SharePoint developer is always a programmer. Not so. Most SharePoint development can be done without writing a single line of computer code. Sure, a really ticklish advanced problem may still need SharePoint programmers to crack open Visual Studio and start writing .NET code. But that's the exception. I see people still furiously writing code to solve problems that would yield to SharePoint tools and *no* code — and I figure it must be force of habit. As they say, when you're a hammer, everything looks like a nail.

Well, I'm here to tell you that you don't need to be a hammer or a nail to develop solutions on the SharePoint platform. You simply need to be a little tech-savvy and able to work with tools that have a look and feel similar to what you find in Microsoft Office Word, Excel, and Visio. The other tools you use to develop on the SharePoint platform are no more difficult to use than the Office tools, and you still won't have to write code. That said, in the next section, you take a look at the range of tasks you can take on as a well-equipped SharePoint developer. . . .

Types of SharePoint Development

SharePoint development spans a broad spectrum. Chances are you've used a Web browser, right? Well, then, you already have the necessary skill set to do a great deal of SharePoint development. Ever used Microsoft Office? Then you already have what it takes to use the SharePoint development tools. (And here's a trade secret: When you're ready to unleash your inner programmer, you'll find it's not as difficult as it's cracked up to be.) So, in essence, you have three general ways to build a SharePoint solution: use the Web browser, using the built-in SharePoint tools, and (only when you have to) write computer code.

Meet your good friend, the Web browser

Here's an approach to development that uses nothing more than SharePoint and your Web browser. That same Web browser you use to read the news, check on the status of your friends, plan and book your vacations, and (oh, yeah) *work* is also the environment for a staggering range of SharePoint development tasks.

This is in fact one of SharePoint's claims to fame. Using only a browser, you can create portals, sites, lists, libraries, and the list goes on. Chapter 4's focus is using the browser to develop SharePoint solutions.

Exploring the SharePoint tools

The second type of SharePoint development involves tools. My grandpa once told me that the secret to making a job easier is having the right tool — that 90 percent of the job was having the right tool. He was, of course, talking about physical handyman tasks such as fixing a car, a shelf, or a fence, but the same wisdom holds true for technology.

When you're developing a SharePoint solution, know your tools — and their roles in the big picture — so you can choose the best tool for the job at hand. Here are some examples:

- ✔ You *could* spend hours in SharePoint Designer hacking out specialized forms using ASP.NET — but if you'd rather not (why, I'm shocked!), then simply open up InfoPath (discussed in detail in Chapter 6) and build the forms you want by clicking through its menus, wizards, and views.

- ✔ What might take days to develop using Dashboard Designer might go a lot faster if you use Report Builder instead, as I explain in Chapter 9.

- ✔ What might require an extensive effort using Visual Studio and .NET custom code might take only a matter of hours if you try it using the Workflow feature of SharePoint Designer (all without writing code)! You discover how to take on SharePoint Designer in Chapter 8.

- ✔ After spending days getting Report Builder to do exactly what you want it to do, you might discover that you could have simply used Excel — and then posted the spreadsheet to the SharePoint site using Excel Services, as Chapter 5 explains. (Ack! Well, live and learn.)

Understanding each tool and where it excels is a critical step in heading off the heartbreak of wasted labor when you could've been watching the game or something.

See the section "SharePoint Development Tools" later in this chapter for an introduction to the tools that do common jobs best.

Getting down to the DNA level with programming

And then there's the kind of SharePoint development that calls for (gasp) computer programming. Relax. The beauty of the SharePoint platform is that it's built on a standard framework known as ASP.NET. You could, of course, hire a gaggle of programmers who are ASP.NET geniuses and have them build a SharePoint-like solution from scratch — but why? Microsoft was kind enough to build both ASP.NET *and* SharePoint with *their* programmers — all to be endlessly poked, prodded, and tweaked using (a whole lot less) computer code.

You can think of programming as tweaking the DNA of the SharePoint platform — and actually getting a *friendly* creature. (Ideally, anyway.)

When you get to the point where you need a highly customized solution and you've determined that using the browser and tools just won't cut it, that's when you can bring in the programmers. SharePoint provides a number of tools and toolkits designed to make programming on the platform easy.

SharePoint Development Tools

A big-picture overview of the types of SharePoint development — and the tools they use — is the best place to start when you're zeroing in on the approach that works for you. Although the SharePoint tools often have overlapping functionality, each excels in a particular development strategy. The tools in your SharePoint development belt consist of

- ✔ Your friendly Web browser (a familiar way to access to SharePoint).
- ✔ Office application such as Excel, InfoPath, Word, and Visio.
- ✔ Standalone tools built in to SharePoint, such as SharePoint Designer, Report Builder, and Dashboard Designer.
- ✔ Programming tools such as Visual Studio and PowerShell.

Cracking open the Web browser

The simple truth is that most people interact with SharePoint only via the Web browser. After all, SharePoint is a Web-based application designed to move the company intranet portal to the center of the organization. In this starring role, the portal has to be accessible from many different environments — and what software is more ubiquitous (and versatile) than a Web browser?

Moving beyond simply browsing a SharePoint portal, you have quite a range of development efforts you can accomplish using only the browser. These include

- ✔ Creating and developing entire sites.
- ✔ Creating and developing individual pages.
- ✔ Developing site and page templates.

✔ Creating and developing lists and libraries.

✔ Developing site columns, views, and content types.

✔ Developing publishing solutions.

✔ Creating a custom look and feel for a site and developing themes.

For the details of SharePoint development using the Web browser, check out Chapter 4.

Microsoft Office tools

Microsoft Office remains a wildly popular and nearly ubiquitous productivity suite. Information workers already spend a lot of time using Office tools such as Word and Excel, so Microsoft decided to tightly integrate these tools with SharePoint. Using the Microsoft Office tools, you can develop solutions that utilize these tools in the SharePoint environment.

Excel

Microsoft Excel is already a very powerful and (some would say) critical tool in data analysis. One of its biggest problems, however, is sharing the results of that analysis with the rest of the organization. A data analyst might create a spreadsheet and then send it to others for feedback before printing it out as a report for the executive team. Seems harmless enough — but that's when it starts mutating. As the spreadsheet is e-mailed and altered and e-mailed again, mistakes have many opportunities to creep in. Not to mention that sharing the document with the rest of the organization becomes a cumbersome task. Imagine sending the report out to everyone who should have it — and then suddenly finding a calculation error that throws off the entire workbook. No fun at all.

SharePoint now includes a featured called Excel Services that provides tight integration with Excel workbooks. Using SharePoint with Excel Services, you can

✔ **Develop document libraries:** Libraries keep track of versioning, check-in and out for collaboration, security, and workflow.

✔ **Edit a document collaboratively:** That's right, you can edit through the Web with one or more colleagues. If you and they have the document open at the same time and are editing it, you'll see whenever they make changes and they'll see when you make yours. It's a way to catch mistakes (and new ideas) quickly — especially while looking at the same document at the same time on-screen and talking through prospective changes on the phone.

> ✔ **Embed Excel documents in a SharePoint Web page:** When a page is embedded, you can limit who can change Excel documents, which helps keep everybody on the same page (so to speak). When it's time to send out the report, you simply publish the final version — the Web page that contains the report is updated automatically. If changes are needed, just change the embedded Excel document and your changes are updated automatically as soon as you publish the new version of the Web page.

Chapter 5 gives you the lowdown on developing solutions with Excel and Excel Services.

InfoPath

InfoPath has been a part of Office for some time but many people don't understand the benefits of the product. The idea behind InfoPath is that people should be able to create their own feature-rich forms easily, without need of a programmer.

Up to now the problem has been the standalone nature of InfoPath: If you created an InfoPath form and wanted to distribute it for input, you'd have to send it in an e-mail message. The recipient would have to have the InfoPath client installed locally to open the form and fill it out. This might work for some internal scenarios but it's much easier to just browse to a Web site and fill out a form without the extra hassle of using e-mail, sending attachments, and having client applications installed locally.

But wait, there's more: SharePoint includes a feature called InfoPath Form Services that integrates InfoPath forms right into the SharePoint platform. Using InfoPath Form Services you can finally build feature-rich InfoPath forms (which can, for example, calculate specified fields automatically) and integrate them right into your SharePoint portal. In fact, whenever you work with forms at all on the SharePoint 2010 platform, you're already working with InfoPath forms. For example, say you develop a custom list and then begin entering items in the list. Voilà — the form you're using to enter the items is an InfoPath form — and you can develop and tweak it further with only a few simple steps, thanks to InfoPath Form Services. For more about what InfoPath Form Services can do for you, check out Chapter 6.

Word and Visio

I've been hard-pressed to find an organization that doesn't use Microsoft Word for word processing. Word has become so ubiquitous that it's almost an assumed part of the software installed on everybody's local computers. Organizations use Word for everything from résumé submissions from new applicants to year-end performance reviews and invoicing. But what happens if you have an invading horde of documents to deal with? Thankfully, the SharePoint platform provides a top-notch Enterprise Content Management (ECM) system for controlling and directing the plethora of Word documents flowing through an organization. When Word documents live in SharePoint, features such as check-in/check-out, security, versioning, and workflow keep the documents' access levels appropriate, versions controlled, and destinations right for the task at hand.

Another component of the Office productivity software is Visio — used for building visual diagrams of everything from the flow of a process to the bones of the organizational hierarchy. SharePoint integrates Visio into the platform so you can embed diagrams right into your pages. In addition, the SharePoint workflow feature is integrated with Visio to provide a real-time visual representation of workflow status without programming.

For more information about developing SharePoint solutions with Word and Visio, check out Chapter 7.

Standalone tools

In addition to using the Web browser and the Office tools, you can apply standalone SharePoint tools that are tailored to SharePoint development: SharePoint Designer, Report Builder, and Dashboard Designer.

SharePoint Designer

The primary standalone tool for SharePoint development — SharePoint Designer — is designed specifically for SharePoint development; it has no other purpose.

The power of SharePoint Designer lies in how the SharePoint platform works. SharePoint is a Web application that was designed to store content and configuration information in a database (or databases). The Web application (SharePoint) pulls the content from the database and builds the Web pages that you interact with on the platform dynamically as you maneuver around the portals built on the SharePoint platform.

When you're doing SharePoint development, you're actually manipulating a complicated database. SharePoint Designer provides a task-based window into this database that provides more power than simply developing using the Web browser.

When you have to develop things such as workflows and Master Pages, you'll need to use SharePoint Designer. When you get really comfortable with SharePoint Designer, you might prefer to do most development tasks in it, even if you could perform those same tasks using the Web browser. SharePoint Designer manages to be a very powerful development tool without requiring that you write a single line of code. For more information about SharePoint Designer, check out Chapter 8.

Report Builder

Understanding the data that flows through an organization is critical to success. Looking at raw data, however, is better left to the computers. What decision-makers need are reports that summarize and easily display the data. When you build a report, you're turning the raw data into information that mere mortals can easily understand and put to practical use.

You can develop reports using a vast number of technologies — but one in particular is specifically geared for just such a feat: a component of SQL Server called Reporting Services that can be integrated with (you guessed it) SharePoint. When SQL Server Reporting Services (SSRS for short) is integrated with SharePoint, the reports themselves live in the SharePoint environment — which means they instantly gain access to all that SharePoint has to offer an aspiring young report on its way to hang out with the honchos.

But end users aren't left out of this equation. Far from it. They have a SharePoint tool that bears a strong family resemblance to Microsoft Office products such as Word or Excel: Report Builder, which can be launched right from a SharePoint-based portal. Wielding Report Builder, users and analysts can develop and publish reports like mad — and base them on a vast arrange of data sources. And because the environment is still within SharePoint, the IT department is happy because it still maintains governance and control. For more information about Report Builder, check out Chapter 9.

Dashboard Designer

Business intelligence may sound like a sci-fi movie set in a Wall Street skyscraper, but actually it's a set of techniques that organizations now employ to make the most of their internal information, in quest of a critical advantage over their competitors (who are using business intelligence too). BI (as it's familiarly known) has spawned new types of databases called *OLAP cubes* (short for OnLine Analytical Processing), refers to the different types of descriptive data as *dimensions,* and has driven the development of self-serve tools for everyday users within the business. (Hm. Still sounds kind of sci-fi.)

Experts might take months to develop a complex analytical database but what should users do with it after it's complete? Dashboard Designer is an end-user tool designed to crunch the numbers and build dashboards and reports based on those new OLAP analytical databases. The SharePoint technology that makes all this possible is called PerformancePoint Services.

In essence, PerformancePoint Services is the engine that runs the *dashboards* (arrays of real-time indicators showing the status of business processes) that you can build in (what else?) Dashboard Designer. It's similar to how Reporting Services is the engine that displays the reports you build in Report Builder. (Yep, there's a pattern here.)

Now, people often confuse the purposes of these two programs and use the names interchangeably. Someone who claims to be building PerformancePoint reports may actually be building dashboards using Dashboard Designer (okay, those are *displayed* using PerformancePoint Services, but you have to build 'em first). By the same token, someone who claims to be working up a Reporting Services report is, um, technically half right; what's really going on is the building of a report in Report Builder. Such reports are *rendered* (presented to the higher-ups) by Reporting Services, just doing its job as a component of SQL Server. Stick with the concepts to keep a clear picture of what's going on:

- ✔ If the thing is being built to display data in PerformancePoint Services, it's a dashboard — think of a high-*performance* sports car's *dashboard,* if that helps. The tool for this is called Dashboard Designer.

- ✔ If the thing is to be shown in Reporting Services, it's a report. The tool being used to build it is (well, yeah) Report Builder.

Hey, you'll know exactly what they're doing. Can't blame them for getting all excited at their newfound powers.

You can launch both Report Builder and Dashboard Designer directly from the SharePoint platform; both are designed for end users. (For more about Dashboard Designer, flip to Chapter 10. For more about Report Builder, check out Chapter 9.)

If you'd like to learn more about analytical databases (and who doesn't?), allow me to recommend *Microsoft Business Intelligence For Dummies* (Wiley) by yours truly.

Programming tools

Okay, although most SharePoint development doesn't involve programming, sometimes you need capabilities so specific that you have to write some computer code. Granted, computer programming is not for the faint of heart; if you have a touch of technophobia, it's okay to let your geek friends wrestle with writing code. But if you already have an understanding of how to write any computer code at all, then you can write code for SharePoint — which comes with tools and libraries to make the whole undertaking easier. These tools include an application called Visual Studio and a command-line language called PowerShell — each worth a closer look.

Visual Studio

You can think of the Visual Studio application as the Swiss Army knife for Microsoft-compatible programming. Visual Studio is a type of software application known as an Integrated Development Environment (IDE). The Visual Studio IDE is used for many types of Microsoft development — not just programming. The power of this approach comes from the modular aspect of the tool. Do you need to develop some OLAP cubes for an analytical database? Visual Studio is your tool. Do you need to write a completely custom application from scratch to run locally on your computer? Visual Studio gets the job done. Do you need to develop a SharePoint feature or Web Part that just isn't available as a standard option? Again, Visual Studio is your tool of choice. For more about Visual Studio, check out Chapters 11, 12, and 13.

PowerShell

Speaking of development tools, this one's a beaut — and yes, it uses the command line. If all that typing seems daunting, consider: Tools that allow you to point and click are popular mainly because they provide an easy-to-use visual representation of an application. The problem with pointing and clicking is that it gets cumbersome when you're trying to automate operations. There are programs that will record your mouse clicks and then replay them, but that becomes a pain in a hurry.

If you've ever used a command prompt such as DOS or an operating system such as UNIX, then you've seen the no-nonsense power of a command-line application: You simply type in a command, check to make sure it's accurate, press Enter, and the computer executes the command. No fuss, no backtalk, no visual ambiguity. For example, in DOS you might type the cd command to change the directory. It may not be blindingly fast, but it's a lot more accurate.

PowerShell is essentially a command prompt that allows you to do just about anything with Microsoft products — right from the command line. You can write a bunch of commands, save them in a file, and then have them executed whenever you need to — or rig them to run on a timer. PowerShell is, accordingly, an indispensable tool for administrative automation. For more about PowerShell, power on over to Chapter 14.

Part II

Developing with Your Web Browser and Microsoft Office

The 5th Wave   By Rich Tennant

"The funny thing is he's spent 9 hours organizing his site directory."

In this part . . .

This part explores how SharePoint development uses your Web browser and Microsoft Office applications — in particular, Excel, InfoPath, Word, and Visio. SharePoint is a Web application, designed to be used with a Web browser — but Microsoft didn't stop with the end users. You have a tremendous amount of development functionality that you can access right from your browser. Here's where you get a handle on using it to develop solutions — first with Excel Services and InfoPath Form Services, and then with Word and Visio — to integrate client-application convenience with SharePoint muscle to solve real-world business problems.

Chapter 4

Developing Sites with Your Web Browser

In This Chapter

▶ Getting into developing sites and pages

▶ Becoming a SharePoint developer guru who can customize SharePoint pages to suit

▶ Creating your own custom templates and views

▶ Making your SharePoint site sparkle with a custom look and feel

As we look ahead into the next century, leaders will be those who empower others.

— Bill Gates

*F*irst, the good news: SharePoint can be customized beyond your wildest imagination. SharePoint is built on Microsoft's .NET platform, so anything is possible — and much of that development can be accomplished right from your Web browser. Because the Web browser is the primary mechanism for most SharePoint interaction, understanding how to use your browser for development is the key to becoming a SharePoint developer guru.

In this chapter, you discover how to create and develop SharePoint sites, pages, custom templates, and views right from your browser. You explore the development of document libraries and lists, and customize content types and site columns. Finally, to give your SharePoint site some flair, you find pointers on how to dress up your development efforts with a custom look and feel.

Creating a SharePoint Site

To a user browsing a SharePoint *site,* it's nothing more than a regular Web site — with some fancy SharePoint capabilities. Those SharePoint capabilities enable easy collaboration, access to business information, and a boost to business intelligence all though the Web. In SharePoint terms a site is a container for SharePoint pages. This entire ball of functionality, also called a *platform* (because you can build on it), is the Microsoft product called SharePoint. One thing that makes SharePoint so exciting is that you don't even have to drop out of your Web browser to tell SharePoint what to do. As long as you have access to SharePoint and a current browser, you're ready to start developing a site.

When you're first starting out with SharePoint development you will need a site that you can develop within. When you create a new site, you can start with a blank site or a *template site* that already has some stuff built into it — such as lists, libraries, and Web Parts developed and configured to do particular tasks. Those templates are available on the Create screen when you create a new site. For example, you might get a request to create a Business Intelligence site in order to consolidate reports, charts, and indicators. Rather than start from scratch you can use a template specifically designed for this task. In this scenario the template site you would use is called the Business Intelligence Center, and is shown in Figure 4-1.

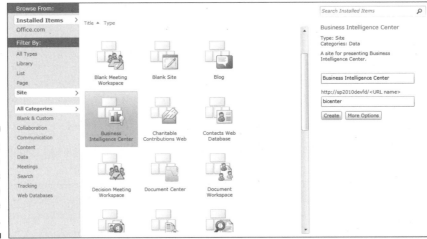

Figure 4-1:
The
Business
Intelligence
Center site
template.

The Business Intelligence Center site template is only available when the PerformancePoint Services Site Collection feature is activated. To activate this feature, choose Site Actions⇨Site Settings⇨Site Collection Features and click the Activate button for the PerformancePoint Services feature.

Before you start building custom applications for SharePoint, having a solid working knowledge of its various components is a good idea. (After all, you wouldn't try to design a house without having some knowledge of how the plumbing works, right?) The best way to get to know SharePoint is to start with a blank site and develop it from scratch so you understand what the templates are doing. Then you can more easily start with a template as a baseline and develop your site from there.

Looking for a wheel instead of reinventing one

When you need to develop a SharePoint site to solve a problem, be sure you start with a solid understanding of the available site templates. It's often much easier to start with a site template that 'almost' does what you want and then develop it from this starting point than to start at ground zero and develop everything from scratch.

Creating a new site is as simple as clicking Site Actions⇨New Site from the parent site and then clicking through the templates to find the site you to create. (A *parent site* is a site that holds another site.)

Table 4-1 lists the available site templates in SharePoint 2010 — along with the description of each site.

Table 4-1	SharePoint 2010 Site Templates
Site Template	*Description*
Assets Web Database	Create a database to keep track of your organization's *information assets* (valuable information), including the details and owner(s) of each asset.
Basic Meeting Workspace	A site on which you can plan, organize, and capture the results of a meeting. It provides lists for managing the agenda, meeting attendees, and documents.
Basic Search Center	A site that provides SharePoint search functionality; includes pages for search results and advanced searches.
Blank Meeting Workspace	A blank meeting site that you can customize to your meeting's requirements. The difference from a Blank Site is that a Blank Meeting Workspace has the components available that you'll need to build out a site geared to meetings.

(continued)

Table 4-1 *(continued)*

Site Template	Description
Blank Site	A blank site with no built-in features; customize it to match your requirements. It sounds funny to create a blank site using a blank site template. What you are actually doing is creating a container for SharePoint stuff, a site, without actually putting any of the SharePoint stuff in there at the time of creation.
Blog	A site that works like an Internet blog; a person or team can post ideas, observations, and expertise that site visitors can comment on.
Business Intelligence Center	A site for presenting business intelligence in the SharePoint environment. Microsoft marketing has dubbed as SharePoint Insights any of the components that make up Business Intelligence. This includes features such as PerformancePoint Services, Reporting Services, and Excel Services as well as tools such as Dashboard Designer, Report Builder, and Excel.
Charitable Contributions Web Database	Using this site, you can create a database that keeps track of information about fundraising campaigns — including donations, contributors, campaign-related events, and scheduled tasks.
Contacts Web Database	Using this site, you can create a database to manage contact information from customers, partners, and other people who work with your team.
Decision Meeting Workspace	A site you can use at meetings to track the status of projects or make decisions. The site includes lists you can use to create tasks, store documents, and record decisions.
Document Center	A site from which you can manage documents centrally for your entire enterprise.
Document Workspace	A site on which colleagues can use that famous SharePoint collaborative capability to work together on a document. The site provides a document library for storing the primary document and supporting files, a list for to-do tasks (is there any other kind?), and a list that can hold links to resources related to the document.

Site Template	Description
Enterprise Search Center	This site provides the SharePoint search capability. The Welcome Page includes a search box that has two tabs: one for general searches and another for searches for information about people. You can add tabs, delete them, or customize them with different search scopes or specified result types.
Enterprise Wiki	A site for publishing knowledge that you capture and want to share across the enterprise. Use this site to edit, co-author, and discuss content, as well as to manage projects.
FAST Search Center	A site for delivering the FAST search capability for information on your server. The welcome page includes a search box with two tabs: one for general searches, and another for searches for information about people. You can add and customize tabs to focus on other search scopes or result types. The FAST Search component provides functionality beyond the Enterprise Search component by providing features such as the ability to preview Office documents within the search results and showing the number of each type of document in the search results.
Group Work Site	This template provides a site that teams can use to create, organize, and share information. It includes the Group Calendar, Circulation, Phone-Call Memo, the document library, and the other basic lists.
Issues Web Database	Create an issues database to manage a set of issues or problems. You can assign, prioritize, and follow the progress of issues from start to finish.
Multipage Meeting Workspace	A site on which you can plan a meeting and make note of the meeting's decisions and other results. The site provides lists for managing the agenda and meeting attendees, as well as two blank pages you can customize to your requirements.
Personalization Site	A site for delivering personalized views, data, and navigation from this site collection to My Site. It includes Web Parts that are specific to personalization and navigation that is optimized for My Site sites. This template is available only at the site level.
Projects Web Database	Create a project-tracking database to track multiple projects and to assign tasks to different people.

(continued)

Table 4-1 *(continued)*

Site Template	Description
Publishing Site	This template offers a starter site hierarchy (grouping of SharePoint sites), for an Internet site or a large intranet portal. You can use distinctive branding to customize this site. It includes a home page, a sample press-releases site, a Search Center, and a logon page. Typically, this site has many more readers than contributors; it's used to publish the Web pages by using a process for approving new content that's known as an *approval workflow*.
	By default, this site enables content-approval workflows to provide more control over the publishing process. It also restricts the rights of anonymous users: They can see content pages but not SharePoint Server 2010 application pages.
	This template is available only at the site-collection level. A site collection is a special SharePoint site that allows you to separate key aspects of the sites contained within the site collection. For example, you turn on features at the site collection level which makes those features available to all sites within the site collection. On a technical level SharePoint separates site collections by using different databases. This allows for separation of security and users since two different site collections use two different databases.
Publishing Site with Workflow	A site for publishing Web pages on a schedule by using approval workflows. It includes document and image libraries for storing Web publishing assets. By default, only sites that have this template can be created under this site.
Records Center	A site designed for managing business records. Records managers can configure the routing table to direct incoming files to specific locations. You can also specify whether records can be deleted or modified after they're added to the repository.
Social Meeting Workspace	A site on which you can plan social occasions and use lists to track attendees, provide directions, and store pictures of the event.
Team Site	A site on which a team can organize, generate, and share information. It provides a document library, as well as lists for managing announcements, calendar items, tasks, and discussions.
Visio Process Repository	A collaborative site on which teams can view, share, and store Visio process diagrams. It provides a document library (with version control) for storing process diagrams, as well as lists for managing announcements, tasks, and review discussions.

The number and type of standard site templates you have available depends on the edition of SharePoint you've installed. For example, if you're running SharePoint Server 2010 Enterprise Edition, then you have access to all site templates. But if you're running SharePoint Foundation 2010, then you only have the templates that come with that edition.

Starting with a blank slate

Often the best way to begin developing a site is to start with a blank site and add the features and functionality you'll find useful. A blank site lets you get familiar with each feature or component you add to the site. When you start with a pre-built template, it's often difficult to get a full grasp of all the pieces.

When you're comfortable with developing SharePoint sites, you can save yourself a lot of time by starting with a template site and then tweaking it for your particular need.

You can create a blank site by following these steps:

1. **After an administrator creates the site collection, it becomes a parent site; in this parent site, click the Site Actions button in the upper-left corner, and then click the New Site button in the Site Actions drop-down menu.**

2. **Select the Blank and Custom filter and then choose Blank Site.**

3. **Fill in a title and URL for the new site and then click Create, as shown in Figure 4-2.**

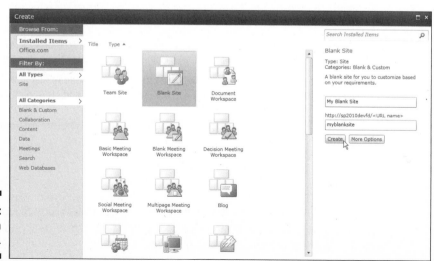

Figure 4-2:
Creating a
blank site.

You can also click the More Options button on the Create page in order to specify a description, adjust permissions, and modify navigation.

You can also create a top-level blank site from Central Administration — the application designed for managing the SharePoint farm and infrastructure. (The practical details of Central Administration and managing a SharePoint farm can be found in *SharePoint 2010 For Dummies.*)

Developing SharePoint Pages

As cool as SharePoint sites are, no Web site is all that interesting without content. A SharePoint site is, in essence, a container for SharePoint pages — which are, in turn, containers for actual content (you know, the stuff people carry around in their brains). Thus developing pages gives you a place to put the content that gives your SharePoint sites a reason to exist.

Introducing the types of SharePoint pages

You can create and develop three primary types of SharePoint 2010 pages (in your browser, no less!) — each with a distinct function:

- **Content page:** Also known as a *wiki page,* this is the Swiss Army knife of SharePoint pages. A content page provides not only a place to put content but also a kind of workshop for collaboration, development, and customization — multiple users can wield a full-featured text editor built right into the browser. A content page is easy to develop and is an extremely powerful and intuitive tool for collaborative authoring, data capture, and documentation.

  For example, if you're in the business of manufacturing consumer products, you might have a content page that allows customer service reps to capture common questions that users ask regarding your products. The page could be dynamically updated as the reps encounter new questions — no need to call in a programmer.

- **Web Part page:** This type of SharePoint page provides Web Part zones where you can drag and drop various Web Parts (reusable pieces of functionality) right onto your pages from the SharePoint Web Part gallery. Although a set of Web Parts comes standard with SharePoint, you can also custom-develop Web Parts to meet your specific business needs. Imagine developing a Web Part for your company that ventures forth to become an everyday tool for nearly all the users in your organization — on their own sites — and to get the tool, all they have to do is simply to drag and drop the Web Part right onto their pages. For example, you might have Web Parts that you have developed for your call center reps. When new Web Part pages are developed the Web Parts that are used by the call center can be added to the page. This lets a programmer package up Web functionality into a reusable component (Web Part) that can be reused on multiple pages.

✔ **Publishing page:** This type of SharePoint page is designed to serve two functions: managing content and managing the look and feel of the page. A publishing page lives in a document library that provides version control and the SharePoint workflow feature (see Chapter 8). It's designed for the management and distribution of content — the essence of publishing content to SharePoint.

Master pages, application pages, and site pages

Three more types of SharePoint 2010 pages give you indispensable ways to standardize the look and feel of a site, boss SharePoint around, and create more sites. Here's a quick look at each of these page types.

Master page

Use this special type of page to give a consistent look and feel to various components on your Web pages across the entire site. For example, imagine you're developing a Web site and you want to have the same navigation, header, and footer across every page on the site. You could put the same information at the top and bottom of every page — but it would require a lot of effort to keep every single page looking the same any time the information (or the layout) changed. A master page works essentially like a template — it's a single page whose design is used throughout a Web site to provide a consistent look, feel, and layout. The master page contains placeholders for other types of pages to be plugged in; as a developer, then the content page you're working on is all you need worry about — not the overall look and feel of the header, navigation, and footer. You can leave the look and feel to a user interface expert.

Application page

Use this type of page to administer the SharePoint environment. For example, when you go to the Site Settings page (by clicking Site Actions⇨Site Settings), the page you're actually viewing is called `settings.aspx` and it lives in the `_layouts` folder on the server (yes, there is an underscore before the name of the folder) as seen in the URL example:

```
http://ServerName/SiteName/_layouts/settings.aspx
```

These administrative pages are called *application pages.* If you want to take a peek at what application pages are available, you can browse to the actual folder that the _layouts virtual directory corresponds to on your SharePoint server; you can find it at the following location:

```
C:\Program Files\Common Files\Microsoft Shared\Web Server Extensions\14\
                template\layouts
```

The application pages that come with SharePoint are often more than an administrator will ever need. If an administrator does need specialized functionality it can be developed by creating a new application page. Developing application pages is beyond the scope of this book but realize that it can be done if it is required.

Site page

This is the typical page you'll be developing from the browser. A *site page* — essentially a home for the actual content that makes up a site — can come in any of three different flavors: a basic content page, a Web Part page, or a publishing page. Although the process of developing and customizing each of these page types with your Web browser is very consistent, you'll run into some important differences. To get a closer look at those (and their crucial details), read on — and behold the cosmic secrets of creating content pages, Web Part pages, and publishing pages.

Grasping page-creation basics

SharePoint pages can be created in a number of different ways, depending on the type of page you want to create. You explore the ways to create specific types of pages in the following sections, but here you find a few basics that apply no matter what type of page you need to make:

- ✔ **You can create all page types by clicking the Create button contained on the View All Site Content page.** To access the View All Site Content page, shown in Figure 4-3, select it from the Site Actions drop-down menu.

- ✔ **A SharePoint page is almost *too* easy to create if you're using the Site Actions⇨New Page button on any site.** Be careful: The default page that pops into existence when you click this button — as well as the document library where the page is saved — will depend entirely on how you've configured the site. For example, if you're working with a publishing site, then the button creates a publishing page automatically. If you're working with a team site, the button creates a content page automatically.

If you get stumped occasionally, don't worry: You have a number of ways to create pages — and to use tools such as SharePoint Designer, Visual Studio, and even the text-based command-line program known as PowerShell.

Figure 4-3:
The Create button is located at the top of the View All Site Content page.

Create button

Creating a content page

A content page, also known as a *wiki page,* is one of the most versatile pages on the SharePoint platform, and it's easy to develop, too. The Enterprise Wiki site (refer to the earlier table) is a site designed to contain and manage wiki pages. Follow these steps to get started:

1. **Create the content page using whichever method you prefer.**

   Here are the four primary ways to create a content page:

   * *Click the Site Actions button and choose New Page from the menu.*

     For publishing sites, this same behavior creates a publishing page by default.

   * *Create a link on your page by using double-bracket wiki syntax and then clicking the new link.* More about wiki syntax in a moment.

   * *Browse to the Site Pages document library and click the Add New Page link.*

   * *Choose Content Page from the Create dialog box.*

   When a content page is created, it's stored in the Site Pages library.

2. **If the Sites Pages library isn't already created, click Create in the dialog box that appears and asks for permission to create the Site Pages library, along with a Site Assets library.**

   When you create a new content page, you're automatically presented with the page in Edit mode.

3. **With the page in Edit mode, you're free to add content as desired.**

   The Ribbon and wiki syntax are the two ways you can add content to a page, as I explain in a moment. Note that wiki syntax is still just adding content to the page. Just like when you are typing text in Microsoft Word you will be typing text in the page in edit mode. The actual text that you type is the content for the page. When you type a special wiki syntax, such as `[[Ruby Red Toothpaste]]`, SharePoint will take note of the special [[and]] characters and create the link page for you automatically as you will see in a moment.

4. **Save your page and exit edit mode.**

Click the Save & Close button located in the Ribbon to exit edit mode and return to viewing mode. In viewing mode you will see SharePoint magically convert the special wiki syntax characters to links.

If you leave your page and want to return to editing it, follow these instructions:

1. **Browse to the page you want to develop.**

2. **Click the Page tab in the SharePoint Ribbon.**

3. **Click the Edit button to switch the Ribbon into Edit mode, as shown in Figure 4-4.**

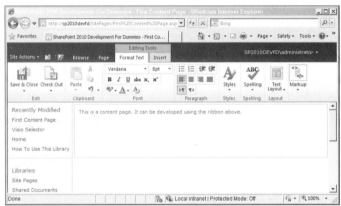

Figure 4-4:
Editing a content page through the browser.

Developing content pages with the Ribbon

The Ribbon is more than just a fancy way to run a Microsoft interface; it's also a powerful development tool. Here's what you need to know to start using the Ribbon for your development work:

✔ **The Ribbon features offered depend on the context of your current development.** For example, if you're developing a content page then you'll see tabs, menus, and sections of functionality geared toward content page development. If you're developing a publishing page you'll see items relevant to a publishing page.

✔ **The Ribbon offers two primary tabs for editing your content page.** The first is the Format Text tab which resembles a rich text editor such as Microsoft Word; the second is an Insert tab for inserting tables, pictures, videos, links, and Web Parts (as shown in Figure 4-5).

Figure 4-5:
The Insert
tab on the
SharePoint
Ribbon.

Creating and linking pages with wiki syntax

In addition to the SharePoint Ribbon, you can use a special Wiki syntax as you type content on the page. The wiki syntax can be used to create new pages of content (and link to existing ones). For example, if you're developing a page to document your toothpaste products and you want to create a link to another product mentioned on the current page, you enclose the words you want to link in double brackets. The double brackets [[and]] represent the wiki page you're creating; they tell SharePoint to use the enclosed text as a link to another page. If that page does not already exist, then the link appears underlined with a dashed gray line when you save the page you're working on. Not to worry: Clicking the link with the dashed gray line creates the page you're linking to — automatically — and opens the new page in Edit mode. Pretty slick.

As you might imagine if you've used well-known wikis (such as Wikipedia) on the Web, wiki functionality is a powerful mechanism for collaboration and documentation. For example, suppose you create a main page that has a number of references to other pages. No need to worry about creating these reference pages up front before you link; SharePoint shows those links as dashed gray underlines, ready for someone to click. If you want (say) to create a list of all your products on the main page, with links to the individual product pages (as shown in Figure 4-6), this automatic page creation helps you create that list quickly.

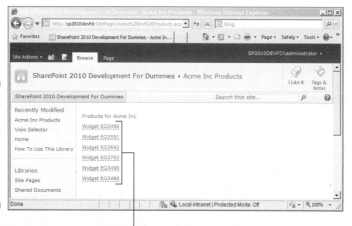

Figure 4-6:
A main wiki
page with
reference
links to
specific
products.

Dashed gray lines

You could then blast out an e-mail to the product groups, asking them to help fill in the content for all those new pages with their individual knowledge of the products. When the product groups' users come to the page, they see a link with a dashed gray line. When they click the link that corresponds to their product, SharePoint waves the automatic magic wand to create a new page in Edit mode, ready to receive the product information. As more and more people add their knowledge to the site, it continues to grow and bloom. The term often used to describe this functionality is *crowd-sourcing* because the site is gathering and capturing the knowledge of the crowd.

Table 4-2 outlines the dynamic linking functionality of a SharePoint 2010 content page.

Table 4-2	SharePoint 2010 Content Page Linking
Syntax	*Description*
`[[MyPage]]`	Creates a link to a page named MyPage in the same document library. If the page doesn't exist already, then a link appears with a dashed gray line. Clicking the link creates the page automatically.
`[[MyFolder/MyPage]]`	Creates a link to a page named `MyPage`, in a folder named `MyFolder`.
	Note that the folder must already exist; otherwise the page is created in Site Pages. (Instructions on how to enable folder creation follow this table.)
`[[List:Announcements/Welcome]]`	Creates a link to the item called Welcome which is contained in the Announcements list of the current site.
`[[File:Shared Documents/Folder1/Hello.docx]]`	Creates a link to a Word document named `Hello.docx` that is contained in the `Shared Documents` library in a folder named `Folder1`.
`[[My Title|MyPage]]`	Creates a link with the text `My Title` that points to the page titled `My Page`. The character in between is called a pipe.

By default, the New Folder option is disabled on the Ribbon for the Site Pages document library. Here's how to enable the New Folder button so that you can use the `[[MyFolder/MyPage]]` option in Table 4-2:

1. Click the Library tab.

The Library Settings page appears.

2. **Click the Library Settings button.**

    A dialog box appears, offering settings for the document library.

3. **Click Advanced Settings.**

    The Advanced settings dialog box appears.

4. **Next to Make New Folder Command Available, click Yes.**

    The Yes radio field is now shown as being selected with a black dot.

5. **Scroll to the bottom of the page and click OK to save the settings and enable the New Folder command on the Ribbon for the Site Pages document library.**

Adding Web Parts to a content page

Even though a special page, called a Web Part page, is set aside as a place to keep Web Parts, you can add them to a content page as well. A Web Part page contains special zones where Web Parts can be dragged and dropped with minimal effort. When you insert a Web Part into a content page, however, the Web Part lives right in the page instead of in the special Web Part zone. Think of a content page as a similar to a Word document but for the Web. You can enter edit mode and just start typing. You can insert images or tables or even Web Parts, but they are just inserted wherever the cursor happens to be at that time. Inserting a Web Part into a content page requires only two steps:

1. **Make sure you're in Edit mode and then select the Insert tab.**

    The Ribbon at the top of the page switches over to show the Insert commands.

2. **Click the Web Part button in the Ribbon.**

    The Web Part gallery appears.

3. **Select the Web Part you want to add to the page and click Add.**

    The Web Part is added to the page at the location of the cursor.

Dragging-and-dropping your way to a Web Part page

Web Part pages represent a versatile and powerful way to add functionality to a SharePoint site. Creating a Web Part page is slightly trickier than creating a content page; a Web Part page requires some decision-making about the layout of the Web Part *zones* that will contain your Web Parts. On a Web Part page, you can drag and drop your Web Parts between zones, depending on where you want them to be.

Follow these steps to create a Web Part page:

1. **Click Site Actions and then select the More Options button.**

   The Create dialog box appears.

2. **Select Page in the Filter By section.**

   The idea is to narrow down the list to Pages.

3. **Choose Web Part Page and then click the Create button.**

   Doing so launches the New Web Part Page dialog box.

4. **Give the page a name and then choose a layout.**

   As you click through the layouts, you see a preview of how the Web Part zones will be displayed.

5. **Choose the document library where the page will be stored.**

   If a document doesn't already exist, a link is provided to create one. (Check out *SharePoint 2010 For Dummies* for more about the ins and outs of document libraries.)

6. **Click Create to create your new Web Part page and save it to the document library you specified.**

After you create a Web Part page. you're ready to begin developing it (using, of course the Web Part Page template). Here's where you see its three signature qualities in action:

- ✔ A Web Part page is a page designed specifically to hold Web Parts.
- ✔ The Web Parts are added to the page in special sections called Web Part *zones.*
- ✔ The Web Part zones allow Web Parts to be dragged and dropped from the Web Part gallery or between zones.

For example, if you add the view of a SharePoint list to a Web Part zone and then later decide you want to move this Web Part to a different zone you simply drag it from the current zone and drop it in the new zone.

Keep in mind that you can add more than one Web Part to the same zone. When a zone contains more than one Web Part, you can drag and drop the Web Parts in order to reshuffle the order in which they are displayed.

To add Web Parts to a zone, follow these steps:

1. **Click the Add a Web Part link in a Web Part zone (as shown in Figure 4-7).**

   When you click Add a Web Part you're presented with the Web Part gallery. The Web Part gallery contains a vast range of Web Parts that are available out of the box. The Web Part gallery is shown in Figure 4-8.

Add a Web Part buttons

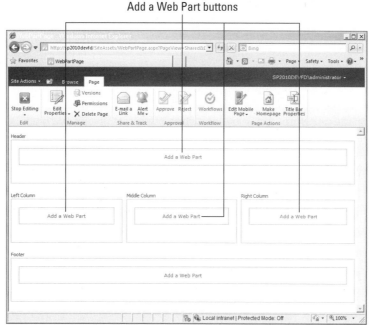

Figure 4-7:
A Web Part
page with
Web Part
zones.

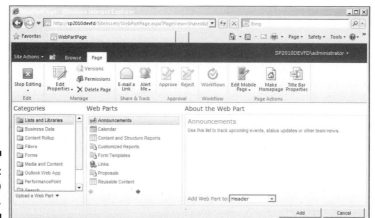

Figure 4-8:
The Web
Part gallery.

2. **Click a category on the left so see the available Web Parts in the middle column.**

If you're unsure what a Web Part does, see the description in the right column.

The Web Parts that are available in the Web Part gallery are determined by the features that have been activated for that particular site. As you activate and deactivate features the list of available Web Parts that

appear in the Web Part gallery will change. If you're looking for a particular Web Part and it is not showing up in the Web Part gallery, then your
first response should be to look at the features that are activated for the
site you're working in.

In addition, any custom Web Parts that have already been developed
and made available to the site will also show up in the Web Part gallery.
(For more about developing custom Web Parts, see Chapter 13.)

3. **Click Add to place the selected Web Part onto your page.**

4. **To begin configuring the Web Part, click the small arrow in the upper
   right corner of the Web Part and choose Edit Web Part.**

   The configuration screen for the particular Web Part opens on the right
   side of the screen and the Web Part can be configured. The properties
   that show up in the configuration window depend on the Web Part that
   is being configured but there are also some properties that are common
   to all Web Parts, such as settings that affect the appearance and layout
   of the Web Part on the Web Part page.

5. **To connect one Web Part to another, click the small drop-down menu
   in the upper right corner of the Web Part while the page is in Edit
   mode and choose Connections.**

   The connections available to the current Web Part will appear and can
   be configured. For example, you might use a filter Web Part to limit the
   list of available data in another Web Part. You would connect these Web
   Parts using the Connections menu.

One of the great things about SharePoint is that every page also contains a
sibling that is designed for a mobile device. If you click Site Actions⇨Site
Settings you'll see the mobile URL for the site in the right hand corner of the
screen. Often, however, you'll need to remove Web Parts that take up to much
screen space for a mobile display. To edit the Web Parts that show up on the
mobile page use the Edit Mobile Page button found on the Ribbon under the
Page tab as shown in Figure 4-9.

Figure 4-9:
The Edit
Mobile Page
button found
on the
Page tab.

Creating a publishing page

A publishing page is part of the publishing functionality of a SharePoint site. One of the key differences between a publishing page and the other page types is that a publishing page is designed to provide a separation of duties between the person entering the content and the person managing the look and feel of the page and site.

In order to develop a publishing page, you must be working with a site that has this feature activated. Here's what you need to know about activation:

- ✔ **If your site was created using the Publishing Site template,** then the feature is already activated for you.

- ✔ **If you're working with another type of site,** you can also use the feature, but it must be activated manually. To activate the feature click Site Actions➪Site Settings and navigate to the Manage Site Features link under the Site Actions section. Search through the available features and click Activate next to the SharePoint Server Publishing feature.

  In order to activate the SharePoint Server Publishing feature for a site it must also be activated for the parent site collection. Activate it by clicking Site Actions➪Site Settings and then clicking the Site Collection Features link under the Site Collection Administration section.

You can create a publishing page in either of the following ways:

- ✔ **Click Site Actions➪New Page.**
- ✔ **Choose Publishing Page from the Create dialog box.**

  The Create dialog box can be accessed by clicking Site Actions➪View All Site Settings and then clicking the Create button.

When a publishing page is created, SharePoint stores it automatically in the Pages document library — which is itself created automatically when the SharePoint Server Publishing feature is activated.

To develop a publishing page, you use the same techniques as a content page and Web Part page. You navigate to the page and then click the Edit button. The Ribbon then transforms to include functionality to develop the page. With a publishing page there is an additional tab in the Ribbon called Publish. The Publish tab provides functionality to begin the publishing process.

Also, when developing a publishing page, you need to know that a publishing page is associated with a content type. For now, here's what you need to know about content types and developing publishing pages:

✔ A SharePoint *content type* is a logical collection of metadata fields. For example, if you're a bookstore, you might have a content type called Book that includes metadata fields related to books. Example fields might include the name of the author, a picture of the book, the title of the book, a description of the book, and the price of the book. A designer might build a custom page layout for the book page. When a store employee needs to create a new Web page (which happens to be called a publishing page in SharePoint terms) they simply click the New button on the Ribbon of the library that will hold the page and then select the Book layout. The new page appears with the look and feel of a book page and they simply need to fill in the content. This forces every book page to look and feel the same since it is using the same content type and page layout. The business user, or person entering the content for the book, doesn't need to worry about the look and feel. They just need to worry about getting the right content on the page. This separation of duties in adding Web content is what makes SharePoint such a valuable platform. Building custom page layouts using SharePoint Designer is covered in Chapter 8.

✔ Because a publishing page is associated with a content type, you can also edit the content of the page by editing the content type fields directly. To view the content type fields, browse to the document library containing the page (usually the Pages document library), click the drop-down context menu for the page, and choose Edit Properties. The Properties dialog box loads, showing you all the content type fields (along with their associated content) for the page.

Developing Your Own Navigation

SharePoint navigation can be a bit overwhelming at first — but it boils down to a pair of primary onscreen zones:

✔ **Global navigation:** These navigation components appear across the top of the screen as a user browses around a particular site. Controls for global navigation usually span multiple sites, offering users the same navigation wherever they browse.

✔ **Local navigation:** These controls are for navigating the current site; usually you can find them arranged down the left side of the screen.

Controls for local navigation change depending on the site the user is currently browsing. Figure 4-10 shows the global and current navigation on a SharePoint application with four sites.

In the figure, the SharePoint 2010 Development For Dummies tab is the home tab. Here global navigation also includes a Company Blog site, a Human Resources site, and a Process Repository site. Notice that the Process

Repository site is active — you can tell because the tab for that site is highlighted. Controls for local navigation (down the left side of the screen) only show you around the currently selected Process Repository site. Whenever you click one of the global navigation tabs, the current navigation controls change to coincide with the appropriate site. (Think of it as one way SharePoint says to you, "You are here. These are the controls you need.")

Global navigation

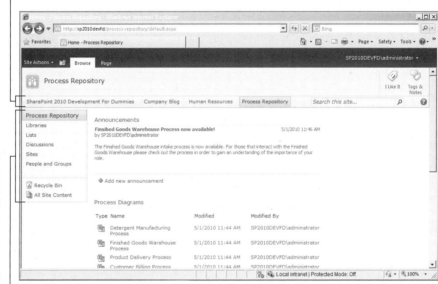

Figure 4-10:
Global and current navigation on a SharePoint site.

Local navigation

One of the great advantages of SharePoint — also one of the challenges — is that the global and current navigation tabs and links can be completely customized. Here how you can develop the navigation controls you offer users:

1. **Choose Site Actions⇨Site Settings⇨Look and Feel⇨Navigation.**

   The Navigation page appears.

2. **Add new headings and links to the global *and* current navigation settings using the buttons titled Add Heading and Add Link.**

3. **If needed, rearrange the order of the links by moving them up and down the list, using the up and down arrows (as shown in Figure 4-11).**

   Be aware of the site for which you're currently developing navigation. You can quickly determine the site for which you're developing navigation by looking at the *breadcrumb* (no, not the one next to your sandwich): At the top of the page is the path to where you are in the

SharePoint system; it has this Hansel-and-Gretel nickname because it leaves a trail — the site name, followed by an arrow, followed by Site Settings, followed by another arrow, and then Navigation Settings (as shown in Figure 4-12).

Up and down arrows

Figure 4-11:
Configuring
the
navigation
settings on a
SharePoint
site.

Figure 4-12:
The
breadcrumb
showing
the site
for which
the Site
Navigation
Settings
page
applies.

Breadcrumb path

SharePoint 2010 also provides navigation-based Web Parts that you can add to a page. Those Web Parts are listed under the Navigation category in the Web Part gallery. The process of adding a Web Part to a page depends on the type of page you are developing as was described in the previous sections. The Web Part gallery, however, is the same regardless of the type of page you are developing. The Web Part gallery shows a listing of all available Web Parts and allows you to select the one you want to add.

Wrangling Data on Your Pages

When you need to present data on your SharePoint pages, lists, libraries, and content types can help. These built-in features help you present different types of data, taking advantage of resources you may already have. Here's a quick introduction to each one:

- ✔ **Lists:** A list is more than just a place to arrange information vertically; to a developer, it's also a basic component that makes up the foundation of the SharePoint platform.

  The idea behind a SharePoint list is the same as for any other type of real-world list. In effect, it's a stack of items — specifically items of data. For example, a cook might have lists of recipes on 3x5 cards in the kitchen (yes, hard copy, even today — have to keep the sauce out of the computer, right?). Each 3x5 card might have designated places on it — always in the same place on each card — to put the recipe name, cooking time, cooking temperature, ingredients, and instructions. Those places-on-the-card become onscreen fields if you develop the same kind of list in SharePoint to capture recipes. Then, whenever you want to enter a new recipe, you simply click the New button and type the data into the appropriate fields. The SharePoint list captures all the information and stores it electronically. Each recipe becomes an item in the list.

- ✔ **Content types:** The whole collection of recipe fields might need to be used on multiple sites and could thus be all bundled together and saved in what is known as a content type. In this example the content type could be called a recipe content type. When a new site has a requirement to track recipes you would simply add the recipe content type instead of going back and entering all of the fields that are required for a recipe into the new list on the new site.

- ✔ **Libraries:** A library is, after all, a special type of list designed to hold files with equally specialized purposes (such as Web pages, documents, reports, forms, pictures, and slides). When people talk about a library they often forget to talk about how it is just a special list. Since a library is a list with the ability to store documents it is common for people to talk about it as only a place to store documents. A library can store documents but it can also store metadata fields associated with each document.

Knowing your list options

SharePoint 2010 comes with a collection of standard lists and libraries. Microsoft has already taken the time to develop these in order to make your life as a developer easier so you might as well use them. The following list introduces the standard SharePoint lists and provides brief descriptions:

✔ **Announcements:** This list is for brief news items, quick status checks, and other quick-and-informative stuff.

✔ **Calendar:** This calendar is strictly business — deadlines, meetings, scheduled events, and the like. A bonus: you can synchronize the information on this calendar with Microsoft Outlook or other Microsoft-friendly programs.

✔ **Circulations:** This list is for sending information around to team members via an email notification; the list includes confirmation stamps so members can indicate that they've seen what you wanted them to see. An example would be an important new company policy. You can use the Circulations list to track that everyone has read and accepted the policy. Note that in order to see this list template you must have the Group Work Lists feature activated.

✔ **Contacts:** If you're a regular Outlook user, you may have developed a list of contacts. If you haven't, here's your chance to list the people relevant to your team (such as partners, customers, or public officials). You can synchronize the SharePoint Contacts list with Microsoft Outlook or other programs that play nice with Microsoft products.

✔ **Custom List:** If you're trying to develop a list but none of the standard list types does what you have in mind, you can start from scratch with a blank list and drop in the views and columns you want.

✔ **Custom List in Data Sheet View:** Here's a familiar twist on the blank list: SharePoint shows it as a spreadsheet so you can set up a custom list as easily as you would in (say) Excel, specifying views and columns as needed. Note that this list type requires an ActiveX control for list datasheets; fortunately, Microsoft Office provides such a control. (Coincidence? I think not.)

✔ **Discussion Board:** If you're a seasoned netizen from the heyday of the newsgroup, this list will be a familiar place for online discussions. Naturally you'll want to keep the discussion businesslike, so this list type helps you manage those discussions (for example, you can require posts to be approved before everybody can see them).

✔ **External List:** Use this list type to create a list of data identified as an External Content Type. An External Content Type is a term used to describe groupings of data that live outside of SharePoint. An example might be data that lives in a backend system such as SAP.

✔ **Import Spreadsheet:** If you have data contained in an existing spreadsheet (created in Excel or another Microsoft-compatible program) that you want to use in SharePoint, you can import it into a list of this type. You get the same columns and data as the original spreadsheet.

✔ **Issue Tracking:** If you want to organize your project team's responses to a problem associated with (say) an important project, this is the type of list you use to set priorities, assign tasks, and keep track of progress toward resolving the issue.

✔ **Languages and Translation:** SharePoint offers a Translation Management workflow (see Chapter 8 for more about workflow) that helps assign translation tasks. This list type is for creating a list of the languages used in those tasks — and of designated translators for each language.

✔ **Links:** This list type helps you organize links. The user can consult a list of Web pages and similar online resources — and simply click to go to any of them.

✔ **Microsoft IME Dictionary List:** Create a Microsoft Input Method Editor (IME) dictionary list when you want to use data in a SharePoint list as a Microsoft IME dictionary. Microsoft IME is a system that allows you to enter characters, such as Japanese or Chinese, not found on your keyboard. When an application that supports these characters is running, a small virtual keyboard appears on your screen that allows you to enter the characters. The Microsoft IME Dictionary List allows you to store the various character values in SharePoint. Note that in order to see this list template you must have the Group Work Lists feature activated.

✔ **PerformancePoint Content List:** This list type is where you put the components of a PerformancePoint Dashboard — scorecards, filters, report views, and the like (see Chapter 10).

✔ **Project Tasks:** If you're a veteran of Microsoft Project 2010 (especially if have Project — or a compatible equivalent — running in your organization), this list type will be familiar. It's essentially a big to-do list organized as a Gantt chart (which you can, in fact, open with Project): A place to track team or individual progress on tasks and keep your eye on allocated resources and deadlines.

✔ **Status List:** This list type offers a big-picture perspective of a project's status. It's a place to display goals for (say) a project and show how close you are to reaching them.

✔ **Survey:** This list type is for gathering information, specifically by crowd-sourcing. Here's where you put a list of questions you want people to answer. A Survey list helps you formulate your questions and can summarize the responses you get back. The responses to the survey are stored in the list and can then be analyzed, charted, or exported.

✔ **Tasks:** This list type is essentially a to-do list for a team or individual.

Checking out the available libraries

When you need a way to organize files so that they're accessible via a SharePoint site, you find a selection prebuilt for the most common types of libraries in SharePoint 2010. Take a gander at these standard libraries and the brief descriptions of what they do:

✔ **Asset Library:** Here's where you store information assets other than documents — ready-to-use information in the form of images, audio files, video files — to make them available and regulate their usage.

✔ **Dashboards Library:** Libraries of this type contain Web Part pages, including those with status lists (Chapter 8), and dashboards created and for use with PerformancePoint Services (see Chapter 10).

✔ **Data Connection Library:** This library type is where you can put and share files that specify and describe external data connections. For example, you might want your users to be able to pull data from a data warehouse. Setting up a connection to the data warehouse and getting all of the server names, usernames, and connection information just right can be tedious. Using a Data Connection Library an administrator could set up the connections and store them in the library. The users would them just use the connection to the data warehouse whenever they wanted to pull data and analyze it.

✔ **Data Connections Library for PerformancePoint:** This library type is for storing information about the data connections that are specific to ODC (Office Data Connection), Universal Data Connection (UDC), and PerformancePoint. ODC files are used to store connection information for database connections, but UDC files can store connection information for nearly any type of connection and can be configured to store information about custom and proprietary systems as well. Keep in mind that a connection file is nothing more than a text file with some specific formatting that is used to connect to the external systems. These text files are in the format of eXtensible Markup Language (XML) which just means the text is formatted and organized in a specific syntax. PerformancePoint can then use these connections to pull in data for building dashboards, scorecards, KPIs, and graphs using Dashboard Designer as described in Chapter 10.

✔ **Document Library:** You run across — and create — a lot of these in SharePoint. Such libraries are for storing documents, organizing them in folders, controlling their versions, and regulating their usage with a check-in/check-out system.

✔ **Form Library:** Here's where you store and manage electronic versions of blank business forms for everyday documentation such as purchase orders and status reports. To create and maintain libraries of this type, you need a Microsoft-compatible XML editor. As it happens, Microsoft provides one — InfoPath. (Coincidence? Well, no, not really.) Keep in mind however that the form library is just a place to store the data that has been entered into the form. To build the actual form you will need to use InfoPath.

✔ **Picture Library:** This library type is for storing and sharing digital images. The difference between the Assets Library and the Picture Library can be subtle since they both store images. The key distinction lies in the name. The Picture Library is designed specifically to store pictures whereas the asset library is used to store images. If you think of a picture as something you take with a camera and an image as something like a logo or graphic that you would use in a Website the differences start to emerge. For example, the pictures in a Picture Library show a thumbnail image when they show up in searches whereas the images in an image library do not.

✔ **Record Library:** Here's where you store business records. There is nothing special on the technical level about a business record. It might be in the form of a Word document, but as for its importance on a business level, it is important. When you create a Record Library you are adding some functionality that allows SharePoint to create record management and retention schedules. This type of functionality is important when you want to make sure you are doing your due diligence in keeping track of your business records by letting SharePoint do the heavy lifting.

✔ **Report Library:** This library type is dedicated to Web pages and documents that keep track of performance (and other such metrics), progress toward business goals, and other information used in business intelligence. For more about reports check out Chapter 9 on Report Builder and Chapter 10 on Dashboard Designer.

✔ **Slide Library:** You can use this type of library to display Microsoft PowerPoint slides (or those created in compatible similar applications) to multiple viewers via the SharePoint system. You can also use this library type to find, organize, and reuse existing slides.

✔ **Translation Management Library:** Libraries of this type store materials that help with the creation and translation of documents in multiple languages. In addition, such libraries provide a workflow (see Chapter 8) for managing the processes and tasks of translation, help you control the versions of files, and help regulate usage of the stored materials with a check-in/check-out feature.

✔ **Wiki Page Library:** Libraries of this type have interconnected Web pages (containing content such as text or images and functionality in the form of Web Parts) that multiple users can edit easily.

The number and types of lists and libraries available to you depend on the edition of SharePoint you've installed. For example, if you're running SharePoint Server 2010 Enterprise Edition, then you have access to the full range of lists and libraries; if you're running SharePoint Foundation 2010, then you'll have only the lists and libraries that come with that edition.

Creating a list or library

Although lists and libraries work differently, the steps to create them are basically the same. You create a lot of lists and libraries in SharePoint, so you might want to bookmark these steps for easy reference.

When you're ready to create a list or library, follow these steps:

1. **Click Site Actions⇨View All Site Content.**

2. **Click the Create button near the top of the screen.**

3. **Click the List or Library filter to see all available lists or libraries.**

4. **Select a list or library template and then give the new list or library a name.**

5. **(Optional) Click More Options to provide a description and configure navigation.**

   Depending on what you are creating the More Options button provides additional configuration options specific to the list or library.

6. **Click the Create button to create the list or library.**

   If you have been reading through the chapter you might remember the process for creating a library earlier in the chapter was different. As with many things in SharePoint, there are always a number of ways to accomplish the same result.

Developing a list

One of the best ways to learn about list development is to start with a blank list. When you create a new list and choose Custom List, you'll be starting with the basic list. You can then add columns, views, bells, whistles, and gewgaws as needed.

Adding columns

To add new columns to the list, follow these steps:

1. **Browse to the new list and click the List tab.**

   Doing so displays the list-specific Ribbon. The List tab is part of the List Tools section of the Ribbon as shown in Figure 4-13.

Figure 4-13:
The List
development
Ribbon.

2. **Click the Create Column button to bring up the Create Column dialog box.**

3. **Configure the new column by giving it a name and choosing the type.**

   Notice how the configuration choices change as you select different column types. Each column has different types of configuration components. For example, a Choice column type requires you to enter the choices presented to the user.

4. **When you've configured the new column, click the OK button to add it to the list.**

Setting up a view

Viewing — and presenting selectively — the data that's part of a list is a common and vital aspect of list development. Some columns in a list might be important to users; others might be better left behind the scenes. To show just the needed information, you can develop a view that shows specific columns in a specific order.

To create a new view, follow these steps:

1. **Browse to the new list and click the List tab to display the list-specific Ribbon.**

   The List tab is part of the List Tools section of the Ribbon.

2. **Click the Create View button to begin the process.**

   You can save time by basing your new view on a standard view format or an existing list. Extending an existing view can be very powerful if you want to take advantage of previous development work you've done and simply modify it to fit a particular group.

3. **For this example, click Standard View to bring up the configuration screen for a new view and provide a name for the view.**

4. **Fill in the configuration details.**

   • You can choose the columns shown in the view, as well as the ordering of the columns across the screen.

   • You can also use this configuration screen to develop a look and feel for the data. For example, you can use the Group By configuration section to organize and group the data into functional chunks that make sense to the target audience. An example might be grouping a listing of recipes by the meals they correspond to (such as breakfast, lunch, and dinner) for an audience of short-order chefs.

5. **When you've configured the view, click OK to return to the list.**

   • If you selected to make your new view the default view, you see the list as it appears in the new view.

   • If you're using some other view as the default, then you can switch to your new view by clicking the drop-down menu under the Current View label on the List Ribbon.

Packaging groups of site columns with content types

Developing a custom set of columns (also known as *fields*) is a time-consuming process. It would be even more time-consuming if you had to repeat the process every time you wanted to use the same grouping of columns anywhere in the site. For example, suppose you put a lot of time into developing a recipe list and fine-tuning it to include all the columns required for a recipe. Then (sure enough), next week, another business group wants to be able to add recipes to an existing list that they use for cooking tips. Now, you *could* modify their current list of cooking tips to include every single column required for a recipe, but remember that old proverb about too many cooks spoiling the broth? Same deal here with columns: Adding the same new columns to every list that needs a certain grouping of columns would make those lists pretty convoluted and hard to use. A better option would be to make use of the same functionality you've already developed — a recipe content type: You could put that content type in the list of cooking tips as a column — so you add only one new type of content, instead of a big batch of columns.

A content type enables you to group columns and use the group throughout your site.

Here's the drill for creating a new content type and attaching it to a list:

1. **Click Site Actions⇨Site Settings to bring up the Site Settings page.**

2. **Click the Site Content Types link under the Galleries section.**

   The Site Content Types screen appears, showing all existing content types.

3. **Click the Create button to bring up the new Site Content Type screen, give the new content type a name (such as** Recipe**), and then fill in a description.**

4. **Choose a content type that you want your new content type to be (that is, inherit).**

   SharePoint divides content types into a hierarchy of *parent* types and their derivative *child* types. Each new content type inherits the fields of its parent content type — and then you add, remove, or modify fields for your new content type. Thus you can tweak and reuse content types instead of starting from scratch.

   For this example, choose the base content type which is Item. To do this, select the List Content Types group from the first drop-down and then choose Item from the Parent Content Type drop-down as shown in Figure 4-14.

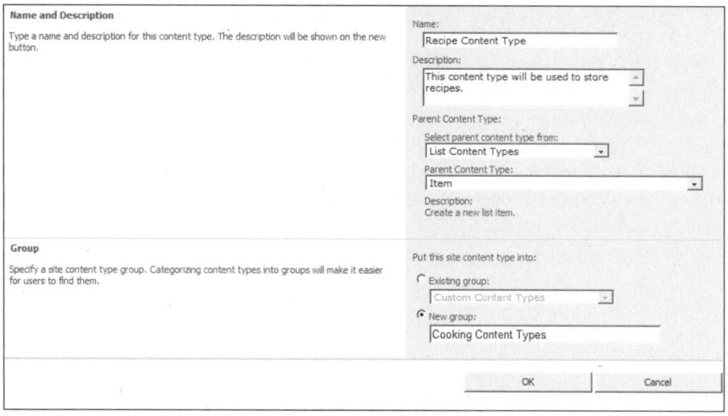

Figure 4-14:
The content
type screen
for the
new site.

5. **Choose the content type group to which you'll add your new content type.**

   You can choose from an existing group or create your own group. If you're developing (say) a number of recipe content types, then you could create a new grouping of content types called Cooking Content Types.

6. **Click OK to create your new content type.**

   When your new content type is freshly created, you're presented with the Content Type Configuration page — where you can behold your newly minted content type already selected. From here, you can continue to develop your content type by adding columns, workflows, and policies. A SharePoint policy is a feature that allows for the managing of things like document retention and auditing. Using the configuration screen, you can also change the name, description, and grouping of the content type, or delete it if it caves in like a soufflé.

7. **When you've finished developing your content type, you can click Site Actions⇨Site Settings and then click Site Content Types to return to the content type listing.**

   There you see your new content type named (for example) Recipe under the Cooking Content Type grouping.

8. **Browse back to the list to which you want to add your new content type; click the List tab and then click the List Settings button.**

9. **Under the Content Types section, select Add From Existing Site Content Types to display the Select Content Types screen.**

10. **Click the drop-down menu and choose the Cooking Content Types grouping; then click the Recipe content type and click the Add button.**

    Doing all that stuff adds the content type to the list, as shown in Figure 4-15.

11. Click OK to finalize your addition of the content type.

- Note that the ability to manage Content Types is disabled by default. You can enable that functionality on the list's Advanced Settings page.

- Now, when you click the Items tab and click the drop-down menu for New Item, you see the Recipe content type (as shown in Figure 4-16). Choosing this new content type adds a new recipe to the list.

Figure 4-15: Adding a custom content type to a list.

Figure 4-16: The Recipe content type is available from the New Item drop-down menu.

Developing a Custom Look and Feel

The total look and feel of a SharePoint site depends on style sheets, master pages, and themes. Developing style sheets (using SharePoint Designer) is covered in Chapter 8; for now, you can create a completely new look and feel for the entire site by changing the master page and theme. Read on.

Applying a theme to your site

Themes offer an easy way to manage the look and feel of your SharePoint site. Ready-made themes have consistent fonts and colors to change how a site looks. Think of a theme as a bundled up look-and-feel for a site. Having a range of themes available makes the entire look and feel of a site pretty easy to change.

Here's how to change a site's theme, step by step:

1. **Click Site Actions⇨Site Settings.**

   Doing so brings up the Settings page for the site.

2. **Under the Look and Feel section, click Site Theme.**

   The Site Theme page appears.

3. **Specify whether you want to have your site inherit its characteristics from the parent site or have a new theme.**

   • Click the different themes and view the color combinations.

   • You can choose to customize a theme by changing its colors and fonts. Be careful, however! Once you start changing an existing theme the changes are permanent for the site and its sub-sites. If you want to upload or create a new theme you can do so in the Themes gallery which can be accessed on the Site Settings page of the Site Collection.

4. **Click the Preview button to see how the newly developed theme will appear in your site.**

5. **To accept the new theme, click the Apply button.**

Importing an Office theme into SharePoint

Often an organization already has a Microsoft Office theme it's using for PowerPoint presentations and as an "official" look for the Office products its users stare at onscreen all day. Why toil to recreate the same theme just for the SharePoint environment? Microsoft has made Office themes easy to import right into the SharePoint environment.

You can export a theme from PowerPoint and then import it into SharePoint. First export your theme from PowerPoint by following these steps:

1. **Open the PowerPoint file that contains the theme.**

2. **Open up the Backstage View by clicking the File tab.**

   The Backstage View contains all the information about the PowerPoint file.

3. **Click the Save As button and then choose Office Theme from the Save As Type drop-down menu.**

4. **Provide a name for the theme and choose a save location that you'll remember such as your Desktop.**

5. **Then click the Save button to export your theme to a file with the** `.thmx` **extension.**

The preceding steps use PowerPoint 2010. If you're using the previous version of Office — that is, PowerPoint 2007 — you can export a theme by clicking the Office button and choosing Save As⇨Office Theme.

When you're ready to import the theme into SharePoint and apply it to your site, here's what to do:

1. **Open your SharePoint site and choose Site Actions⇨Site Settings.**

   Doing so brings up the Settings page.

2. **Click the Themes link located in the Galleries section.**

   The Themes gallery contains all the themes available on the SharePoint site.

3. **Click the Add New Item link at the bottom of the screen.**

   Doing so opens the Upload Document dialog box.

4. **Browse to the theme you saved from PowerPoint, select it, and then click OK.**

5. **Provide a name and description for the new theme and then click Save to upload your theme to the Theme gallery.**

   With your theme ensconced in the Theme gallery, you can apply it to an entire SharePoint site. (Savor the moment of sheer power.)

6. **Click Site Actions⇨Site Settings and then choose Site Theme under the Look and Feel section. Select your new theme from the list of themes and then choose Apply.**

   Your SharePoint site now has the same look and feel as the theme defined in your PowerPoint file. (Looks official as the dickens, doesn't it?)

Creating themes with Theme Builder

If you find themes more fun than painting rooms, here's the good news: Microsoft has created a tool you can use to develop your own Office themes. The tool is called Theme Builder; you can find it here:

```
http://connect.microsoft.com/ThemeBuilder
```

Any themes you whip up with Theme Builder you can then use with all Office applications — PowerPoint, Word, Excel, Outlook, the whole shebang — and import the same theme into SharePoint to maintain a consistent look and feel throughout the organization. (Wonder what's next — snappy uniforms?)

Changing the master page

A master page functions as a container for actual content pages: You design the master page once and then use it to hold components found on every page in the site, making the master page a natural tool for tinkering with look and feel. For example, a master page includes navigational components, as well as header and footer information, that appear in the same place on all pages. Because the content pages all use a single master page, all pages in the site look the same except for the content that appears on them. Figure 4-17 shows a visual overview of how a master page serves as a container for content pages.

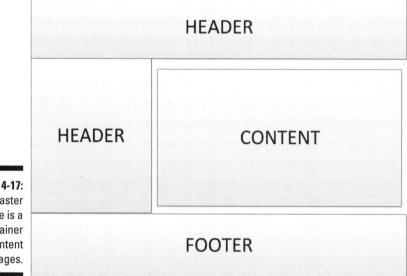

Figure 4-17:
A master
page is a
container
for content
pages.

If you're chomping at the bit to develop your own custom master page using SharePoint Designer, flip ahead to Chapter 8.

All master pages have the file extension of .master — and you can find them by clicking Site Actions⇨Site Settings and then looking in the Galleries section. The name of the gallery containing the master pages will either be Master Pages and Page Layouts or just Master Pages depending on whether the publishing feature is activated for the site. The reason for this is that page layouts are specific to the publishing feature and when it is activated the same gallery for master pages is used for the page layouts.

If the site you're working with has the SharePoint Server Publishing feature activated, you can browse to a page that allows you to change the master page. The following example demonstrates changing the master page on a publishing site:

1. **Click Site Actions⇨Site Settings.**

   The settings page for the site appears. Make sure that you are on the Site Settings page for the site collection and not a sub-site. You can check this by looking under the Site Collection Administration section of the Site Settings page. If you are on the Site Settings page for a sub-site then there will be a link under the Site Collection Administration section to take you to the Site Settings page for the site collection. If you are already on the Site Settings page for the site collection then you will have links for managing the site collection.

2. **Click the Master Page link under the Look and Feel section of the site.**

   The Site Master Page Settings page appears, as shown in Figure 4-18. Here are some points to keep in mind about this page:

   • If the link doesn't show up, then it's likely that the SharePoint Server Publishing feature hasn't been activated. (If that's the case, then you've gone about as far as these steps can take you until you activate Server Publishing.)

   • The Site Master Page Settings Page allows you to change the master page for the site as well as for the SharePoint system.

   • The site master page is used for all publishing pages — and for all forms and View pages within the site.

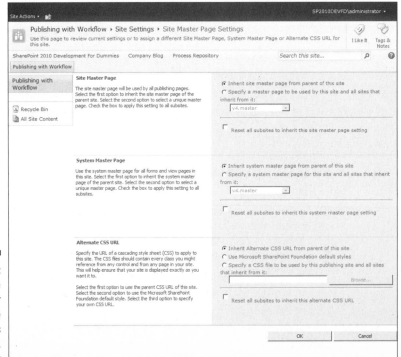

Figure 4-18:
The Site
Master
Page
Settings
page.

3. **Select a radio button to specify a master page, and then choose one of the available master pages (such as** `nightandday.master`**) from the drop-down menu.**

4. **Click OK to change the master page.**

   The new master page changes the look of the site (maybe even drastically — are you *sure* you want to use *those* colors?) but the content remains the same.

Reusing Your Development Efforts with Templates

Templates are an easy-to-use feature of SharePoint that are great for consistency: You can capture and reuse your development efforts as templates whether they're sites, pages, or lists.

Developing a site by adding Web Parts, pages, libraries, lists, themes, and content takes a lot of work. Saving a finished site as a template allows you to create a brand new site based on the one you've already developed. In addition, you can export the new template to a file and then upload the site-template file to a different SharePoint environment. Fortunately, the process of saving is much the same for a list, library, or site as a template. The difference lies in where you go to begin the process. For example, to save a site as a template you need to start on the Site Settings page for the site. To save a list or library as a template you need to start on the settings page for that particular list or library. The following sections walk you through the steps.

Saving a site as a template

To save a site as a template, follow these steps:

1. **Click Site Actions⇨Site Settings, and then click Site Actions⇨ Save Site As Template.**

   Note that this link only appears if the site is not a publishing site; the content on a publishing site cannot be saved as a template. The reason for this is that publishing sites rely on content types that might not be available in the site you are moving the template into.

2. **Provide a name for the template file and a name for the site template (this is what shows up in the Create dialog box when you create a new site based on this template).**

3. **Choose whether to include the actual content of the site or just the structure.**

4. **Click OK to create the site template.**

   When the site template is fully created, you see a dialog box that tells you the Web site has successfully been saved to the Solutions gallery — and that you can now create new sites based on this template.

   If you save a list as a template, then that template is stored in the List Template gallery. See "Saving lists and libraries as templates" at the end of this chapter for more details.

   Note that if you want to create new sites that use this template, first you must activate the new site template you just created. See the upcoming section, "Activating a site template," for details.

5. **To view all the solutions in the Solutions gallery (including the new site template you just created), click Site Actions⇨Site Settings, and then choose Galleries⇨Solutions.**

   The name you provided in the Filename field when you created the template is now shown in the Solutions gallery.

6. **Create a new site based on this site template by clicking Site Actions⇨New Site and then choosing your site template from the list.**

   Note that the name that shows up under the Create screen is the name you provided in the site template name field when you created the site template.

You can export a site template solution to a physical file by clicking the name in the Solutions gallery. Clicking the name pops up a dialog box to save the solution to a file with a .wsp extension. You can then import this file by uploading it to the Solutions gallery in another SharePoint environment.

The Save Site As Template feature doesn't save Publishing feature content (such as content types and page layouts) — thus it's not available if the SharePoint Server Publishing feature is activated for the site. In a test environment, you can check this by activating and deactivating the SharePoint Server Publishing feature — and checking to see which functionality is turned on and off. The Save Site As Template feature is a perfect example; it appears and disappears as the feature is activated and deactivated.

Activating a site template

It can be a little frustrating to *know* you've seen some SharePoint functionality before but wonder why it's not showing up when you need it. Well, that's actually a feature, not a bug: The dynamic nature of SharePoint functionality (such as the Save Site As Template link) means it appears and disappears in response to the features that are activated on the site. For example, turning off the SharePoint Server Publishing feature removes a number of links on the Settings page for the site.

If you've imported a site from a different environment, then you'll have to activate it before you can create a new site using the template. To activate the site-template solution, hover your mouse pointer over your new site-template solution, click the down arrow, and choose Activate from the drop-down menu. A dialog box appears and warns you that you should only activate features that you know are safe. Click the Activate button at the top of the dialog box.

Saving lists and libraries as templates

A list or library can also be saved as a template. List and library templates are stored in the List Template Gallery. To save a list or library as a template, simply click the link to save the template found in the Settings page of the list or library (it's under the Permissions and Management section of that page). Remember that not every library can be saved as a template. If you do not see the link under the Permissions and Management section of a library then it is likely that the library cannot be saved as a template. For example, the Site Pages library that is used by a team site to store wiki pages cannot be saved as a template. If you create a new library based on the Document Library template however and then go to the same Permissions and Management section of the library you will see the link to save as a template since this library has the capability to be saved as a template.

You can get to the Settings page of a list or library by browsing to the list or library you have in mind and then selecting the List or Library tab to bring up the Ribbon specific to that list or library. (You can find that tab under the List Tools or Library Tools primary tab, as shown in Figure 4-19.) When the list or library Ribbon appears, click the List Settings or Library Settings button, whichever one you have on-screen.

Figure 4-19:
The List and Library Ribbons.

Chapter 5

Taking Excel to a New Level with SharePoint

Once a new technology starts rolling, if you're not part of the steamroller, you're part of the road.

— Stewart Brand

The Microsoft Office Excel product has to be one of the most beloved — and most used — programs in data analysis history. As a consultant, I'm always amazed when I walk into a client's office and discover how vital Excel is to the organization. Excel provides an easy way for anyone to become a data analyst — but keeping the analysis consistent is difficult if everyone in an organization uses Excel in isolation.

Recognizing the importance (and familiarity) of Excel, Microsoft has taken the tool to a new level by integrating it with SharePoint. Using Excel and SharePoint in unison results in a powerful — and governable — solution that both the business and technology departments can embrace. (Okay, you guys, break it up. Back to work.)

This chapter explores Excel and the business magic you can perform with Excel Services — including developing and publishing Excel content to the SharePoint environment.

Providing a Home for Spreadsheets in SharePoint

The traditional place to save an Excel document is either on your local computer or a network drive. Because Excel documents are self contained files, your users can easily e-mail the files to other people. The problem however is that the context, and even data, of the original Excel document is lost as the document passes from person to person and mutates along the way. As the Excel document is e-mailed around, users save various versions on their local computer, which they then tweak. To capture their own versions of the document, users often modify the filename — resulting in long-as-your-arm filenames like this:

```
MyCompany fiscal 2012 forecast - v12_3 - Joe Reviewed-final- Bob
          Edited_02_06-2011_FINAL.xlsx
```

Imagine the team members — all sitting at their desks, looking at different versions of the forecast, and trying to discuss the results. Even in the best case (such as it is), confusion prevails — the team realizes the documents they're looking at are all different. The more likely result is that everyone agrees on what's in the document they're looking at — without realizing that everyone has a different understanding of the forecast details — and everyone moves confidently forward into (surprise!) confusion.

When spreadsheets live in a SharePoint environment, the Attack of the Mutant Spreadsheets is nipped in the bud. Every Excel spreadsheet gets an automatic gift: all the SharePoint document-management capabilities such as versioning, check-in/check-out, security, and workflow. Another huge advantage is the existence of only one document. To maintain control SharePoint allows people to check the document in and out for editing; SharePoint also saves versions and allows all the people with access to view the current version of the document at the same time in a read-only mode.

Moving Excel into your SharePoint site

Microsoft has integrated its Office products so tightly with SharePoint that you can create and store an Excel document in your SharePoint site without ever opening your Web browser. It's as close to seamless as saving gets.

As a developer implementing the capability to save a document to SharePoint, your first step is to set up a library to hold your Excel documents by following these steps:

1. **Click Site Actions⇨New Document Library to bring up the Create dialog box.**

2. **Provide a name and description and then decide whether you want the new library to show up under the local navigation for the site.**

3. **Decide if you want to turn on versioning for this library, and if you do, select the Yes radio button in the Document Version History area.**

    By default, versioning is disabled. You can imagine how much space in the database all of those different versions of documents would take up. Be sure to check with your administrators before you assume that versioning is in effect.

4. **Select Microsoft Excel Spreadsheet from the Document Template drop-down list and then click the Create button, as shown in Figure 5-1.**

    When the library is created, you can connect it to Office so you can easily save to the location right from your Office applications.

5. **Connect the library to Office by clicking the Connect To Office tab (on the Ribbon on the Library tab, as shown in Figure 5-2).**

    The library is now created and ready to hold Excel documents. In addition, the library is available right from the Office applications themselves, as I explain in the upcoming steps.

Choose to enable versioning here

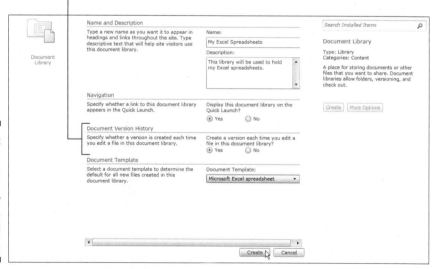

Figure 5-1:
The configuration screen of a new library to store Excel documents.

Figure 5-2:
The Connect
To Office
button on
the Ribbon
of the
Library tab.

Although you don't need to create documents in Excel and save them via SharePoint features in order to develop a site, knowing how the process works can help you understand what results your work produces and explain how users can work within a newly developed site. Follow these steps to create and save an Excel document in SharePoint:

1. **Fire up Excel and create a spreadsheet.**

2. **From within Excel click the File tab to enter the Backstage View.**

3. **Click the Save & Send tab and then the Save to SharePoint tab, as shown in Figure 5-3.**

   The library you set up in the previous exercise (and then connected to Office) shows up under the Locations section.

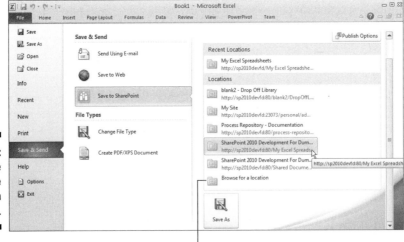

Figure 5-3:
The
Backstage
View in
Excel 2010.

Click to browse for a location

4. Under Locations, click the existing library.

In my example, the existing library is called My Excel Spreadsheets.

The Save As dialog box appears.

- Notice that saving to the library is very similar to the traditional process of saving to a folder on your local computer, as shown in Figure 5-4.

- If the library does not show up as an option, you can select Browse for a Location from the listing of libraries located under Locations (Figure 5-3) and enter the URL when saving the file.

5. Provide a name for the spreadsheet and then click the Save button.

Doing so saves the spreadsheet in the SharePoint library.

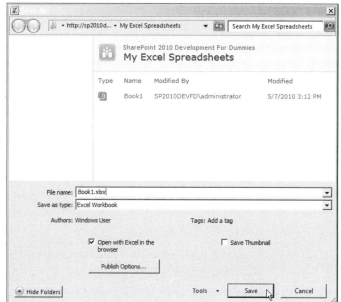

Figure 5-4:
Using the Save As dialog box to save a document to a SharePoint library.

If your local computer is running a server operating system such as Windows Server 2008 R2 (as opposed to a desktop operating system such as Windows 7), then you can't browse SharePoint sites from within Excel. If you try it, you receive an error message such as

```
Could not open <library name>
```

or

```
You can't open this location using this program. Please
              try a different location.
```

Before you can work in Excel from the server environment, you have to turn on the Desktop Experience feature. To do so, open Server Manager, click the Features tab, and then choose Add Features➪Desktop Experience.

Publishing only pieces of Excel

Although it's pretty cool to have entire Excel documents living in SharePoint, you can also publish only specific pieces of a spreadsheet. For example, suppose you have a very large spreadsheet, chock-full of sensitive information — that only a few people are allowed to view in entirety — but it also has a graph or summary page that should be shared with a larger group. You could always copy and paste the information for the larger group into a new spreadsheet and then save this new spreadsheet to a library with more access — but that's a lot of work. Excel Services offers a better way: Publish only specific pieces of the spreadsheet to a SharePoint library where the larger group can access it. You always have the option to publish the entire spreadsheet, specific sheets from the spreadsheet, or any item in the workbook to SharePoint.

To publish a specific piece of your Excel spreadsheet — say, a chart — to a SharePoint library, follow these steps:

1. **In Excel, open the spreadsheet that contains the chart you want to publish.**

2. **Click the File tab to enter the Backstage View.**

3. **Click the Save & Send tab and then the Publish Options button, in the upper right (refer to Figure 5-3).**

   The Publish Options button is also available on the Save dialog box, which appears after you click the Save As button.

4. **Choose Items In The Workbook from the drop-down menu.**

   You can also choose the entire workbook or specific sheets from the workbook.

5. **Select the chart that you want to publish to the SharePoint library and then click OK.**

6. **Click the Save As button launch the save dialog box.**

7. **Provide a name for the chart and then click Save.**

The chart is published to the SharePoint library and a browser window opens to show you the chart in the browser, using Excel Services (as shown in Figure 5-5).

Before you can create a new Excel document or edit an existing Excel document using the Web browser, you must have Office Web Apps installed in the SharePoint farm. For more about editing an Excel document in the browser, read on.

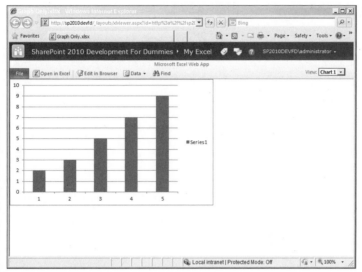

Figure 5-5:
A single chart from an Excel spreadsheet shown in the browser, using Excel Services.

Editing an Excel Spreadsheet from the Browser

Storing Excel documents in a SharePoint library and viewing them through the Web browser is great. But wouldn't it be nice if you could edit the Excel document right from the browser as well? (If you dream about such things, it's a hint that you might be a developer.) Microsoft has finally released a product to make this dream a reality — a product called Office Web Apps — and you can install it with SharePoint to provide in-browser editing.

An administrator must install Office Web Apps in the SharePoint environment. After installation, the Office Web Apps component shows up as a feature of a SharePoint site collection and must be activated for each site collection that uses it. For installation instructions, point your Web browser to the following URL:

`technet.microsoft.com/en-us/library/ee855124(office.14).aspx`

After the Office Web Apps product is installed on the SharePoint server, a magic Edit in Browser button is available in the Ribbon when you view an Excel spreadsheet in the Web browser, as shown in Figure 5-6.

Click to edit in the browser

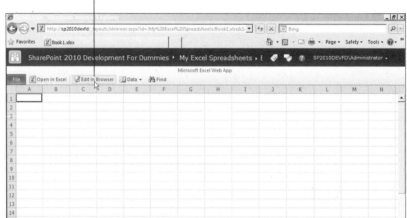

Figure 5-6: With the Office Web Apps, you can edit documents right from the browser.

When you click the Edit in Browser button, the Excel spreadsheet switches to Edit mode and allows you to make changes right from the browser. In Edit mode, an Excel Ribbon appears at the top of the screen, providing some of the functionality available in the standalone client application (as shown in Figure 5-7).

Another great feature of the Office Web Apps is that multiple people can edit the same document at the same time. As you're editing the document, your changes show up automatically on the other persons' screens — and their changes show up on your screen. Changes to the spreadsheet are processed in the order received.

At first glance, having multiple people edit the same document might seem like the royal road to confusion and conflict. Because the edits show up almost simultaneously, however, you can immediately see what the other people are doing — and communicate with them should you disagree with an edit. The benefit to the functionality is that no matter what happens, there is always just the one spreadsheet — so only one source of the truth about what's in it. I'm sure you've experienced a single spreadsheet e-mailed to various people who tweak it, save it, and then e-mail it on again. The number of slightly different spreadsheets grows exponentially as it's passed around. The process is a bit like taking gremlins on an outing to a water park — suddenly the critters are everywhere, and some are getting ugly. Keeping the single spreadsheet in a SharePoint library allows everyone to work on and view the same document with no need to e-mail the actual file.

You can see how many people are currently editing the document by viewing the label in the lower right-hand corner of the screen. You can see who is editing by clicking the small arrow in the lower right-hand corner of the screen next to the 2 People Editing label, as shown in Figure 5-8.

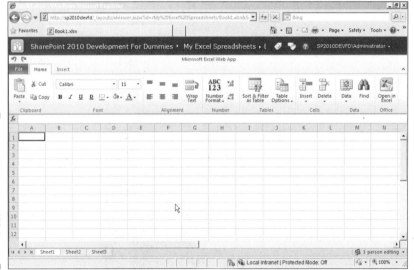

Figure 5-7:
The Excel Ribbon is available when editing a spreadsheet in your browser.

Figure 5-8:
Multiple people can edit the same Excel spreadsheet at the same time.

Developing Data-Analysis Applications with Excel

Microsoft Excel is one of the most powerful data-analysis applications in use today. Excel is easy to use, installed on a very large number of computers, and has a very large user base. Someone who works with numerical data but *hasn't* used Excel would be hard to find. In fact, many of the organizations I have worked with as a consultant use Excel for everything from project management to forecasting.

Microsoft is hip to all those uses of Excel, and so continues to beef up the features and functionality to put the power of data analysis — the essence of business intelligence — in the hands of normal users. Business analysts need no longer go to developers to get convenient access to data and perform the analysis that their jobs require. This shift in power goes by the name *self-serve business intelligence:* In effect, decision-makers can help themselves to what they want to know and then analyze it — anytime. Using SharePoint to share and communicate self-serve business information results in (all together, now!) truly collaborative business intelligence.

Flipping data around with PivotTables

For a quick analysis, the good ol' Excel PivotTable is one of the favorites. Entire books extol the power of the PivotTable in data analysis. The Excel PivotTable goes all the way back to the early '90s.

A PivotTable allows you to group and summarize data in an easy-to-read format. You can then re-group, or *pivot,* data you want to see arranged and summarized in a different way. For example, let's say you have sales data that you want to analyze. Here's a sweet example: Table 5-1 contains some fictional data for a company that sells honey-related products. The company has two sales people and two offices. As a manager, you want to be able to analyze the data and determine what exactly is going on. You might want to answer questions such as "Which salesperson is better at selling various products?" or "What products are the top sellers in each city?" As you analyze the data, you're likely to come up with additional questions on the spot — so you want the right tool for this *ad-hoc analysis* without having to ask a developer to build a new report. A simple Excel PivotTable provides an easy solution.

Table 5-1	Excel PivotTable Sample Data		
Office	*Sales Person*	*Product*	*Amount*
Seattle	Rosemarie	Gift Baskets	$1,254
San Francisco	Ken	Honey Straws	$845
San Francisco	Rosemarie	Honey Candies	$2,982
Seattle	Ken	Honey Straws	$1,312
Seattle	Rosemarie	Gift Baskets	$3,823
San Francisco	Rosemarie	Honey Straws	$459
Seattle	Rosemarie	Gift Baskets	$2,138
San Francisco	Ken	Gift Baskets	$983
San Francisco	Rosemarie	Honey Candies	$2,854

The following example walks through developing a simple PivotTable in Excel to analyze the data in Table 5-1:

1. **The first step in any analysis is getting the data into Excel.**

   In this simple example, you can just key in the data or use the prebuilt Excel document available on the *SharePoint 2010 Development For Dummies* Web site. (See the book's Introduction for details.)

   In a real-world scenario, you'd likely be importing the data from a database that has already captured the information. Then you'd use a section of the Data tab called Get External Data to import the data (and it can do so from a number of sources).

2. **With the data nicely tucked into Excel, click the Insert tab and then click the PivotTable button, as shown in Figure 5-9.**

   Here's what you need to know about selecting data to analyze:

   - If a cell within the data was selected when you clicked the PivotTable button, then Excel guesses that the selected section of data is the only stuff you want to analyze with the PivotTable.

   - If a cell outside the data was selected, then a dialog box appears and asks you to select the data you want to analyze.

     Make sure that your target data is selected and that the headers are included.

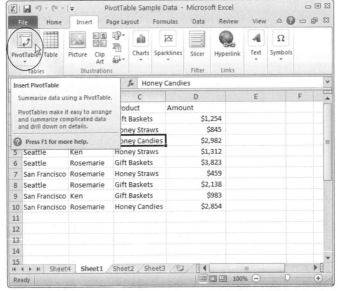

Figure 5-9:
The
PivotTable
button is
located on
the Insert
tab in the
Tables sec-
tion of the
Ribbon.

3. **Decide whether you want the PivotTable to show up in the same work-sheet as the data or a new worksheet; then click OK to generate the PivotTable.**

   For this example, I chose a new worksheet to make the PivotTable more easily visible.

   The newly generated PivotTable includes a graphic as a placeholder for the PivotTable and the PivotTable Field List on the right side, as shown in Figure 5-10. The Field List contains all the data fields from the sample data.

4. **To begin analyzing the data, simply drag the chosen fields and drop them in the Filter, Row, Column, and Values boxes.**

   The PivotTable updates automatically to show the results of the new computations. The Values box should contain a numeric value that will be summarized. In this example, we want to summarize the Amount field and pivot among the fields that hold the data for stores, sales persons, and products.

5. **Drag the Office field to the Columns box to create the range of offices across the top of the pivot.**

6. **Drag the Amount field to the Values box and the Sales Person and Product fields to the Rows box.**

   You can drag the fields between boxes to see a different grouping of the data. As you drop the field in the new box, the data instantly recalculates and you see the new result. If you have to reorder a grouping in the same column simply drag the fields to the order you'd like to see. Figure 5-11 shows an example analysis.

Placeholder graphic   PivotTable field list

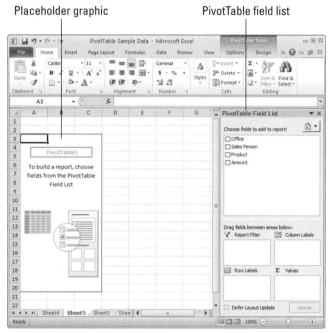

Figure 5-10:
A newly created Excel PivotTable.

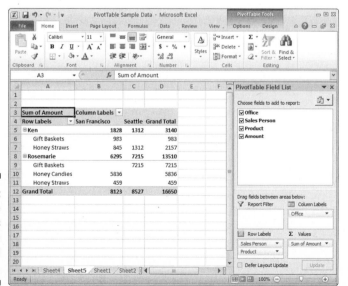

Figure 5-11:
A sample analysis using an Excel PivotTable.

Slicing up the data

If you've ever viewed a printed report and thought of a way you'd like to tweak the data to answer a new question, then you already have an idea of what PivotTables can do — namely, pivot the various data categories to get instant answers to your questions. PivotTables provide real value because you're actively analyzing the data instead of staring at a static or printed report and wondering how it would look if you could shuffle around some categories and come at the analysis from a different angle.

Taking the PivotTable a step further is a feature known as a Slicer. Imagine in the sample data that you've pivoted your data between Sales Person, Product, and Office but you still need tighter control over viewing the data. A Slicer lets you click the various pieces of data to filter them out instantly. It slices! It dices! It cuts through irrelevant data like butter!

But wait, there's more! The following example walks you through adding slicers to your PivotTable analysis (watch your step, please):

1. **With your PivotTable open in Excel, click the Options tab under the PivotTable Tools section of the Ribbon, as shown in Figure 5-12.**

   Note that to display the PivotTable Tools tab, you have to click to select any cell within the PivotTable.

Figure 5-12:
The PivotTable Tools Ribbon in Excel — now with Slicers!

2. **Click the Insert Slicer button and then select the columns you want to filter from the Column Selection dialog box.**

   The result is a button-like component for each column you selected. You can then click those buttons to slice out or filter the data. For example, if you click the Gift Baskets button on the Product slicer, the PivotTable instantly changes to show only Gift Baskets, as shown in Figure 5-13. You can click and unclick buttons to "slice out" or "slice in" data, narrowing or broadening it for your analysis.

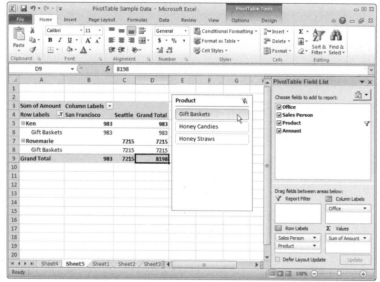

Figure 5-13:
Slicing the
PivotTable
using
Slicers.

You can select multiple slices of the data by holding down the Ctrl key on your keyboard and clicking the buttons in the Slicers to select or unselect as many as you need to.

Gorging on data with PowerPivot

The PivotTable has been good to data-analysis experts for years — but as the amount of data to analyze has exploded, they've needed an industrial-strength tool to analyze larger and larger sets of data. Microsoft has developed a new feature called PowerPivot in Excel 2010 that is specifically designed to handle the glut of data coming in from disparate sources.

The PowerPivot functionality is hefty enough that it requires separate installations. To get the PowerPivot tab in Excel 2010 you have to install the PowerPivot for Excel Add-In. Microsoft has provided detailed instructions on install this add-in at

```
msdn.microsoft.com/en-us/
          library/ee210599(SQL.105).aspx
```

In addition, to publish and work with PowerPivot in your SharePoint environment, you have to install PowerPivot For SharePoint, a separate product. Microsoft has provided detailed instructions here:

```
msdn.microsoft.com/en-us/
              library/ee210708(SQL.105).aspx
```

After the PowerPivot for Excel Add-In is installed, you get a new tab called PowerPivot on the Ribbon in Excel — and it contains a launch button, as shown in Figure 5-14. (That humongous mass of data had just better look out.)

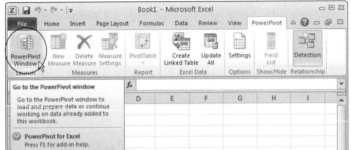

Figure 5-14: The PowerPivot tab in Excel 2010.

PowerPivot gives Excel the capability to import and analyze tens of millions, even hundreds of millions, of rows of data. PowerPoint data can come from all over the place, from disparate sources — including traditional databases, multi-dimension databases, files on your computer, data feeds, and reports. The different methods of importing data into PowerPivot include copy and paste, wizards, and queries — and even links to data that are already in your Excel spreadsheet.

The minute you see the data in the PowerPivot window, you can create relationships between the tables — and you're on your way to organizing data from disparate sources. With the data organized, you can create PivotTables and PivotCharts, just as you would in a typical Excel analysis.

Finally, when you're ready, you can share and collaborate on your analysis by uploading the Excel document to SharePoint (as described earlier in the chapter). SharePoint gives the *consumers* of your analysis (those who see and use it) a way to view and interact with the spreadsheet without ever having to leave their Web browsers.

With an Excel PivotTable, you can just key data into an Excel spreadsheet. PowerPivot, on the other hand, is designed to work with massive amounts of data. You could, of course, key a ton of rows into Excel to get a feel for the power of PowerPivot (finger cramps, anyone?). Instead, Microsoft has provided a free project on CodePlex that fills this specific need. To download the data, navigate to `powerpivotsampledata.codeplex.com` and then click the Downloads tab. Choose Other Available Downloads⇨Power Pivot Sample Data. The files will be downloaded in a `.zip` file called `IndustryBikeSales.zip`.

A PowerPivot analysis on the sample data provided by Microsoft is actually pretty straightforward. The first step in performing a dazzling analysis on vast amounts of data is getting the data into the PowerPivot tool; then you have to tell PowerPivot how to import the data. Here's the process, step by step:

1. **Open the PowerPivot window by clicking the PowerPivot tab and then clicking the PowerPivot Window button.**

2. **Click the Home tab, and in the Get External Data section of the Ribbon, choose From Database⇨From Access button, as shown in Figure 5-15.**

   The Table Import Wizard opens, ready to walk you through the process of importing data.

Figure 5-15:
Choosing
to import
data into
PowerPivot
from an
Access
database.

3. **Click the Browse button to browse to the Access database named** AW_CompanySales **and then click Open.**

   Note that the database is included in the PowerPivotSampleData project from CodePlex.

4. **Click the Next button to continue moving through the wizard.**

5. **Select the option labeled** *Select from a list of tables and views to choose the data to import* **and then click Next.**

6. **Select all the tables and views from the list by selecting the check box in the upper-left corner of the dialog box.**

7. **Click the Finish button to begin importing the data from the Access database into PowerPivot.**

   Importing data into PowerPivot takes time. Now's your chance to get some coffee and catch up on your mobile games.

8. **After the import operation has finished, click the Close button.**

   Notice the (enormous) amount of data available for analysis in Excel.

9. **Click the Total Sales tab to view the record count.**

Just this single sheet holds more than 1.3 million records (rows) and there are 24 columns — which equates to more than 33 million data points on this single spreadsheet tab (1.3 million times 24 columns).

10. **Create a PivotTable by clicking the PivotTable button and choosing a PivotTable and PivotChart combination.**

11. **Choose a single PivotTable for the example, choose to create the PivotTable in a new worksheet, and then click OK.**

    The PivotTable appears and the data is ready to be analyzed by dragging and dropping fields into the pivot boxes.

12. **Scroll down to the TotalSales table and click the plus sign to expand it and view the fields within the table.**

13. **Drag the SalesAmount field into the Values box to view a sum of all sales.**

14. **Expand the SalesTerritory table and drag the SalesTerritoryRegion into the Row Labels box.**

    Notice that the PivotTable instantly reshuffles and breaks out the total sales figure into regions.

15. **Expand the Quarter table and drag the Quarter field into the Column Label box.**

    Notice that the sales figures split again into quarterly figures, as shown in Figure 5-16. You can continue to analyze the data by dragging and dropping fields to instantly reshuffle the data.

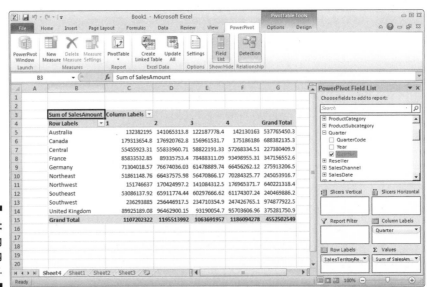

Figure 5-16:
Analyzing
data using
PowerPivot.

Often viewing the data one way leads to additional questions. These additional questions can be answered in real time by simply dragging the fields into different boxes to view the data in a different way that will answer a specific question.

16. **(Optional) Drag fields into the horizontal and vertical Slicer boxes to create Slicer buttons, as described in the earlier section "Flipping data around with PivotTables" in this chapter.**

You must have a cell in the PivotTable selected before you can view the tables, fields, and pivot boxes. If the task pane disappears, then you've probably clicked a cell outside the PivotTable. That's by design; after all, when you're working with other parts of your spreadsheet that are outside the PivotTable, you don't want the PivotTable view pane cluttering up the screen.

Analyzing OLAP cube data with Excel

Pulling data into Excel and then analyzing it using PivotTables is a great technique, but not the only possible approach by far. Often you run into a special type of data construct called an OnLine Analytical Processing (OLAP) cube that some development team has already built and tucked into a database. An OLAP cube works much like a PivotTable — but on a much larger scale. It's not uncommon for an OLAP cube to be pulling data from *billions* of data points. Prior to PowerPivot, even small organizations had to hire expensive developers to build OLAP data-analysis cubes because the Excel client application couldn't handle the huge scads of data by itself.

In a SharePoint environment, however, Excel can attack the data-overload problem on two fronts:

✔ You can connect Excel to PowerPivot, which extends the capabilities of Excel to hundreds of millions of rows of data.

✔ You can connect Excel to an OLAP cube running in a data center and analyze the data in much the way you would local data contained in Excel.

The technology that runs OLAP cubes is a component of Microsoft SQL Server; it's called SQL Server Analysis Services (SSAS). You can connect Excel to an SSAS cube, which provides a PivotTable interface for analysis.

For more information (and a detailed walk-through on using Excel to connect to, and analyze, an SSAS cube), check out *Microsoft Business Intelligence For Dummies* by yours truly.

Creating visualizations with Excel

The Excel PivotTable is a powerful tool for data analysis, but life just isn't the same without pictures. Building data visualizations is an important aspect of any analysis, and Excel makes the task a cinch.

A PivotChart is a chart that is based on a PivotTable. A PivotChart allows you to dynamically view the PivotTable using a number of different charting techniques. For example, you might have a PivotTable grouped just the way you want it, but you have to put the information in a nice pie chart or column chart. To add a chart based on your PivotTable, simply click the Options tab under the PivotTable Tools tab and then click the PivotChart button.

Excel comes with a set of ready-made charts; selecting one adds it to your spreadsheet automatically, with the PivotTable already designated as a data source. One of the nice things with the Excel PivotChart is that it updates automatically as you drag the fields between boxes in the PivotChart while performing an analysis. You might like the data in a certain grouping when you're analyzing the numbers in the PivotTable, but for the chart, you might want to see the data in a way that makes better sense as a chart. The PivotTable and PivotChart objects update dynamically in response to each step of your analysis.

Charts can be created on the basis of any data set, but here they're tightly integrated with the PivotTable functionality that data analysts find so useful. To create a chart based on data that isn't in a PivotTable, simply select the data and then click the Insert tab and choose a chart from the Chart section.

A chart is a powerful way to visualize data, but sometimes all you really need is a basic spreadsheet with rows and columns. Excel 2010 has implemented a hybrid technique — Sparklines. A *Sparkline* is simply a very small chart embedded directly into a cell of a spreadsheet to provide visual guidance to each row. For example, say you've developed a sales spreadsheet that lists all the stores and their respective sales. You might find it very helpful to have a small graphic in each row that shows the one-year sales average in relation to the number. The graphic would supplement the data with a small visualization, as shown in Figure 5-17.

The available Sparklines include a line chart, a column chart, and a win-loss chart. A *line chart* plots values along a line, a *column chart* plots values in groupings represented by columns, and a *win-loss* chart shows wins and losses over time by placing a data point either above the center line (win) or below the center line (loss). Figure 5-18 illustrates the different types of charts.

Sparklines

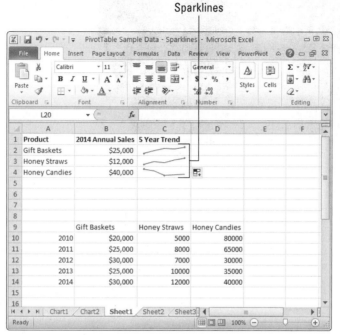

Figure 5-17:
Sparklines
supplement
spreadsheet
data by
providing a
small visu-
alization in
a cell in the
row.

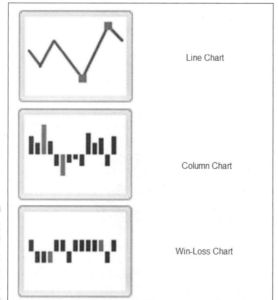

Figure 5-18:
Types of
Sparklines
available in
Excel 2010.

Revving Up SharePoint with Excel Services

SharePoint Server contains a feature called Excel Services — which in turn includes three powerful tools: Excel Calculation Services, Excel Web Access, and Excel Web Services.

SharePoint Server is a different edition from the free SharePoint Foundation. For more information about how SharePoint Server differs from SharePoint Foundation, check out Chapter 1.

Tallying results with Excel Calculation Services

The Excel Calculation Services (ECS) component of SharePoint Server introduces a powerful relationship between Excel and SharePoint. The ECS feature is the "engine" behind Excel calculations in the SharePoint environment: ECS loads an Excel document, performs the needed calculations, and then presents the results to the Web browser.

You can think of the ECS engine as providing Excel functionality for the rest of the Excel Services components. To divide up the processing power, the ECS component is generally run on a server that does not handle Web requests from users. This special server is called an application server because its only job is to process requests for the applications (such as Excel Calculation Services) running in the SharePoint farm. Here *farm* simply refers to the collection of all the servers that are required to run SharePoint (each one in its stall, mooing contentedly . . . never mind). For example, if you work at a large organization that has thousands of users, then SharePoint might need 10 different servers, each performing a specific duty. Figure 5-19 illustrates what ECS does for Excel in a SharePoint environment.

Embedding a spreadsheet with Excel Web Access

Excel Web Access provides the capability to embed an Excel spreadsheet in a SharePoint Web page. Then, when users browse to the SharePoint page, they see the Excel sheet as part of the page instead of hanging around as a standalone document. This distinction may seem subtle but the implications are enormous. A producer of Excel documents might build an analysis or reporting document that could made easily available to hordes of users; all the users would have to do is navigate to a designated SharePoint page using their Web browsers. They wouldn't have to use Excel (or even know that it was the tool used to build the analysis or report) to see the information they need. Quick in, quick out, no problem.

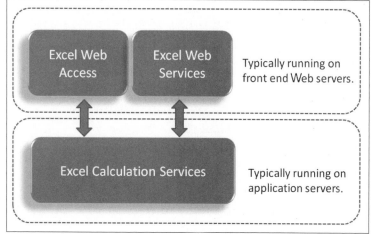

Figure 5-19: Excel Calculation Services powers Excel functionality in the SharePoint environment.

An Excel document can be embedded in a Web page using the Excel Web Access Web Part (for more about Web Parts, see Chapter 4). A Web Part can either be embedded directly into a page or it can be added to a Web Part zone in a Web Part page. The Web Part is located in the Web Part gallery under the Business Data category, as shown in Figure 5-20.

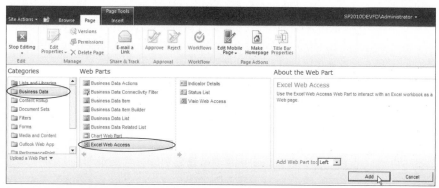

Figure 5-20: The Excel Web Access Web Part in the Web Part gallery.

The advantage of placing a Web Part in a Web Part zone on a Web Part page is that you can simply drag and drop Web Parts between zones to change the look and feel of the page.

When a Web Part is placed on a page directly, it takes up the entire area to which it was added — you can't move it to other parts of the page by dragging and dropping.

You can add the Excel Web Access Web Part directly to a page by following these steps:

1. **Browse to the page where you'd like to embed the Excel document.**

2. **Click the Page tab and then the Edit button to put the page in Edit mode.**

3. **Click the Insert tab and then the Web Part button.**

   The Web Part gallery appears.

4. **Under the Categories group, choose Business Data and then choose the Excel Web Access Web Part.**

5. **Click the Add button.**

   Doing so adds the Excel Web Access Web Part to the page.

6. **Click the link labeled** *Click here to open the tool pane.*

   Doing so gets you started configuring the Web Part by pointing it to a specific Excel document.

7. **In the configuration screen, click the ellipsis button next to the Workbook field and browse to an Excel document.**

   The Web Part Configuration dialog box is also where you can configure other look-and-feel aspects of the embedded Excel document. For example, you can choose the type of Excel toolbar that appears above the embedded spreadsheet. Those choices include a Full, Summary, or Navigation Only toolbar. In addition, you can choose to turn off the toolbar completely.

8. **Click the OK button to return to the page.**

   The Excel Web Access Web Part displays the Excel document that was configured in Steps 6 and 7.

9. **Click the Page tab to return to the page Ribbon; then click the Save button.**

   The saved and finished page appears as shown in Figure 5-21.

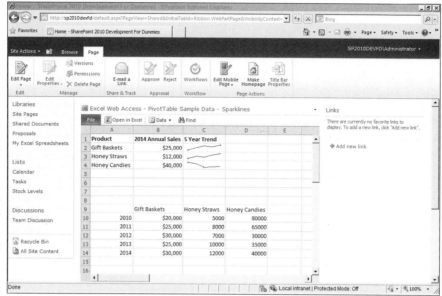

Figure 5-21:
An Excel
document
embedded
in a page.

Adding the Excel Web Access Web Part to a Web Part zone on a Web Part page is very similar to adding the Web Part directly to a page. The difference is that when you add the Web Part to a Web Part zone, you can simply drag the Web Part between zones. To access the Web Part gallery from a Web Part page, simply click the Add Web Part button located in the zone where you want to add the Web Part.

Excel Web Services

The Excel Web Services (EWS) component of SharePoint Excel Services consists of three different application-programming interfaces (APIs): User Defined Functions (UDFs), ECMAScript (JavaScript), and REST-based Web services.

An *application programming interface* (API) is a way to interact with a specific bundle of code that interacts with or manipulates an application. For example, the Excel Calculation Services (ECS) API consists of a bundle of code from Microsoft, and it enables developers to interact with the ECS engine through their own programming code.

User Defined Functions

A *user-defined function* is a function that lives within Excel and performs some special operation. Standard functions in Excel include SUM(), AVERAGE(), VLOOKUP(), and COUNT(). When you need something very specific, you can create your own function. When an Excel document with UDFs is uploaded to SharePoint, you can continue to use these UDFs through the Web services.

ECMAScript

ECMAScript is a scripting language standardized by an international non-profit standards organization known as Ecma International. ECMAScript has a number of different *dialects* (essentially versions of the language); the most prominent of these dialects are JavaScript and JScript.

In SharePoint Excel Web Services, the ECMAScript Object Model enables developers who work in one of the ECMAScripting dialects to use the Excel Calculation Services.

Working in SharePoint 2010 with an especially famous ECMAScript dialect — JavaScript — is covered further in Chapter 12.

RESTful Web services

A *Web service* is a piece of programming logic that lives on a server. Using the HyperText Transfer Protocol (HTTP), a Web service provides clients with access to the Web service's programming logic. A client in this context is another computer application that wishes to use the services of the Web service. When a Web service is built using a set of guidelines known as Representational State Transfer (REST), then the Web service is known as a REST-based Web service (or RESTful, though it never really gets a chance to snooze).

SharePoint Excel Services provides a rich set of REST-based Web services targeted at Excel spreadsheets. With Excel Services running, you can build your own applications using any platform and any programming language, and these applications can issue commands to Excel Services. Simply call into the REST-based Excel Web services, as shown in Figure 5-22.

The SharePoint 2010 REST-based Web services are not only new but powerful: You can use them to access the parts of an Excel spreadsheet with nothing more than a standard URL to go on. In essence, you can enter a URL into your Web browser and see the parts of a spreadsheet immediately.

Much of the power of a REST-based Web service lies in the simplicity of the architecture: Any programming language or programming environment that allows you to open an HTTP URL can be used to work with Excel if you're using SharePoint Excel Services. In a nutshell, you can boss around any Excel spreadsheets that live in SharePoint with nothing more than your Web browser.

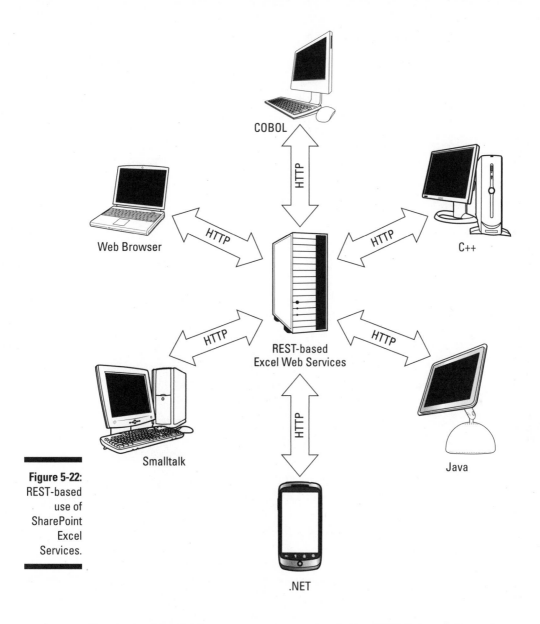

Figure 5-22:
REST-based
use of
SharePoint
Excel
Services.

Here's an example that assumes a very simple Excel 2010 spreadsheet, shown in Figure 5-23. The spreadsheet is stored in a default Shared Documents folder of a SharePoint 2010 site.

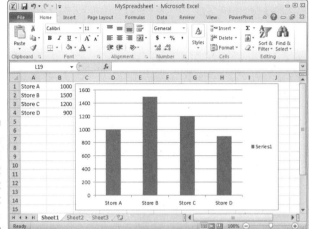

Figure 5-23:
Basic Excel
spreadsheet
in a default
SharePoint
library.

Because a REST-based Web service is all about the URL you enter into the browser, think of the URL as the tool for accessing the various portions of the Excel document. The basic format of a Web-service request looks like this:

```
servername/_vti_bin/ExcelRest.aspx/
          Shared Documents/My Spreadsheet.xlsx/
          Model/Charts('MyChart')
```

Actually the request has three parts:

- The first is the address to the Excel Services REST page:

  ```
  servername/_vti_bin/ExcelRest.aspx
  ```

- The second part is the path to the Excel document stored in the SharePoint site:

  ```
  /Shared Documents/My Spreadsheet.xlsx
  ```

- The third part is the path to the particular chunk of the spreadsheet you want to view; single quotes surround the name of the actual chart:

  ```
  /Model/Charts('MyChart')
  ```

You can change the name of a chart in Excel 2010 by clicking the chart to select it and then clicking the Properties button (located on the Layout tab under the Chart Tools main tab).

When you enter the full URL into your browser and press Enter, the chart in the Excel spreadsheet loads right into the browser, as shown in Figure 5-24.

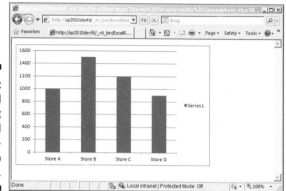

Figure 5-24:
An Excel
chart
viewed
using REST-
based Web
service.

When you're programming with the Excel Web services in mind, you often want to access a specific piece of data such as a chart or range. At other times, however, you might want simply to browse the available components of the Excel document that can be accessed via the URL. To browse through the available components of the spreadsheet, simply point your code to the /Model of the spreadsheet. For example, if you enter the following URL into the browser, you get a screen in which you can to browse through the components of the spreadsheet:

```
server/_vti_bin/ExcelRest.aspx/
        Shared Documents/My Spreadsheet.xlsx/Model
```

You can then click through the different components of the spreadsheet and take note of the URL used for each component.

When you're using the Web services, the default format of the data coming back to the browser is a form of XML called Atom. If you browse to a named range and see an error message, it's because Internet Explorer doesn't know how to read a single entry of the Atom format. If you look at the very last piece of the URL in your browser, you'll see that Atom is the format as noted by the syntax 'sformat=atom'. Change the Atom format to HTML by simply changing 'sformat=atom' to 'sformat=html' in the URL in your browser — and then the range will show up in the browser properly.

You can also specify a specific range of cells in your Excel document by specifying them in the Ranges function. For example, if you wanted to view cells A1 through B4, you enter /Model/Ranges('Sheet1!A1|B4') at the end of the URL in your browser.

More information about the Excel REST-based Web services can be found at the following URL:

```
msdn.microsoft.com/en-us/
        library/ee556413(office.14).aspx
```

Chapter 6

Collecting Information with InfoPath

Civilization advances by extending the number of important operations which we can perform without thinking about them.

— Alfred North Whitehead

Collecting data is a fundamental need of any organization. The technology behind data collection has gone through a number of different phases. The process of gathering data was relatively simple when paper forms ruled the world. The hard part came in actually doing something with the data after it was trapped on a piece of paper. The usual process was to hire an army of people to sift through the papers and file them. If a head honcho needed a report on the data, then the army would have to spend weeks or months going through every piece of paper to count and track the data. The (eventual) result was a report.

The digital revolution managed to fast-forward that process; people could enter their information into a digital format directly. Highly technical developers would have to spend considerable time creating the electronic forms — which were often clunky (as well as expensive) but much more efficient than paper forms.

InfoPath and SharePoint have changed the game again by tightly integrating form development and use. InfoPath gives the less technical folks an efficient way to develop forms — with no computer science degree required. In fact, you can whip up a dazzling form and upload it right into SharePoint for end users to fill out — all without writing a single line of code. Any user who knows the ropes of other Office products (such as Word or Excel) can work this kind of magic with InfoPath.

This chapter covers developing forms using InfoPath and integrating those forms with SharePoint using InfoPath Form Services.

Designing Dazzling Forms with InfoPath

InfoPath is a component of Microsoft Office designed to provide non-developers with a handy way to create forms for data capture. InfoPath is designed for the same user base as the other Office applications (such as Word, Excel, PowerPoint, and Outlook) — you know, the masses of non-developers who just want to get some everyday work done. In the same manner that Word is for documents, Excel for data analysis, PowerPoint for presentations, and Outlook for e-mail, InfoPath is designed to build electronic forms to capture data.

As with many software tools, InfoPath has had its difficulties in the past — mostly having to do with user confusion over how to use the product. A form is a very basic and specific kind of document, familiar to users after all the paper forms they had to fill out during the last century. They don't need to wonder about the nuances of technology when they're just filling out a form. They simply enter the data and "pay no attention to the man behind the curtain." *Designing* a form, on the other hand, is a bit more complex and requires some additional thought — you're trying to anticipate what the users need to make filling out the form routine and easy.

In its current incarnation, InfoPath has thus been divided into two different applications — a client application (InfoPath Filler) and a designing tool (InfoPath Designer).

- ✔ **InfoPath Filler** is designed for end users who simply need to fill out and submit a form.
- ✔ **InfoPath Designer** is more of an industrial-strength tool used to develop forms.

InfoPath Filler and InfoPath Designer can be found by clicking Start⇨ All Programs⇨Microsoft Office, as shown in Figure 6-1.

An InfoPath form developer isn't the same thing as a programmer. The intuitive InfoPath interface enables non-programmers to develop InfoPath forms. If you're comfortable working in Office products such as Word, Excel, PowerPoint, or Outlook, then you can add InfoPath form developer to your résumé with minimum hassle. The following sections walk you through the basics of designing InfoPath forms.

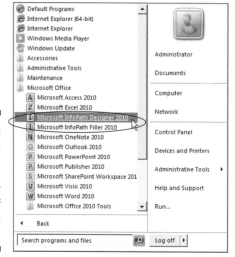

Figure 6-1: InfoPath Filler and InfoPath Designer are part of the Office grouping.

Starting with the InfoPath Ribbon

The InfoPath Ribbon is designed to provide an easy visual path to functionality; the idea is to streamline common tasks — in a way that's consistent throughout Office. Of course, if you're used to the older-style Office interface, then the Ribbon will take some getting used to. (If you've only made that change recently, maybe the "Menu or Ribbon?" sidebar can provide solace.)

The InfoPath Designer Ribbon is divided into five tabs, including the File tab that provides access to the Backstage View. Left to right, the tabs are Home, Insert, Page Design, Data, and Developer. Each tab provides a visual representation of specific set of commands. For example, the Home tab contains the commands you use most often as you develop InfoPath forms — they're for formatting text, adding controls, creating rules, and previewing the form, as shown in Figure 6-2.

Menu or Ribbon?

Having worked with the Ribbon for years, I like it. I was recently at the office of a client who still used the 2003 (pre-Ribbon) version of Office; going back to the old style was more painful than I could have imagined. When you get used to just looking for the command you want on a tab, you may never again want to click down through menu items to find it. Even if you're hunting for a feature you've never used before, clicking through the tabs on the Ribbon is simpler. Granted, the Ribbon might be a change (and an imposed one at that) but if you give it a chance, you may come to love it — or at least use it well.

The Developer tab is not shown by default in Office 2010 applications. If you do not see the Developer tab, you can activate it by navigating to the Options page located on the File (Backstage) view. Click the Customize Ribbon category and then select Developer in the list of main tabs.

Figure 6-2:
The
InfoPath
Designer
Ribbon
with the
Home tab
selected.

The Ribbon is also dynamic: The more screen real estate you have available, the more functionality shows up visually. You can view this behavior by dragging the InfoPath Designer window wider and narrower and watching the available commands change as the window width changes.

Making a form Web-capable

Not all InfoPath functionality is available when a form is uploaded to a SharePoint site. To ensure that your form is Web-capable, be sure to select Web Browser Form as the form type.

Here's how to set your form type:

1. **Click the File tab to enter the Backstage View.**

2. **Click the Info category.**

3. **Click the Form Options button.**

   The Form Options dialog box appears.

4. **Select Compatibility on the left and then choose Web Browser Form from the Form Type drop-down list, as shown in Figure 6-3.**

   Note that if you are developing a SharePoint List form, you won't be able to change the form type.

5. **Click OK.**

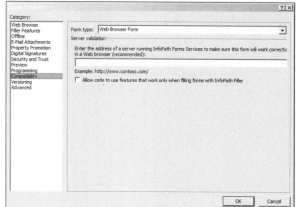

Figure 6-3:
Be sure to
set the form
as Web-
compatible
if you plan
to use it on
the Web.

Designing a form's look and feel

Page layouts provide a quick way to give the overall page of the form a consistent look. After you have the overall page designed, you can add tables to the page — and then add controls to the tables.

Here's an example that outlines the process of creating a simple form:

1. **Start with a blank form by choosing File⇨New⇨Blank Form and then click the Design This Form button.**

   The form opens in Design view. Notice that the default blank form already has a place to enter a title and insert a table, as shown in Figure 6-4. (This layout is the same as the Title Only page layout you find on the Page Layout Templates drop-down button located on the Page Design tab.)

2. **Select the entire page layout by clicking the small box in the upper-left corner of the page layout.**

   If the selection box isn't showing up, click somewhere in the page layout to get the selection box to appear.

3. **With the default page layout selected, press the Delete key on your keyboard to delete the default layout.**

4. **Click the Page Layout Templates drop-down button (located on the Page Design tab) and choose your desired template, such as the Color Bar page layout, as shown in Figure 6-5.**

5. **Choose a theme for the page layout by clicking a color theme from the Themes section of the Ribbon.**

   The Themes section also appears on the Page Design tab. You can expand the view to show all available themes by clicking the small arrow in the lower-right corner of the Themes section.

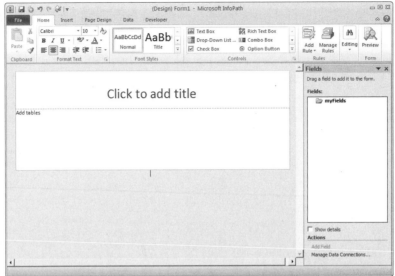

Figure 6-4:
A new
InfoPath
form using
the Blank
template.

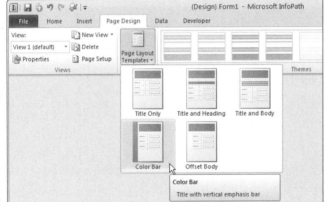

Figure 6-5:
Choosing
the Color
Bar page
layout for
the form.

6. **Type in a title for the form and then click the Add Tables section to move the cursor to the Tables section.**

7. **Click the Insert tab and then choose a table to insert into the form.**

- In this example, I chose Four Column with Emphasis 1 as the layout for my table.

- You can also choose to insert a Custom Table and define the exact number of rows and columns the table contains.

- With the page layout and table in place, you're ready to add controls to the form.

8. **From the Controls section of the Ribbon (on the Home tab), drag the controls you want over to the form and drop them where you want them.**

   When you have the controls arranged the way you want, you've designed your form.

InfoPath has an impressive arsenal of controls available for form design; Table 6-1 provides a handy list. Note, however, that not all controls are Web capable, which means the controls won't work in a form embedded on a Web page. Only Web-capable forms work when filling out a form using the browser. Controls that are not web capable must be filled out using the InfoPath Filler application that is installed and runs locally on a desktop or laptop computer.

Table 6-1	InfoPath Controls		
Control	*Description*	*Type*	*Web-capable?*
Text Box	Captures a single line of text.	Input	Yes
Rich Text Box	Captures *rich text* (that is, formatted text) with its formatting intact, including such features as bold, italics, underlining, font size, colors, bullet points, and so on.	Input	Yes
Drop-Down List Box	Provides a drop-down list of items so a user can select a single item from the list. Users cannot type in their own values (as is the case for the similar Combo Box control).	Input	Yes
Combo Box	Provides a drop-down list of items so a user can select a single item or type in an item.	Input	Yes
Check Box	Provides a box that can be checked or unchecked to toggle a command.	Input	Yes
Option Button	Groups options to allow selection of only a single option at a time.	Input	Yes
Date Picker	Provides a small calendar that's used to select a specific date.	Input	Yes

(continued)

Table 6-1 *(continued)*

Control	Description	Type	Web-capable?
Date and Time Picker	Provides a small calendar and a time-entry box, used to select a specific date and time.	Input	Yes
Multi-Selection List Box	A grouping of Check Box controls to allow users a choice among multiple boxes in a single control.	Input	Yes
List Box	Presents a list of items in a list so the user can select multiple items by holding down the Control key and clicking items.	Input	Yes
Bulleted List	Used to enter a list of repeating data in a bulleted format.	Input	Yes
Numbered List	Used to enter a list of repeating data in a numbered format.	Input	Yes
Plain List	Used to enter a list of data in a plain format without bullets or numbers.	Input	Yes
Person/ Group Picker	A control that allows users to pick a person or group from the directory.	Input	Yes
External Item Picker	An *external item* is a component of Business Connectivity Services (BCS) in SharePoint 2010. Using this control, users can select items that BCS makes available in Line Of Business (LOB) applications.	Input	Yes
Button	An onscreen control that acts like a pushed button when clicked, providing users a familiar way to make selections and launch commands.	Object	Yes
Picture Button	A Button control that uses a picture instead of a standard button as the place for users to click.	Object	Yes
Calculated Value	A field that can use values from multiple fields and/or built-in formulas to create a calculated value.	Object	Yes

Control	Description	Type	Web-capable?
Vertical Label	A label displayed vertically on the form instead of horizontally.	Object	No
File Attachment	Allows the attachment of a file to the form.	Object	Yes
Picture	Allows a picture to be inserted into a form as a link or embedded in the form itself. A user can insert a picture set, or the form designer can set the control as read-only to display a picture.	Object	Yes
Ink Picture	A control designed for Tablet PC users. The person filling out the form can draw on the control, using the virtual ink associated with tablet computing.	Object	No
Hyperlink	Accepts the insertion of a hyperlink into the form. Can allow users to insert links or can be set to read-only (only the form developer can insert links).	Object	Yes
Signature Line	Provides a place to sign the form digitally. Users do so by clicking this control and then signing the form electronically (by uploading a signature file or typing a name).	Object	No
Section	Used to group related controls in a designated area of the form.	Container	Yes
Optional Section	A Section that offers more options and is hidden by default; users can click a link to open the Section and display its controls. Useful when you want to provide more options for users but still save space on the form.	Container	Yes

(continued)

Table 6-1 *(continued)*

Control	Description	Type	Web-capable?
Repeating Table	A Repeating Table allows users to add rows to the table dynamically. In an invoicing form, for example, the number of rows is not predetermined, so a Repeating Table can accommodate as many rows as the table needs.	Container	
Scrolling Region	Provides a fixed range of screen space that includes scroll bars if the data size exceeds the size of the Region. For example, an invoicing form could provide a Repeating Table inside a Scrolling Region to maintain the overall size of the form within a specified limit.	Container	
Horizontal Region	A Region that reaches across the screen and can wrap as the window is resized. For example, you might have a First Name field and a Last Name field next to each other and each within its own horizontal region. If the window width is narrowed, the Horizontal Regions wrap so that they stack, one on top of the other, which moves the Last Name field down below the First Name field.	Container	
Repeating Recursive Section	Similar to a Repeating Section, this control adds new Sections as rows at the bottom of the stack — even within newly-added Sections. The result is a hierarchy of Sections.	Container	
Horizontal Repeating Table	Similar to a Repeating Table but allows additional columns to be added instead of rows.	Container	

Control	Description	Type	Web-capable?
Master/Detail	Links controls so that one control shows the details on another. For example, the Master control might show a single customer and the Detail control might show all the orders that customer has completed.	Container	
Choice Group	Allows users to select a Section to display. For example, you might have an Address Section for the United States, Canada, and Mexico. The default section might be the U.S. Address field. Users who live in Canada or Mexico could hover the mouse pointer over this Section and choose to replace it with a Canada Address or Mexico Address section.	Container	
Repeating Choice Group	Similar to a Choice Group, except it allows users to insert multiple Sections. For example, if a user has an address in the U.S. and Mexico they might fill out the U.S. address and then choose to insert an address in Mexico as well.	Container	
Choice Section	A Section added to a Choice Group or Repeating Choice Group that enables the user to choose an option within the group.	Container	

Making forms smarter using rules and views

One of the powerful things about InfoPath is that a form developer can create extensive functionality without having to do advanced programming. Two InfoPath features that make this boon possible are rules and views.

A *rule* is simply a piece of logic that you set up in InfoPath. For example, you might have a rule that tells the form to do something specific when a user fills out a text box or clicks a button. Rules include such functionality as data validation, conditional formatting, and actions. If you've ever used rules in Office applications such as Outlook (say, to automatically send an e-mail message to a folder if the message meets certain criteria), then you're already familiar with how InfoPath rules work.

You can find the rules commands on the Home tab in (logically enough) the Rules section. The following steps walk you through the basics of setting up a rule in an InfoPath form:

1. **Select a control.**

   Because a rule must be associated with a control, you must have a control selected before you can add a rule.

2. **Click the Add New Rule button on the Home tab of the Ribbon.**

   The rules and actions that are available depend on the control you select. For example, if you select a button and then click the Add Rule button in the Ribbon, only one rule is available: Perform an action when the button is clicked. If (on the other hand) you select a text box and then click the Add Rule button, you see various rules and actions associated with a text box, as shown in Figure 6-6.

3. **Choose an action.**

   A dialog box pops up to guide you through the logic of setting up the rule. After you set up the rule, when InfoPath encounters a rule in the form, InfoPath performs the action associated with that rule.

An InfoPath view is another feature at your disposal. You can think of a form as a collection of fields. A view is simply a way of displaying the available fields. For example, you might have a set of fields for an address form. The fields might include `FirstName`, `LastName`, `Address1`, `Address2`, `City`, `State`, and `ZipCode`. The first view of these fields might include a text box for each field so the user can input a name and address. The next view, however, might be a confirmation view of the same fields, showing them as read-only. The confirmation view might also contain a Back button (so the user can go back to the input view if a change is required) or a Submit button (to submit the data if everything looks correct). In "Building an address submission form" later in this chapter, you find steps that walk you through the creation of an example form, which includes views. Check out that section for more details about how views work.

Figure 6-6:
The rules
associated
with the
Text Box
control.

Making forms communicate with data connections

A form is just a presentation mechanism for collecting data. The data collected from the user needs to be submitted and stored.

A form might also need to query for data to present information to the user. For example, a user might need to choose a product from a list that resides in a database. The form must query the database and present the list of products.

After the user fills in the form, the information goes to a storage mechanism, usually a logical container such as a SharePoint list.

InfoPath has a number of different data connection types available. A form can query data from the following locations:

- ✔ SOAP- or REST-based Web Service (see Chapter 12)
- ✔ SharePoint List or Library (see Chapter 4)
- ✔ SQL Server (the Microsoft database product)
- ✔ XML File (a text file based on the eXtensible Markup Language formatting rules)

An InfoPath form can submit data to the following locations:

- ✔ Web Service
- ✔ SharePoint List or Library
- ✔ E-mail (Sends the form data in an e-mail message.)
- ✔ Hosting environment such as an ASPX page or a Web server

You might wonder why you cannot submit data to a database. This is by design. Every database should have the ability to present Web services for interaction. This conforms to a way of structuring system interaction known as Service Oriented Architecture (SOA). When you're working with SOA, everything you might want to do as a developer — such as receive or submit data to a database — should be available as a service. This middle layer of services is best practice when working in complex computing environments.

The commands that control data connections are located on the Data tab, as shown in Figure 6-7. The Get External Data section is used for querying data and presenting it in the form. An example would be pulling a list of customer names from a SharePoint list. The Submit Form section of the Ribbon is used for submitting the information collected in the form.

Figure 6-7:
Set up
your data
connections
on the
Data tab.

There is a difference between submitting a form to a SharePoint Form Library and submitting the data itself to a SharePoint list. When you set up a form to be submitted to a library, you're storing the form data in a file with the extension .xml in the library. When you submit the data to a list, the InfoPath form simply acts as a user interface for the list. The actual data is stored in the SharePoint list and the form is just a mechanism for getting the data into the list.

Understanding form templates

When you develop a form in InfoPath Designer, you're actually developing a form template. The template file has an .xsn extension and contains all the controls, rules, views, and data connections that make up the form. When users open the form and fill in the data, they're actually opening an instance of the form *template* — that is, the .xsn file.

The actual data that's collected in the form can be submitted to different data connections — in particular, libraries or lists in SharePoint, which are two very different destinations — because of the difference between an InfoPath form template and the actual data that's generated:

✔ If the form submits its data to a SharePoint library, the result is a file with an extension of .xml — containing the data that the user filled out using the form template.

 • When you fill out a form using InfoPath Filler and then save it, the result is an XML data file.

 • You can view the raw data by right-clicking the XML file and choosing to open it with the Notepad application.

 • If you submit the form to a SharePoint library, then this .xml file is the actual container for the data that's submitted.

✔ If the form submits its data to a SharePoint list, then the data ends up in the list as a new item. The form simply acts as the interface that's used to collect the information for the list. The form might also submit data to a Web service. The Web service might live in an environment such as SAP, in which case the InfoPath form template is just an interface for the Web service.

InfoPath is a pretty way to collect data but at some point you will want to report on the data collected. The reporting mechanisms you have available depend exclusively on where you're storing the collected data. For more about reporting, check out the discussion of Report Builder in Chapter 9.

Building an address submission form

The following example walks you through creating a simple address form using rules and views:

1. **Start by creating a blank form and then adding a table to the form with 8 rows and 2 columns.**

    You can add a custom table by clicking the Insert tab and then clicking the Custom Table button.

2. **Add a series of Text Box controls onto the form to set up fields for** FirstName, LastName, Address 1, Address2, City, State, **and** Zip Code, **and then add a Button control, as shown in Figure 6-8.**

    The Text Box and Button controls are located on the Ribbon in the Controls section of the Home tab. To add a control to the form, simply click it in the Ribbon, and it appears on the design surface wherever the cursor was located. You can also move an existing control to a different location by clicking and dragging it.

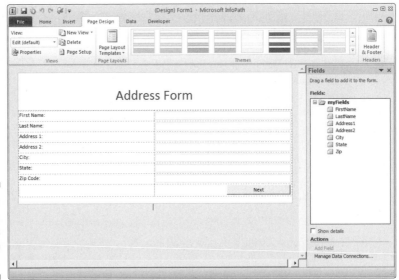

Figure 6-8:
A simple
address
form in
InfoPath.

Note that adding a Text Box control automatically creates a field called `Field1`. Subsequent fields are called `Field2`, `Field3`, and so on.

- You can view the fields by clicking the Data tab and then clicking the Show Fields button.

- You can rename the fields by right-clicking a field, choosing Properties, and then giving the field a name that's more intuitive.

Up until this point you've been adding everything to the default view. This form needs a confirmation page, so you need to add another view; that's the next step.

3. **Click Page Design tab, click the New View button in the Views section, give the new view a descriptive name (such as Confirmation), and then click OK.**

The new view appears and looks like a brand new form — which it isn't. Not yet, anyway. That's because the same fields that you added earlier are still part of the form.

4. **Switch between views by selecting the view you want to design in the drop-down menu in the Views section of the Page Design tab of the Ribbon.**

On the Confirmation view, you want to display the input that the user provided — but in a read-only format.

5. **Add a custom table to the Confirmation view page, with 8 rows and 2 columns, just as you did in Step 1.**

6. **Click the Show Fields button located on the Data tab.**

   The Fields window appears.

7. **Drag the fields from Fields window to the table one at a time to match the user input view.**

8. **Right-click each Text Box control, choose Text Box Properties, and (on the Display tab) check the Read-Only box.**

9. **Change the shading of the text box to light gray to provide a nice read-only visual:**

   a. Right-click the Text Box control and choose Borders and Shading.

   b. On the Shading tab choose a light gray color.

10. **Add a couple of buttons to the form — one to navigate Back and one to Submit the completed form.**

    To add a button simply click the Button control located in the Controls section of the Home tab in the Ribbon.

    The finished Confirmation view is shown in Figure 6-9. The next step is to add rules to the buttons so the user can switch between the views and submit the data.

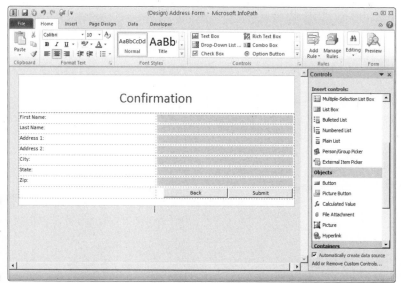

Figure 6-9:
The address confirmation view.

11. **On the Page Design tab, use the view selector drop-down list in the Views section to switch back to the default view.**

12. **Click the Next button to select it, click the Add Rule button on the Home tab, and select Switch Views from the list of available actions.**

    The Rules Detail dialog box appears for switching views.

13. **Make sure the Confirmation view is selected and then click OK.**

14. **Preview the form by clicking the Preview button located on the Home tab of the Ribbon.**

    Notice that clicking the Next button on the first view will bring up the second view.

    The Text Box controls on each view reference the same set of fields. Result: Whatever the user enters on the first view is shown on the second view as well.

15. **Repeat Steps 12–13 with the Confirmation view and the Back button to allow users to navigate back to make edits.**

    What's needed next is a mechanism for submitting data.

16. **Select the Submit button and then choose Submit Data from the Add Rule drop-down menu.**

    The Rule Details dialog box appears, offering a list of data connections.

17. **Click the Add button to create a new data connection, step through the Data Connection Wizard, and choose As An E-mail Message for the destination, as shown in Figure 6-10.**

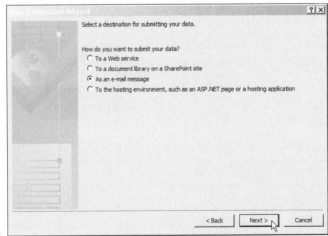

Figure 6-10: Creating a data connection for submitting form data as an e-mail.

18. **Fill in the e-mail information for To, Cc, Bcc, Subject, and Intro, and then click Next.**

19. **Decide whether to send the form as an attachment or as the current view embedded in the e-mail itself, and then click Next.**

    - If the form is submitted as an attachment, an .xml file is attached to the form.

    - If you send the current view, then the Confirmation page will be embedded in the e-mail.

20. **Provide a name for the data connection, click Finish, and then click OK.**

21. **Finally, do a few tweaks to clean up the user experience:**

    a. Add a third view that thanks the user for submitting the form.

    b. Add a second rule to the Submit button that switches to the Thank You view after the user submits the form to the data connection.

    c. Preview the form by making sure the first view is in the Design window and then click the Preview button located on the Home tab.

Starting out the easy way with templates

Designing a form seems like the simplest of tasks — a few labels and boxes for people to enter data — how hard could it be? Often, however, all you need is a very standard form and you don't want to reinvent the wheel. Well, InfoPath may have the form you need, practically ready-made, sitting in its built-in set of form templates. You can even save time by starting with a template to get you 80 percent of the way and then customizing it to meet your specific needs.

If you want to explore form design, Microsoft has a vast number of templates available for download at office.microsoft.com. Here are a few tips on navigating the site:

- ✔ Click the Templates tab to view all the available Office templates. Of course, that's a lot to take in, so you might want to narrow the list. . . .

- ✔ If you want to see only the InfoPath form templates, you can click the Product Categories tab and then the Microsoft Office InfoPath link.

- ✔ Each template page has a thumbnail image of the template, along with information such as the version of InfoPath the template supports.

- ✔ When you click a template, you see a full-page sample view of the template, the additional information, and a download button, as shown in Figure 6-11.

Click the Download button for a copy of a template

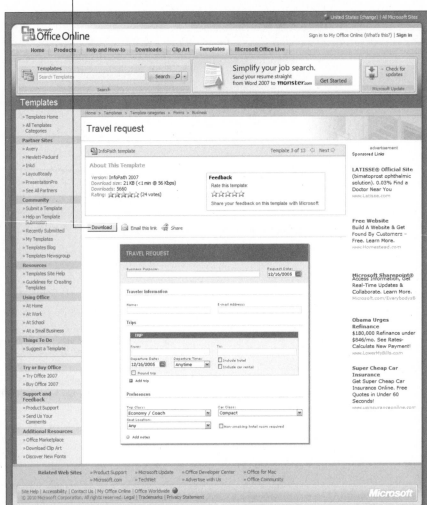

Figure 6-11:
An InfoPath template that can be down-loaded from Microsoft.

In addition to downloadable templates from Microsoft, you have a slew of templates built right into InfoPath — using everything from a database table to a SharePoint list for the initial generation of the form. You can get to the InfoPath templates by clicking the File tab to enter the Backstage View and then clicking the New tab.

The available templates (along with their associated descriptions) are shown in Table 6-2.

Table 6-2	InfoPath Templates
Template	*Description*
SharePoint List	A starting point for SharePoint List forms.
SharePoint Form Library	A starting point for capturing data to a SharePoint form library.
E-mail	Designed to be distributed and submitted through e-mail.
Blank	A blank form that can be customized.
Blank (InfoPath Filler)	A blank form that can only be filled out in the InfoPath Filler application.
Database	Based on a database schema. InfoPath can create this form automatically, basing the form on the fields in a specific database table.
Web Service	Designed to interact with a Web service. InfoPath can pull data (such as the options in a drop-down menu) from a Web service and also submit data to a Web service.
XML or Schema	Based on an XML or schema file. An InfoPath form can be created automatically, based on the fields contained in the file.
Data Connection File	Based on a SharePoint data-source file stored in a SharePoint connection library. An InfoPath form can be created automatically, based on the file.
Convert Existing Form	Designed to convert an existing form in Micro-soft Word or Excel into an InfoPath form.
Document Information Panel	Based on the Properties form of a Microsoft Office document stored in a SharePoint library. An InfoPath form can be generated automatically, based on the columns of the library holding the documents.
Blank 2007 Form	A blank form based on InfoPath 2007.
Blank 2007 Form (InfoPath Filler)	A blank form based on InfoPath 2007 that can be filled out only using InfoPath Filler.
Blank Template Part	A blank template part that can be reused in multiple forms.
Blank (InfoPath Filler) Template Part	A blank template part that can be reused in multiple InfoPath Filler forms only.
XML or Schema Template Part	A template part based on an XML or schema file that can be used in multiple forms.

Reusing form functionality with template parts

A template part is a reusable component of a form that you can use in multiple forms. A template part can contain any component of InfoPath that you might want to use in other forms. Say a template part is specific to a particular section of a form — an address, for example. The address template part contains controls, data connections, data sources, data validation, rules — everything needed for a form that requires address information. The form developer (you) need only insert the template part into the form.

You can create a custom template part by choosing a template-part template and then developing it to meet your form's needs, just as you would with any other form.

Creating a template part

The following example walks you through the process of creating a basic template part:

1. **Open InfoPath Designer by clicking Start⇨All Programs⇨Microsoft Office and then choosing Microsoft InfoPath Designer 2010.**

2. **Create a new template part by clicking the File tab to enter the Backstage View and then clicking the New tab.**

3. **Select Blank Template Part from the list of available templates.**

   If any form using this template part is intended for the Web, make sure you've selected the Web Form type in the Compatibility box, as described previously in the chapter. (See "Making a form Web-capable" for details.)

4. **Design the template by building the form just as you would any other form.**

5. **When you've finished designing, click the File tab and then click Save to save the template part.**

6. **Choose a name for the new template part, specify a location, and then click Save.**

Inserting a template part in a form

When you need to use a template part you've created in a new form, follow these steps:

1. **Create a new form by clicking the File tab and then choosing the New tab. For this new form, choose a simple blank form.**

   The template part you just created is considered a control.

2. **Click the Home tab and then expand the Controls box by clicking the small arrow in the lower-right corner of the Controls section.**

   The arrow points down and to the right; when clicked, it pops the Controls section out into its own box on the right side of the screen. Because the template part you created is brand new, however, it won't show up in the Controls box until you've finished adding it.

3. **Click Add or Remove Custom Controls at the bottom of the Controls box.**

4. **Click the Add button to add a custom control to the list of available controls.**

5. **Select Template Part as the control type.**

   Note that you can also choose to add a custom ActiveX control through this same dialog box. In addition, a link to the Office Marketplace provides access to a place where you can purchase the controls that others have developed.

6. **Click the Next button to continue.**

7. **Browse to the template part that you saved (following the steps in the preceding section) and then click Finish.**

   The template part now shows up at the bottom of the Controls box under the Custom section. Now you can drag and drop the template part onto a form, just as you would any other control.

Making InfoPath Available in SharePoint with Form Services

If you've used SharePoint, then you've almost certainly used electronic forms. Although Microsoft designed and developed the forms that come with SharePoint, you can customize the existing forms — or design and develop your own — to fit your SharePoint implementation. In fact, InfoPath is tightly integrated with SharePoint — which makes form development in SharePoint easier than ever.

The component of SharePoint that's responsible for InfoPath integration is called InfoPath Form Services, a component of SharePoint Server 2010 Enterprise edition. Form Services provides a tight integration between the Office InfoPath product and SharePoint. InfoPath forms integrate with SharePoint in a variety of ways: A form can be embedded directly in a SharePoint site using the InfoPath Web Part, published as a template for a form library, or even used to customize the Web forms used to create and edit list items. You discover how these integration options work in the following sections.

Embedding forms in SharePoint pages

A *Web form* is simply a form that's displayed over the Web — specifically by using a Web browser. You have probably filled out hundreds (or even thousands) of Web forms on your treks across the Web. Whenever you're browsing a Web site and a form asks you to enter data, you're looking at a Web form.

Now, creating InfoPath forms for the Web (as explained earlier in the chapter) is a fine place to start, but what if you want to embed those forms directly into a SharePoint page you've developed? Doing so is easy when you use the InfoPath Form Web Part.

The InfoPath Form Web Part can be added to any page by either embedding it directly in a wiki page or adding it to a Web Part zone on a Web Part page. When you add the Web Part to your page, you simply configure it to point to an InfoPath form template. The end result is that a user sees a Web form on a SharePoint page.

A Web form built using InfoPath looks the same as any other Web form; that's because the form is displayed using HTML. The difference is that InfoPath forms are easier to produce; anyone who can use InfoPath can become a SharePoint form developer without having to write code.

If your form needs functionality that InfoPath doesn't already contain, then you can always write .NET code to go beyond the built-in capabilities of InfoPath — but that's not a requirement for basic form development.

The InfoPath Form Web Part is located in the Forms category, as shown in Figure 6-12. (For more information about adding Web Parts to SharePoint pages, check out Chapter 4.)

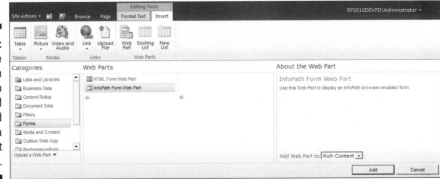

Figure 6-12: The InfoPath Form Web Part is used to embed a form in a SharePoint page.

Creating form libraries

A *form library* is a SharePoint library that stores InfoPath form data in an XML format. The form library uses an InfoPath template form to present the form to the user but the actual data is stored in an XML file with an .xml extension. Each time the form is filled out, a new XML file is stored in the library.

Users can fill out the form using either of the following methods:

✔ **InfoPath Filler:** Users who have the InfoPath Filler application installed locally on their computers can use it to fill out the form. The form is then saved to the SharePoint form library in which they opened the form. This arrangement accommodates the use of some advanced InfoPath features, such as digital signatures.

✔ **Web form:** The form can also be filled out as a Web form. In that case, the form loads in the user's Web browser. The result is the same: The user data from the form is saved in the form library as an XML file. A specific form can be revised simply by clicking the saved form in the form library, making modifications, and then saving the form again.

In addition, when you publish the form, you can specify which fields in the form should be tied to columns in the library that holds the form. For example, if you add a field to your form called City, you could specify that a column be created in the form library that associates the City field in your form with a City column in the library. The distinction here is that the XML file itself holds the form data. The columns for the form library hold metadata about the XML file. When you associate a form field with a form library column, you're actually creating two places to store the data for that particular field. The first is in the XML file itself and the second is in the metadata column in the form library.

The entire process — including developing a form, creating a form library, and publishing the new form to the new library — can be accomplished without having to leave the InfoPath Designer application. Follow these steps to create a new form and form library using InfoPath Designer:

1. **Open InfoPath Designer by clicking Start⇨All Programs⇨Microsoft Office⇨Microsoft InfoPath Designer 2010.**

2. **Choose SharePoint Form Library as the starting template and then click the Design Form button.**

   InfoPath Designer provides a template you can use or you can start from scratch. Designing a form library template is no different from designing any other type of form.

3. **Drag text boxes onto the form to create a simple recipe form, as shown in Figure 6-13.**

   The next step is to publish the form to the SharePoint library.

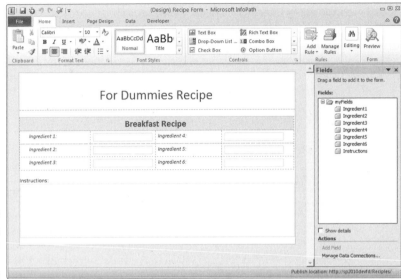

Figure 6-13:
A simple
recipe form.

4. **Click the File tab, click the Publish tab, and then click the SharePoint Server button.**

   The Publishing Wizard dialog box appears.

5. **Enter the Web address of the SharePoint site and then click Next, as shown in Figure 6-14.**

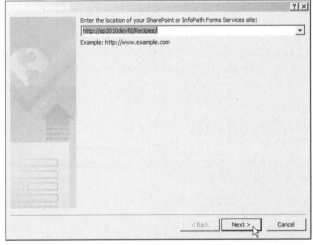

Figure 6-14:
Enter
the Web
address
of the
SharePoint
site in the
Publishing
Wizard.

6. **Choose to create a Form Library and click Next.**

   The other option is to create a Site Content Type that allows a form to be used in multiple sites and libraries.

7. **Choose to create a new form library and click Next.**

   You can also choose to update a template in an existing form library. Then, when you want to modify the template, you can choose to update it instead of creating a brand new library.

8. **Provide a name for the new form library and click Next.**

   The next screen allows you to specify whether a field should also be used as a column in the form library.

9. **Add the** `Ingredient1` **field as a column field (as shown in Figure 6-15), and click Next.**

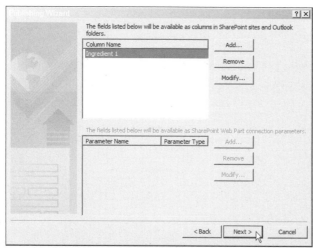

Figure 6-15: Add Ingredient1 (first ingredient) as a column for the form library.

Result: The `Ingredient1` field becomes a metadata field, or column, for the form library. The data for this field shows up not only in the columns for the form library, but also in the form data itself. The benefit is that the field can now be used with the default capabilities of a SharePoint library, such as using this field for filtering when you're viewing the library.

10. **Click Publish to create the new form library and upload the form as a template for the library.**

You can specify how the users fill out the form — whether by using InfoPath Filler or directly in the browser — in the Advanced Settings section of the Library Settings page, as shown in Figure 6-16.

Figure 6-16:
InfoPath forms can be configured to open in InfoPath Filler or in the browser.

Customizing SharePoint list forms

Whenever you create or edit an item in a SharePoint list, you're using a form. In SharePoint 2010, the list forms are easy to edit and customize with InfoPath.

To customize a list form, follow these steps:

1. **Navigate to the list for which you wish to edit the form.**

   Remember that you can see a listing of all lists and libraries in a SharePoint site by choosing Site Actions⇨View All Site Content. To navigate to one of the lists simply click it in the View All Site Content page.

2. **Click the Customize Form button (located on the List tab), as shown in Figure 6-17.**

Figure 6-17:
The Customize Form button is located on the Ribbon in the Customize List section of the List tab.

If the Customize Form button doesn't appear on the List tab, make sure you have the SharePoint Server Enterprise Site Collection feature enabled.

InfoPath Designer opens on your computer and the form will be loaded in the tool and ready for you to edit.

3. **To edit your form, either start with the default form or delete it and create your own form from scratch.**

   To see the fields associated with the SharePoint list, click the Show Fields button located on the Data tab of InfoPath Designer.

4. **To publish the form back to the SharePoint server, click the Quick Publish button.**

   The Quick Publish button can be found by clicking the File tab and then selecting the Info tab. After the form has been published, it will be used by anyone adding or editing an item in the list.

Choosing List forms versus Library forms

The difference between a list form and library form might seem confusing but it's a difference worth a closer look:

- ✔ **A list form submits data directly to a SharePoint list.** When you create a new SharePoint list and then add an item you're using to the default list form, you can customize the list form or even create a brand new form that can be used to create new items or edit existing items. In either case, however, the list form is just an interface into the SharePoint list. When you enter data into the form and submit it, you send the data to the SharePoint list. The form data lives as an item in the list.

- ✔ **An InfoPath library form serves as the template for a SharePoint library that stores forms**. In other words, it's the basis for a form library: The form template submits the filled-out form data to a file with an .xml extension. The data lives in that XML file, and the XML file lives in a SharePoint library. A library form can include complex functionality (such as the digital-signature control) that's only available when the form is filled out using the InfoPath Filler application. The actual data that the form submits, however, ends up in an XML file stored in a SharePoint library.

When you're deciding whether to use a List form or Library form, you can use these guidelines:

- ✔ **Use a List form when**

  - You have a simple form and need to collect data.

  - You want your data to live in a SharePoint list so you can use default list features such as views and filtering.

  - You want your form to be available in offline mode, using SharePoint Workspace (the application formerly known as Groove).

✔ **Use a Library form when**

- You have a complex form that uses InfoPath functionality such as Repeating Sections or nested data.

- You need forms that can be signed digitally.

- You're developing custom code that will be included in your form.

- Your form itself won't live in SharePoint but submitting an XML file that lives in SharePoint will suit your purposes better.

Here are some characteristics of InfoPath Filler that are worth keeping in mind:

✔ Some of the most advanced functionality of InfoPath is only available when the form is designed to be filled out using InfoPath Filler. In such a case, users must have this application installed locally on their machines.

✔ Any InfoPath Filler form can still submit its data to a SharePoint form library as an .xml file.

✔ For a specific list of functionality available only when the form is filled out using InfoPath Filler refer to Table 6-1.

Requiring approval for forms

Form deployment can be as simple as ⌐   ⌐ and pointing to a SharePoint server. Such easy de⌐   ⌐sult in a lack of governance and control for the S⌐   ⌐That's why SharePoint provides a feature to rein in ⌐   ⌐ing frenzies: *administrator-approved forms* that ca⌐   ⌐adminis-trator to a template library through Cent⌐   ⌐ntralized storage location gives administrators mo⌐   ⌐over the InfoPath forms that will be used througho⌐

Central Administration is the name of the SharePoint administrative application. To access Central Administration, click Start⇨All Programs⇨Microsoft SharePoint 2010 Products⇨SharePoint 2010 Central Administration on the server running SharePoint. Because Central Administration is a Web Application, and thus nothing more than a specialized Web site, it can also be accessed by navigating to the Web address directly. Remember, though, that Central Administration is the main interface for managing the entire SharePoint environment. For this reason it is usually restricted to only SharePoint administrators. Working with Central Administration warrants its own book, but if you are looking to get into SharePoint administration Central Administration is the place to start.

Adding Code to InfoPath Forms

You can extend the capabilities of any Microsoft Office application by adding code written using the .NET Framework. If you haven't written code for Office yet, you need an optional Office component called Visual Studio Tools for Applications (VSTA). If Office is already installed, you can add VSTA by choosing Control Panel⇨Programs⇨Programs and Features. VSTA, as you might imagine, makes vigorous use of the Visual Studio development environment (for more about Visual Studio, see Chapter 11).

The Ribbon's Developer tab, shown in Figure 6-18, is your go-to spot for programming InfoPath forms. The primary programming technique is to develop event handlers using a .NET language such as Visual Basic or C# (pronounced "C-Sharp"). For example, selecting a Text Box control and then clicking the Loading Event button on the Developer tab opens Visual Studio and creates an event handler. (Shazam! Just like that.) Then you add the code you want to run to the Loading Event handler, as shown in Figure 6-19.

One problem with letting code like this run in the past was that SharePoint didn't provide an isolated environment for specific code. For example, if you wrote some bad code, you could very well bring down the entire SharePoint environment. Oops. To mitigate this scenario, SharePoint 2010 provides a mechanism known as Sandboxed Solutions (see Chapter 11). In a nutshell, Sandboxed Solutions allows you to break only your Site Collection instead of the entire SharePoint environment. The difference is that you have only your Site Collection Administrator mad at you instead of the SharePoint Administrator.

Figure 6-18:
The
Developer
tab in
InfoPath
Designer.

Some events are compatible with Web forms and some require InfoPath Filler. To help you keep track of which is which, Table 6-3 contains a compatibility list (provided by Microsoft) of all InfoPath events.

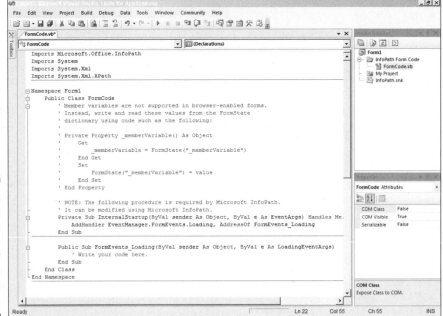

Figure 6-19:
Adding
custom
event-
handler
code to an
InfoPath
form.

Table 6-3	InfoPath Event Compatibility	
Event Name	*Event Type*	*Web-Form Compatible?*
ContextChanged	Form	No
Loading	Form	Yes
Merge	Form	No
Save	Form	No
Sign	Form	No
Submit	Form	Yes
VersionUpgrade	Form	Yes
ViewSwitched	Form	Yes
Changed	Data	Yes
Changing	Data	No
Validating	Data	Yes
Clicked	Button	Yes

Chapter 7

Integrating Visio and Word with SharePoint

Productivity and the growth of productivity must be the first economic consideration at all times, not the last. That is the source of technological innovation, jobs, and wealth.

— William E. Simon

Microsoft Office Visio has always been great at creating visualizations and diagrams of complex data interactions and processes — and Microsoft Office Word is arguably the most popular program around for creating and editing documents. SharePoint sits at the center of an organization and provides centralized access to information, communication, collaboration, and content management. It's no surprise, then, that SharePoint integrates tightly with both Word and Visio.

In this chapter, you discover how to develop Visio and Word solutions that take advantage of this integration with SharePoint. You take a closer look at workflows, Web pages, libraries, and content types while exploring Visio Services, the SharePoint technology that brings Visio into the SharePoint world. You also get pointers on how to develop Word documents for a SharePoint world — including how to let users create and edit Word documents themselves, without ever having to leave their browsers.

Making Visio Diagrams Available to Everyone with Visio Services

If you've ever used Visio, then you know how powerful visualizations of a process flow or diagram can be. As a Microsoft Office product, Visio has been around since the early '90s. Then (suddenly, it seems) SharePoint exploded into the business world as a world-class content-management system. You'd think Visio would be a natural fit with SharePoint — and (fortunately) it is. Although it wasn't always safe to say that one Microsoft product would work well with another, in the case of Visio, the integration is impressive.

In many scenarios, you might want to integrate Visio into your SharePoint environment. One example is embedding Visio diagram in a SharePoint page. Visio has the capability to create data-driven diagrams that pull from a data source. As the data source changes, the Visio diagram is updated accordingly. Using Visio Services allows you to embed this data-driven diagram right into a company portal. Users can then see a visualization of the process as it's happening in real time, using nothing more than their Web browsers.

Before you can work with Visio Services, you must have the SharePoint Server Enterprise Site Collection feature activated. For more information about activating features, check out Chapter 4.

Embedding a Visio diagram

Embedding a Visio document in a SharePoint page first requires that the diagram live in a SharePoint library. To save a Visio diagram to a SharePoint library, follow these steps:

1. **Open Visio and design a sample process-flow diagram.**

2. **Click the File tab in order to enter the Backstage View.**

3. **Click the Save & Send tab.**

4. **Click the Save To SharePoint button.**

5. **Click the Browse For A Location button to find a location and choose Web Drawing for the file type, as shown in Figure 7-1.**

6. **Click the Save As button to bring up the Save dialog box.**

Click to browse for a location   Choose the Web Drawing file type

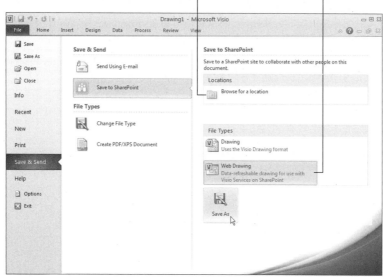

Figure 7-1:
Saving
a Visio
form to a
SharePoint
library.

7. **Type the URL of the SharePoint site in the Filename dialog box and then press Enter.**

   • If you know the entire URL to the document library, then you can provide the entire URL and append a name for the specific file you want to save.

   • If you don't remember the entire URL, you can get right to the SharePoint site by entering a shorter format for the URL: `http://<site>`. Remember to replace `<site>` with the URL of your actual site.

8. **Browse to the SharePoint library where you want to store the Visio drawing and then enter a name for the file in the Filename dialog box.**

9. **Click the Save button to upload the document to the SharePoint library.**

After the Visio diagram is stored in the library, you can easily embed it in a page by using the Visio Web Access Web Part. To add the Web Part and then associate it with a Visio diagram, follow these steps:

1. **In SharePoint, on the page to which you want to add the Visio drawing, click the Insert tab and then click the Web Part button.**

   The Web Part gallery opens. Note that the Insert tab does not appear in the Ribbon unless the page is in Edit mode.

2. **Select the Visio Web Access Web Part (located in the Business Data category) and then click Add, as shown in Figure 7-2.**

3. **Open the Web Part Configuration tool pane by clicking the link labeled** *Click here to open the tool pane.*

4. **Click the blue ellipsis to browse to the Visio drawing and then click OK to close the tool pane.**

   The Visio diagram is now embedded in the SharePoint page, as shown in Figure 7-3.

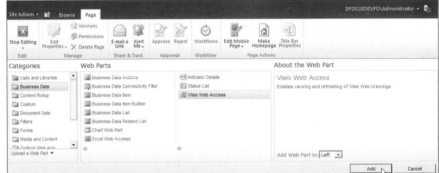

Figure 7-2: Adding the Visio Web Access Web Part.

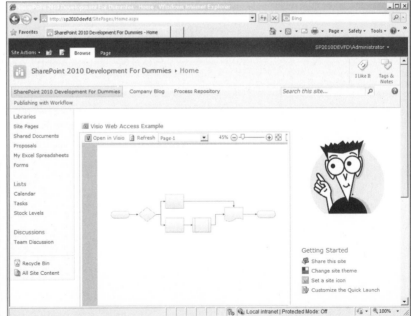

Figure 7-3: A Visio drawing embedded in a page using the Visio Web Access Web Part.

You can also add a Web Part to a Web Part page or a publishing page. Just click the Add Web Part button in the Web Part zone in which you want to add a Visio drawing. Developing different types of pages in the browser is covered in greater detail in Chapter 4.

Linking Web Parts in a Visio diagram

A Visio diagram that is visible in a SharePoint page using the Visio Web Access Web Part is more than just a pretty diagram in a box. You can link Visio Web Parts, and thus the underlying Visio diagram, with other Web Parts in ways that improve the user experience — largely because the Visio Web Part can both send *and* receive connections from other Web Parts. To connect a Web Part to other Web Parts, click the drop-down menu for the Web Part when the page is in Edit mode, and then choose Connections, as shown in Figure 7-4.

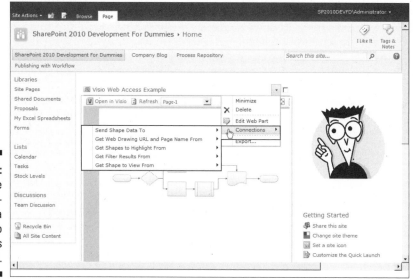

Figure 7-4: Available connections for a Visio Web Access Web Part.

The connections available for the Visio Web Access Web Part include

✔ **Send Shape Data To:** Use this connection to send shape data to a different Web Part. For example, you might want to click a shape and have the details about that shape load in a different Web Part.

✔ **Get Web Drawing URL and Page Name From:** Use this connection to receive a Visio Web drawing URL and page name to load from a different Web Part. For example, you might have a Web Part for viewing Visio diagrams and make the diagram that loads dependent on the item selected in a list. It's one way to load a diagram dynamically in response to a user's interaction with a different Web Part.

✔ **Get Shapes to Highlight From:** Use this connection to receive the shapes that should be highlighted in the diagram. For example, a list might contain a grouping of shapes that represents a certain product group. When the user selects the product group from the list, the Visio drawing updates automatically to show the shapes in that product group highlighted. If the user selects a different product grouping from the list, the shape refreshes to highlight the shapes contained in the new product group.

✔ **Get Filter Results From:** This connection is similar to the Get Shapes to Highlight From connection; however, this connection highlights shapes that correspond to items in a SharePoint list that is being filtered. When the SharePoint list is filtered, only the shapes that correspond to the visible items in the list are highlighted in the Visio diagram. For example, you might have a large list of individual products in a list. You might have one page containing a Visio drawing using the Get Shapes to Highlight From connection so users can select a product group and see the products associated with that product group. You might have another page containing a Visio drawing that allows users to filter the large list of products using various criteria. The products in the Visio drawing would be updated to match the visible items in product list. Result: users can visualize the products dynamically, according to the filter criteria set up for the product list.

✔ **Get Shape to View From:** This connection allows a Visio drawing to be positioned from an external Web Part. If you have a very large and detailed diagram, you want to be able to center in on a specific shape and zoom to an appropriate level of detail. For example, you might have the large diagram zoomed out when a user first comes to the page. When the user clicks an item in a SharePoint list, the diagram zooms in and centers on the corresponding shape from the list.

Extending a Visio Web Drawing Using JavaScript

You can do a lot with Visio and SharePoint Designer without writing a single line of code. At some point, however, one of your SharePoint site requirements will call for functionality that is simply not available out of the box. When this happens, it's time to turn to the infinitely flexible Visio Services JavaScript Mashup API. (No, really, that's what it's called.)

An *application programming interface* (API) is a programming window, or interface, into a particular application. An API provides a mechanism for programmers, who use the application's built-in features to expand what the application can do. In the case of Visio Services, the JavaScript API is a window into programming Visio Web drawings using JavaScript.

The API provides a programmable view of a Visio Web drawing that JavaScript can manipulate. The different components of the Web drawing are called *objects;* the API gives you access to them and organizes them as a hierarchy that's arranged like boxes within boxes:

- ✔ `VwaControl` is the main object, which represents an instance of the Visio Web Access Web Part. The `VwaControl` object contains `Page` objects.

- ✔ The `Page` objects represent the pages within the Visio diagram. Each `Page` object contains `ShapeCollection` objects.

- ✔ Each `ShapeCollection` object contains `Shape` objects.

Using this hierarchy, you can find your way down to specific shapes — and, in effect, tell them what to do — when you're using JavaScript to program a Web diagram.

Here's a taste of what you can do with a Visio Web diagram by using JavaScript to call the shots:

- ✔ **Rich interaction with users:** For example, you can pop up an image overlay when a user moves the mouse pointer over a shape. The image might be dynamically based on a value in the Visio diagram that was pulled from a database — putting the mouse pointer over a picture of a truck that represents current deliveries to a particular store might bring up an overlay of the products being delivered in that particular truck at that moment.

- ✔ **Mashups:** JavaScript can connect parts of your Web page with parts of the Visio diagram. When you combine information from inside the Visio diagram with information outside the diagram but contained in the Web page, the result is called a *mashup*.

Mashups provide a separation of duties between Web page developers and diagram developers. A diagram developer might be focused on the details of building a particularly complex diagram. When the diagram is complete, the diagram developer can hand it over to the SharePoint developer who can then tie the diagram into the rest of the SharePoint page using JavaScript. For example, you might have engineers building a complex diagram with a dizzying array of shapes, lines, and text. The developer really doesn't care about what is in the diagram. The developer's role might be to simply wire up the diagram to highlight different shapes depending on where someone clicks text on the Web site.

JavaScript is a Web programming language that provides access to the components of a Web page. For more information about JavaScript in SharePoint, check out Chapter 12.

Collaborating on Workflows with Visio and SharePoint

Communicating throughout the process of developing a SharePoint workflow can be difficult.

A workflow is the routing of a document through various stages of development and feedback. For example, you might start a document and then want the workflow to send out emails for feedback. After the document is complete, you might want to publish it to a SharePoint site dedicated to policies and procedures.

The workflow developer works with SharePoint Designer in order to build a workflow. A business user would likely walk away muttering if a workflow developer tried to explain the workflow in the SharePoint Designer environment. A business user needs a simple process-flow diagram in order to make sense of the workflow. Because Visio is such a superstar in creating process diagrams, it's a natural marriage to combine Visio and SharePoint workflows.

The integration between Visio and SharePoint workflow flows both ways. You can create the sequence of the workflow using SharePoint Designer, and then export the logic to a Visio diagram to turn the workflow into a pretty visual image. You can also develop a workflow using Visio and import it into SharePoint Designer. The Visio-and-SharePoint workflow marriage is truly a mutual give-and-take.

Keep in mind that you might lose some of the data associated with a workflow when you import or export it. For example, if you develop a workflow in SharePoint Designer and then export it to Visio, you will have the picture of the diagram. But if you then import it back into SharePoint Designer, you might need to reconnect the tasks to the names of the components in the SharePoint site.

To get this kind of integration between workflows in Visio and SharePoint, you must be using the Visio Premium 2010 and SharePoint Designer 2010. Earlier (and/or lower-end) versions just won't cut it.

Creating a picture from a workflow

Keep in mind that the path from Visio image to SharePoint workflow runs both ways; you can create a workflow in SharePoint Designer and turn it into a Visio image. A SharePoint workflow consists of a series of conditions and actions that must correspond to either a `True` or `False` logical value to determine the next condition or action in the sequence. A condition might include checking to see whether a document has been approved. If the condition is `True`, then that result would lead to an action such as sending an e-mail. (For more about designing workflows using SharePoint Designer, check out Chapter 8.)

The series of conditions and actions that make up a workflow can get fairly complicated. In SharePoint Designer, the workflow is depicted as a mazelike series of stages represented by text and lines, as shown in Figure 7-5.

A Visio workflow, on the other hand, starts out as a pretty diagram with pictures, lines, and arrows showing the flow of the process. If you export a SharePoint workflow and then import it into Visio, what you get is a diagrammed view of the workflow that mere business mortals can readily understand. (You can almost hear the lights switching on in their heads.)

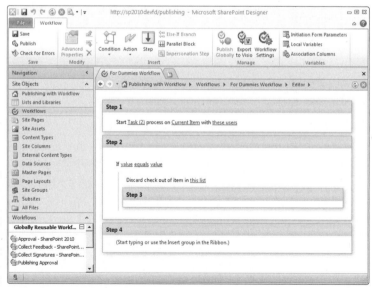

Figure 7-5:
A SharePoint workflow in SharePoint Designer.

To export a workflow from SharePoint Designer and then import it into Visio, follow these steps:

1. **In SharePoint Designer, click the Export To Visio button.**

   You can find the button on the Workflow tab in the Manage group, as shown in Figure 7-6.

Figure 7-6:
Export a
SharePoint
workflow to
Visio.

2. **Provide a name and location for the exported file and then click Save.**

   The exported file is in a format known as Visio Workflow Interchange, and its filename has the .vwi extension.

3. **Open Microsoft Visio 2010 by clicking Start and then typing** Visio **in the Search Programs box.**

   Next, you need to create a new SharePoint workflow flowchart to host the workflow diagram.

4. **In Visio, click the File tab to enter the Backstage View and then select the New tab.**

5. **Choose the Flowchart category from the Template Category list.**

6. **Choose Microsoft SharePoint Workflow from the template list and then click the Create button, as shown in Figure 7-7.**

7. **Click the Process tab and then click the Import button, as shown in Figure 7-8.**

8. **Select the** .vwi **file that was exported in Step 2, and then click Open.**

   The SharePoint workflow appears onscreen as a visual process diagram in Visio, as shown in Figure 7-9. You now have a diagram you can print and share with business users so they can easily visualize the workflow developed in SharePoint Designer. The printout can be helpful if you need to present the workflow in meetings, where users can review it and make changes.

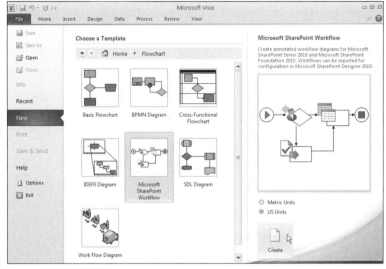

Figure 7-7:
The
Microsoft
SharePoint
Workflow
template in
Visio 2010.

Figure 7-8:
The Import
button is
located on
the Process
tab in Visio.

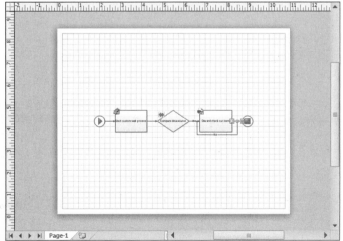

Figure 7-9:
A
SharePoint
workflow
imported
into Visio.

Creating a workflow from a picture

Turning a SharePoint workflow into a picture is useful for communication purposes but what is more valuable is empowering a business user with an understanding of SharePoint workflows in general — what's possible *and* what to ask for from the workflow developer.

Visio provides a template that gives a business user an easy way to map out a SharePoint workflow. Then the diagram can go to the workflow developer, who can simply import the diagram into SharePoint Designer and wire it up to make it a functioning workflow that SharePoint users can use.

Here's how to import a Visio workflow into SharePoint Designer:

1. **Export the SharePoint workflow from Visio by clicking the Export button on the Process tab.**

    Before exporting, Visio checks the workflow to make sure it's valid. If it finds any problems, you get an error message and an Issues box appears, highlighting each issue in the diagram. (For example, if you have a condition, then you must also include a connector with a Yes label that points to an action to run if the condition is True. If you don't, Visio will tell you about that.) When you've addressed any and all of the issues, you're good to go; the file can be exported.

2. **Provide a name and location for the exported file and then click Save.**

    The exported file has a format known as Visio Workflow Interchange with the .vwi extension.

3. **Open SharePoint Designer by clicking Start and then entering** SharePoint Designer **in the Search Programs box.**

4. **Select Workflows in the Site Objects window and then click the Import From Visio button located in the Ribbon, as shown in Figure 7-10.**

Figure 7-10:
A Visio workflow can be imported using the Import From Visio button.

5. **Browse to the workflow that was exported in Step 2, and then click Next.**

6. **Provide a name for the workflow, choose the workflow type from the drop-down menu, choose a list to associate with the workflow, and then click Finish, as shown in Figure 7-11.**

   The workflow is imported into SharePoint Designer where you can configure it for the specific fields and users available on the SharePoint site. The reusable workflow type allows you to attach a workflow to multiple lists instead of just a single list. (For more information about working with workflows in SharePoint Designer, check out Chapter 8.)

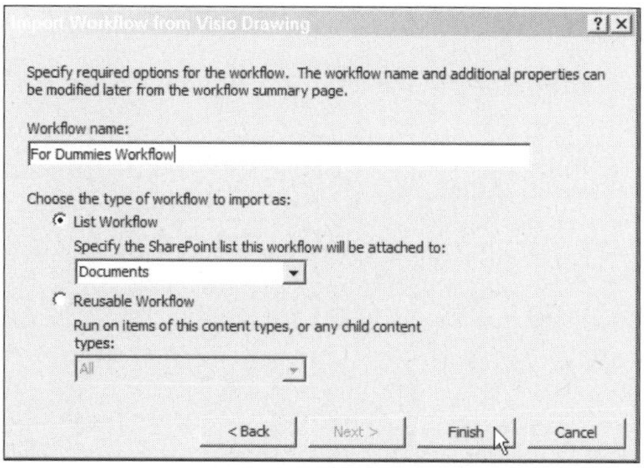

Figure 7-11:
The Visio
Workflow
Import
Wizard.

Visualizing the progress of a workflow

Using Visio in order to better communicate with business users in the workflow development process is important, but the integration between SharePoint and Visio does not stop there. After the workflow has been developed and is being used by users, you can continue to use Visio. Visio Services provides visualizations of workflows in progress, as shown in Figure 7-12. The diagrams include the stages of the workflow, pictures indicating which tasks have been completed, and even the people involved in the particular workflow stages. Understanding the status of a workflow is important on many levels. For example, if you are the Chief Financial Officer (CFO) of an organization, you no doubt want to know where your team is in the final accounting close process. The workflow that depicts an accounting close process probably involves numerous people and tasks, but using Visio Services, you could simply browse to a secured dashboard on your company portal and see exactly what steps have been completed. You might be surprised to find out that the legal team has taken a week longer than they should have!

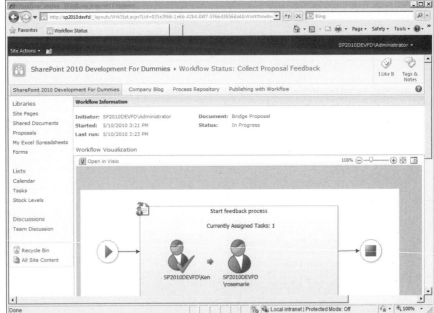

Figure 7-12:
Workflow
progress
visualiza-
tion in
SharePoint,
using Visio
Services.

You can turn on visualizations in the Workflow Settings page of SharePoint Designer, as shown in Figure 7-13. To access this page, make sure the workflow is open in SharePoint Designer and then click the Workflow Settings button (located on the Workflow tab in the Manage section of the Ribbon). Select the Show Workflow Visualization option to display the workflow in progress. A user can then see the status of an item using the workflow by clicking on the workflow column in the list where the workflow is running.

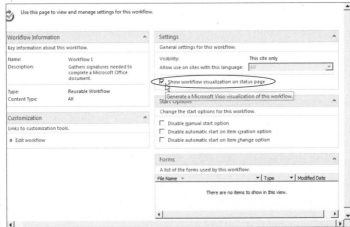

Figure 7-13:
The
Workflow
Settings
page in
SharePoint
Designer.

Creating a Visio Process Repository in SharePoint

As a consultant, I am all too aware that processes are the most important aspect of any business. Having a set of defined, efficient, and effective processes — whether for creating and delivering goods or managing the flow of information inside the company — can make a business kick into the next gear. Without them, the business will likely die as other businesses adopt better processes. An important part of having good processes is documenting them. You can have the best process in the world but if the one individual who understands all the moving pieces leaves the company, then the process walks right out the door with them.

Visio is a powerful tool for documenting processes, easily combined with SharePoint content management. In fact, SharePoint includes a site template designed to create a repository for processes (could it be a subtle hint about getting 'em organized?). The SharePoint Process Repository site template includes a library for storing process diagrams, a discussion board for discussing processes, and a task list for assigning tasks. (Nope, that's no hint. It's more like an engraved invitation.) A SharePoint site created using the Process Repository template is shown in Figure 7-14.

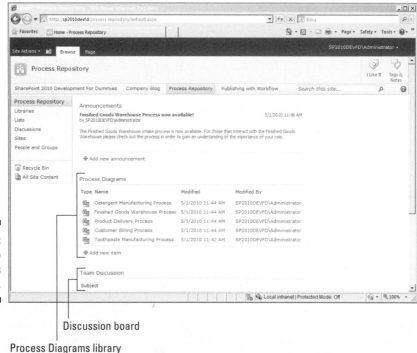

Figure 7-14: The Visio Process Repository.

Discussion board

Process Diagrams library

The SharePoint Process Repository site template includes a series of Visio templates for processing diagrams, as shown in Figure 7-15. Each one serves as a starting point for creating new Visio diagrams that represent processes. If none of the stock templates quite does the job, you can create your own Visio template files to fit your organization, save them under new names, and add them to the Process Repository. Storing the diagrams in a library bestows some SharePoint content-management features on them automatically — in particular, workflow, versioning, security, and check-in/check-out. One of the best features of all, however, is that you can view Visio-based process diagrams right from the browser. You might have a few skilled process folks creating the diagrams but the rest of the organization can simply browse to an intranet portal to view the documented processes in all their glory — no need to install Visio on their local computers.

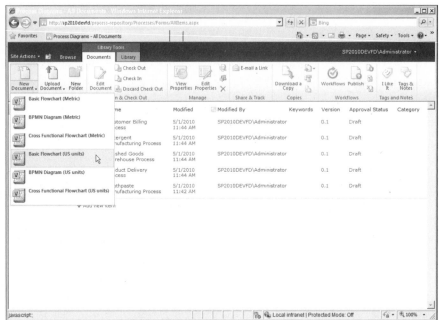

Figure 7-15:
The Visio templates included in the Visio Process Repository.

Using Word in a SharePoint World

In case you've been away on a tour of the solar system and haven't heard, Microsoft Word is one of the most popular word-processing applications in use today — around the world. It's handy for creating and editing everything from simple documents to advanced checklists. But as the sheer amount of digital content grows — much of it in the form of word-processing documents — the need for content management becomes glaringly apparent. Those documents need some sort of governance and overall order, or they spawn versions of themselves all over the place — and keeping track of the real content quickly becomes overwhelming.

And then there's the Attack of the Giant Filenames. You've probably seen a document that attempts to track document versions by using a naming convention in the file — initials, dates, and identifiers such as "draft 1" or "final." What usually ends up happening to the filename is something like this:

```
2010 Financial Forecast - Ken edited 02-06_Rosemarie-revised-03-09_final-RSW_
              FINAL.docx
```

In a word, *yikes.* But doom is not yet imminent. An Enterprise Content Management (ECM) system (such as — you guessed it — SharePoint) solves this problem by using these features to keep track of documents:

- **Versioning:** This process tracks changes to each new version of a document. When a document is checked out, edited, and checked back in, a new version is created. Be careful though, because versioning can be turned on and off for a document library. Make sure it is turned on before you assume versioning is taking place.

- **Check-in/check-out:** Much like checking a book in and out of a library, this process locks the document so that only the person that has it checked out can edit it. When the user completes his changes, he checks it back in so others can have a chance to check it out as well.

- **Security:** Applying document security restricts which users have the ability to read or edit documents in a library. This is important for highly confidential documents that, say, only the finance people should see.

- **Workflow:** The whole process of creating SharePoint workflows (described earlier in this chapter) helps route documents through a specific process. For example, you might need to get feedback from just about the entire company and approval from every boss within a 10,000 mile radius. Using workflow, you can let SharePoint do the work of routing that document and obtaining feedback and approval for you while you grab a coffee.

Using SharePoint as your ECM system, you can avail yourself of the tight integration between Word and SharePoint — especially in these areas:

- SharePoint Libraries
- SharePoint Templates
- Word properties
- SharePoint content types
- SharePoint Line Of Business (LOB) connectivity

The upcoming sections of this chapter look at how each of these features can help tame the chaos of documents.

Setting up libraries for Word documents

A SharePoint library is simply a place to store files. You can think of a library as a virtual file cabinet that nobody has to lift. A SharePoint library is often referred to as a document library because the purpose of many libraries is to store documents.

When a user needs to add a document to the library, she can either save it to the library directly from within the Word application or browse to the library using a Web browser and click a button to upload it manually.

Even though a library is great at storing Word documents, it can also store many other types of files — such as Excel spreadsheets, PowerPoint presentations, text files, PDF documents, SQL Server Reporting Services (SSRS) reports, InfoPath forms, PerformancePoint dashboards, pictures, Web pages, and even data-connection files.

The SharePoint Create page includes a number of different types of libraries you can create. (To access the Create page, choose Site Actions➪More Options.) To whip one up for Word documents, choose Document Library, give the library a name, and then click Create, as shown in Figure 7-16.

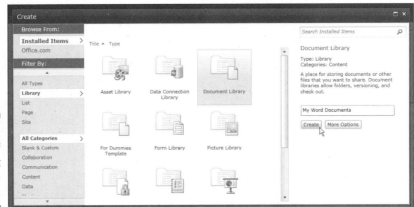

Figure 7-16:
The types of SharePoint libraries you can create.

When developing a library, you need to associate it with a template. The default template is simply a blank Word document. When a user clicks the New button to add a new item to the library the template is used as a starting point for the new document. The Word template is in essence the base document, or starting point, for the new Word document.

You can have more than one template associated with a library but only one template set as the default. Users who click the New Document drop-down menu to add a new item to the document library will see a menu with a list of available templates. For example, you might want to build a document library for storing project proposals, and create templates for various different types of proposals. If you're in the road-construction business, for example, you might have several such types — say, Road Repair Proposal, New Road Proposal, Road Widening Proposal, and Bridge Proposal — as shown in Figure 7-17.

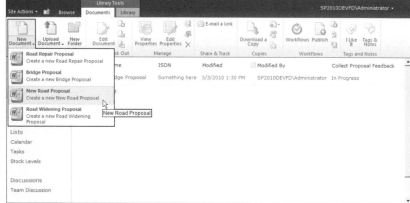

Figure 7-17:
Multiple Word templates can be associated with the same SharePoint library.

Developing Word templates for a document library is as simple as developing a document using Word. After you have the base document set up the way you want it, save it as a template by selecting Word Template in the Save As Type dialog box. (A Word template file has the .dot file extension.)

In the SharePoint world, each Word template is associated with a *content type* — a logical grouping of fields within SharePoint. One of the fields within the content type grouping is the template file that generates a specific type of content. Multiple content types can be associated with a document library. When users click the New Item button and choose a template from the drop-down menu, they are actually choosing a content type for the new item — and the content type is associated with the Word template. For example, if you are creating a proposal you might need to start from a specific template that has already been developed by an expert. The proposal templates might be geared towards different government agency requirements or the type of work that is being proposed.

Associating a Word template with a content type

Creating a new content type and associating a custom Word template with it for use in a library is simply a matter of following these steps:

1. **Open the Site Settings page by clicking Site Actions⇨Site Settings.**

2. **Click the Site Content Types link located under the Galleries section.**

3. **Click the Create button to create a new content type.**

4. **Provide a name and description for the content type.**

   This name will appear on the New Item drop-down menu when users create a new document using the Word template you associate with this content type.

   Content types are hierarchical and a new one must stem from a parent content type. Remember that a content type is a logical collection of metadata fields; when you choose a parent content type, you're starting with metadata fields already associated with your chosen content type.

5. **To associate this content type with a Word document, select Document Content Types and then select Document.**

   You can choose to have the new content type show up in an existing grouping of content types or you can create your own. In this example, I chose to create a new grouping and enter **For Dummies Content Types**. The completed configuration screen is shown in Figure 7-18.

6. **Click OK to create the new content type and enter the Settings page for the content type.**

7. **Choose Advanced Settings⇨Upload A New Document Template under the Document Template section of the Settings page.**

   By default, a blank Word template is associated — but we want to associate our own custom Word template with this content type.

8. **Click the Browse button and select the custom Word template.**

9. **Click OK to save the settings.**

Figure 7-18: Creating a new content type.

Adding a content type to a library

After you've created a new content type and associated a custom Word template with it, you're ready to add your new content type to a library. By sheer coincidence (just kidding) the following steps do just that:

1. **Browse to the document library and then click the Library Settings button (located on the Library tab).**

2. **Make the content types associated with this library modifiable by clicking Advanced Settings⇨Allow Management of Content Types⇨Yes.**

   Note that the section title on the left is called Content Types and the text above the checkboxes is asking if you want to allow management of content types.

3. **Click the OK button to save the settings and return to the Library Settings page.**

   You now have a new section called Content Types.

4. **Click the Add From Existing Site Content Types and select the custom content type you created previously.**

5. **Return to the library and then click the Documents tab.**

   When you click the New Document drop-down menu, you'll now see your custom Word template as an option for creating a new document.

Server properties in Word

When a Word document lives in a SharePoint library, it's associated with a SharePoint content type. A content type has fields that provide metadata (data about the document). You can edit these fields while working with a Word document opened on the local computer. When a Word document that lives in SharePoint is edited, the fields that correspond to the content types are available in a special area called the *document information panel,* which appears as Document Properties – Server, as shown in Figure 7-19.

The document information panel shows up by default when a document is being saved to a SharePoint library. If you close the panel accidentally — or it's not appearing when it's supposed to — you can open it by clicking the File tab to enter the Backstage View and then clicking the Info tab. The right side of the screen shows the properties for the document. You can show the panel by clicking the drop-down menu next to the Properties header and selecting Show Document Panel.

Document information panel

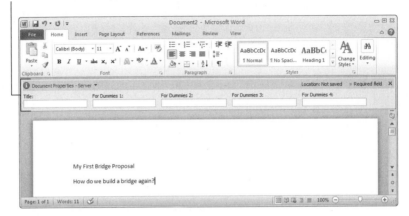

Figure 7-19:
The
document
information
panel is
where you
can update
content type
fields with-
out leaving
Word.

The user can flip between the *local* properties (which are part of the document) and the *server* properties (which are part of the content type) by using
a drop-down menu located in the document information pane. The server
properties that show up in the document information panel are those defined
in the Columns section of the content type settings, as shown in Figure 7-20.
The content type settings page can be accessed by clicking Site Actions⇨
Site Settings and then clicking Site Content Types under the Galleries section.
From this page, you can click a content type in order to access its settings
page.

Figure 7-20:
The col-
umns of a
content type
show up
as server
fields in the
document
information
panel in
Word.

Columns		
A column stores information about each document in the document library. The following columns are currently available in this document library:		
Column (click to edit)	Type	Required
Title	Single line of text	
For Dummies 1	Single line of text	
For Dummies 2	Single line of text	
For Dummies 3	Single line of text	
For Dummies 4	Single line of text	
Created By	Person or Group	
Modified By	Person or Group	
Checked Out To	Person or Group	

The document information panel is simply an InfoPath form; in fact, you can
use InfoPath to customize the panel that is displayed in Word — using settings
for the document information panel that you can access through the Content
Type Settings page.

Using Word as a Line of Business Front End with Business Connectivity Services

SharePoint 2010 provides many features that you can make accessible within Word to provide a better user experience. One of the most powerful of these is Business Connectivity Services (BCS) — which gives you a read/write connection to Line Of Business (LOB) applications such as SAP, Oracle, and Microsoft Dynamics. (An LOB system is a software system that is used to manage some function of business such as accounting or HR.)

SharePoint can provide the connectivity to the LOB systems so the information that comes from them becomes accessible within Word — which result in a Word document that provides a seamless experience for a business user. For example, you might have a Word document template for filling out proposals, with one of the fields designated for client-contact information normally stored in an SAP system; using SharePoint and BCS, Word could pull the client information into the Word document.

The Word document actually pulls the information from SharePoint — and SharePoint does the errand of pulling the information from SAP — but to the user, the entire process is seamless. The user just notices that the information needed in the document information panel for the proposal is incorporated right into the document — Presto! No silk hat and rabbit required.

The importance of accessing the metadata associated with a document library from a Word document may not be blatantly apparent. The importance lies in the location of where the metadata (data about data, or in this case, data about a Word document) lives. If the data is embedded in the local properties of a Word document, then it is not accessible to the rest of the SharePoint system. It is self-contained within the Word document. If the data is contained as a column in the SharePoint library, however, then it is accessible to SharePoint and can be used for all sorts of business functions. For example, you might want to filter the library of documents based on certain metadata fields. If the data is in the Word document, you couldn't do it, but if the metadata is in the library column, you can simply add a filter Web Part and connect it with the library.

Being able to access the library metadata columns from within SharePoint is important because it is a major hassle to leave the Word document and fill in columns on the SharePoint library. In fact, most users won't do it, and you end up with a system that is both painful and inefficient. If a user sees a couple boxes at the top of their Word document that are required they are much more likely to fill them out without feeling annoyed. The result is that the metadata is now captured in a format that is usable to the SharePoint platform with minimal disruption to users.

Working with Word from the Browser

Web portals have rapidly become the information hubs of organizations. A company Web portal is a central location where users can quickly find information relevant to their jobs, the company's products, and the life of the company itself. SharePoint dominates the Web-portal market; Microsoft is pressing this advantage by constantly beefing up the functionality of the product. One of the exciting new features is the ability to work with Word documents right from the browser. No longer does Word have to be installed on the local computer. The documents live in SharePoint and can be edited right from the Web browser.

Making applications available on the Web as services is the technology that enables Word and Excel editing in the browser. The Microsoft product that provides this advantage is called Office Web Applications (Web Apps for short). Office Web Apps must be installed in the SharePoint environment by an administrator. After it's installed, the Office Web Apps component shows up as a site-collection feature and must be activated individually for each site collection that uses it. Installation instructions are available here:

```
technet.microsoft.com/en-us/library/
        ee855124(office.14).aspx
```

After Office Web Apps is installed and activated, you can browse to a SharePoint library containing Word documents and click to view any of those documents in the browser. Two buttons are available for editing the document, as shown in Figure 7-21. The first allows you to edit the document using the full Word client application installed on your local computer; you just click the Open In Word button. The second allows you to edit the document right in the browser by clicking the Edit In Browser button.

Click to open in Word

Click to edit in browser

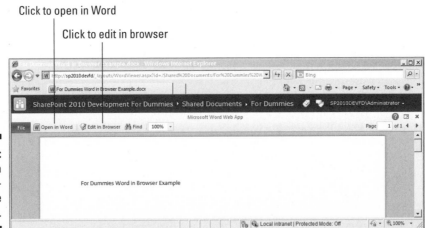

Figure 7-21: Viewing a Word document in the browser.

The Edit In Browser mode uses its own version of the Ribbon that is very similar to the Office Ribbon used when Word runs on your local machine. Figure 7-22 shows a Word document in Edit mode. The familiar Word Ribbon is available, and you can use it to make edits right in the browser.

Word Ribbon in the browser

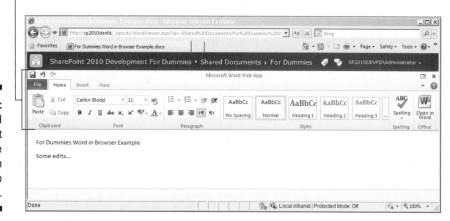

Figure 7-22: A Word document can be edited from a Web browser.

If someone is already editing a Word document in the browser and another user tries to edit the same document, the second user gets an error message, as shown in Figure 7-23. Sounds like a traffic jam, doesn't it? But not to worry: If both users are editing the document using the traditional standalone Word application (installed on their local computers), then both users can be editing and collaborating on the same document — an example of some advanced SharePoint-and-Word functionality that's only available when the locally installed, standalone version of Word is running on the local computers. When one user saves the Word document, he is notified of any changes, the document refreshes, and he sees the changes from the other user immediately. This functionality is ideal when working on a large document at the same time but in different sections. SharePoint manages the versions as they are saved so at any point the team can choose to roll back edits by other members of the team. The process might sound complicated, but SharePoint handles the heavy lifting. The alternative is for each team member to work on her sections of the document individually and email the content or word documents to a designated complier of the sections, who manually copies and pastes each section into a single document. Trust me, letting SharePoint handle it is much easier.

If you have turned on the functionality of a document library that requires a document be checked out for editing, then collaborative editing is not supported. This makes sense because how could two people work on the same document if it is a requirement that someone checks out a document in order to work on it? They couldn't, and SharePoint makes sure of it.

Figure 7-23:
If someone
is already
editing a
Word docu-
ment in the
browser,
a second
user who
tries to edit
receives
an error
message.

Introducing Word Automation Services in SharePoint

Word Automation Services provides the Save As functionality of the Word client — but on the SharePoint server. Users can save (that is, export) Word documents to other formats without leaving the browser. For example, a Word document might be developed through the browser by someone in the Human Resources department. When the document is complete, its creator might save it as a PDF file (to cement the contents) and store the PDF file on the company's SharePoint intranet portal for the entire organization. That whole process is possible without leaving the Web browser.

The interface that enables a user to save a Word document in PDF format is not a standard SharePoint feature. That's where you, the developer, enter the picture: A developer would have to provide this capability by working up a custom event or Web Part that interfaces with Word Automation Services. For that matter, much of the work of Word Automation Services happens behind the scenes. For example, your users know that they create Word documents in a document library. What they don't know (and don't particularly need to) is that each such document is also converted to PDF format, using a custom event — and then saved to an archiving library as well.

But you can also carry this process a step further: The conversion of a Word document to PDF can be automated so it runs without user interaction. For example, you might use Word Automation Services when a company policy completes an approval process. The final document might need to be saved as a PDF and loaded into a library that is accessible by the entire organization. You can automate this final saving and make it the last stage of the approval process; that way business users don't have to save the final document to PDF manually on a local computer and then upload it to a SharePoint library. Instead, saving to PDF and uploading to the library would happen automatically when the document reaches an approved state.

Developers can access Word Automation Services functionality in a Visual Studio SharePoint project by adding the `Microsoft.Office.Word.Server` assembly. For more information about writing .NET code for SharePoint (of which this assembly is an example), check out Chapter 12.

Because Word Automation Services is a Service Application, you can configure it in SharePoint Central Administration on the Manage Service Applications page (located under the Application Management category).

Part III
Exploring Standalone SharePoint Development Tools

The 5th Wave   By Rich Tennant

"I'm not saying I believe in anything. All I know is since it's been there our server is running 50% faster."

In this part . . .

In this part, you leap fearlessly into some of the more advanced development techniques: Using standalone SharePoint development tools, you craft solutions in SharePoint Designer, use Report Builder to develop reports (deployed, managed, secured, and viewed right in your SharePoint site) for SQL Server Reporting Services, and tinker up business dashboards with Dashboard Designer to provide content (such as Scorecards and Key Performance Indicators) to PerformancePoint Services. Then (or maybe a little later) you go forth to conquer the world.

Chapter 8

Using SharePoint Designer to Make Your Sites Sing

I used to think that cyberspace was fifty years away. What I thought was fifty years away, was only ten years away. And what I thought was ten years away . . . it was already here. I just wasn't aware of it yet.

— Bruce Sterling

SharePoint Designer provides an intuitive interface into the underlying SharePoint platform — and a staggering range of development possibilities. You can, of course, develop and configure sites, pages, lists, libraries, and content types — for openers — but you can also build custom page layouts, develop workflows, and create branding (just to name a few). Aside from using the browser, SharePoint Designer is one of the most useful tools for developing on the SharePoint platform — and a place you will likely spend a great deal of time.

That's why this chapter shows you how to navigate SharePoint Designer and gives you a look under the hood at how the Ribbon works. You get pointers on using the various editor programs to develop workflows, pages, lists, libraries, and content types. You get a look at developing pages by adding controls, Web Part zones, and styling. Finally, you get to style your page the easy way — with style sheets.

Peering into the Looking Glass with SharePoint Designer

To exercise all its well-muscled capabilities, SharePoint relies heavily on another Microsoft product: SQL Server, a database application that's designed to store data. The SharePoint platform stores its content and configuration information in a number of SQL Server databases. Because those databases hold all the crucial goods, you can't just crack open Windows Explorer and start looking at files in SharePoint. You need a tool that allows you to peer into the databases and work with the SharePoint platform. SharePoint Designer is just such a tool.

Some good news: You can download, install, and use SharePoint Designer for free. After installation, launch SharePoint Designer by pressing the Windows key and typing **SharePoint Designer** into the search box. You can also open SharePoint Designer by selecting Start➪All Programs➪SharePoint➪Microsoft SharePoint Designer 2010.

Whenever SharePoint Designer opens, it begins with the Backstage View as shown in Figure 8-1. Because SharePoint Designer is designed to work only with SharePoint (well, yeah), you must connect SharePoint Designer to an existing site or create a new site in an existing SharePoint environment. If you've already connected to a site, then that site shows up in the Recent Sites section — you can simply click the name of the site to connect and start developing.

Figure 8-1: SharePoint Designer must connect to a site or create a new site when opened.

When you've connected to a site, the Ribbon activates, the navigation comes to life, and you have all the SharePoint Designer capabilities at your disposal, as shown in Figure 8-2.

If you're a newcomer to SharePoint Designer, check out the following tips on what SharePoint Designer can and can't do:

- ✔ **You can use SharePoint Designer to work with SharePoint.**

- ✔ **You can't use SharePoint Designer as a more general Web development tool.** If you don't have a SharePoint site to develop, then you have no need for SharePoint Designer (or, really, anything for it to work on). If you need a more general Web-development tool, check out Microsoft Expression Web. Expression Web is similar to SharePoint Designer but isn't tied to SharePoint sites.

- ✔ **You can develop a horde of SharePoint components** — pages, lists, libraries, data sources, content types, views, forms, workflows, and external content types — all without having to write any code. SharePoint Designer spans a large swath of development capabilities.

- ✔ **You can keep using Designer when you go deeper into SharePoint development** and start working up master pages, page layouts, CSS, and JavaScript.

- ✔ **You can't write .NET code.** When your SharePoint site calls for .NET code, switch to Visual Studio, which is covered in Chapter 11.

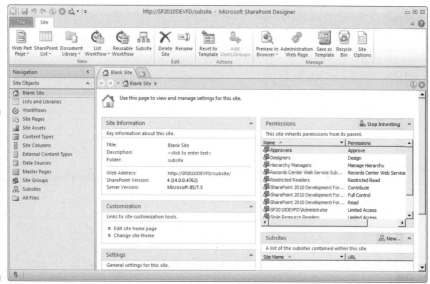

Figure 8-2:
When SharePoint Designer is connected to a site, the Ribbon and site navigation become active.

SharePoint Designer 2010 works only with SharePoint 2010. If you're working with SharePoint 2007, install SharePoint Designer 2007 instead. The two versions of SharePoint can be installed side by side on the same machine — but each has its own specific tools; you can't mix and match them.

Taking a Spin around SharePoint Designer

Any piece of software can be overwhelming at first glance — and SharePoint Designer is no exception. Microsoft has gone to great lengths to make the tool as intuitive and user-friendly as possible — but it still helps to take a spin around the user interface. The screen is divided into three main sections: the Ribbon across the top of the screen, a navigation window on the left side of the screen, and a design surface at the right of the screen, as shown in Figure 8-3.

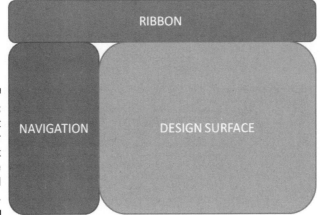

Figure 8-3:
SharePoint
Designer
is split
into three
functional
components.

Finding site-creation tools

You can use SharePoint Designer in several different ways to create a site. The easiest way is to use the SharePoint Designer File tab, also known as the Backstage View. The Backstage screen is what appears when SharePoint Designer is opened for the first time; after all, you have to either create or connect to a site or Designer has nothing to work with. The base templates that are available include a blank site, a blog site, and a team site. Depending on which features you activate for a particular site collection, additional templates are available. Clicking the More Templates button allows you to connect to a site collection in order to view the range of templates you have available (based on the activated features).

SharePoint Designer cannot be used to create Web Applications or SharePoint site collections. You can use any of three tools to do that job: the Central Administration application called PowerShell, the command-line utility STSADM, or .NET custom code.

Unwrapping the Ribbon

SharePoint Designer incorporates the visual arrangement of controls that you find in other Office applications in a feature known as the Ribbon. The Ribbon runs across the top of the screen; it's where you go to activate the commands you use as you develop your custom programs in SharePoint. You'll likely find the following Ribbon features handy as you begin using it:

- ✔ **The Ribbon is dynamic;** it changes to match the component of SharePoint you're currently using. For example, if you're working on a workflow, the Ribbon displays options for developing workflows (as shown in Figure 8-4). If you're developing a page, the Ribbon displays the commands you need for page development (as shown in Figure 8-5).

- ✔ **You can customize what's on the Ribbon** (beyond its standard functionality), and even add new Ribbons that are your own creations. All you have to do to customize a Ribbon tab — or add a new one — is right-click the standard Ribbon and choose Customize The Ribbon.

Figure 8-4:
The SharePoint Designer Ribbon when a workflow is being developed.

Figure 8-5:
The SharePoint Designer Ribbon when a page is being developed.

Steering the navigation features

In addition to the Ribbon across the top of the screen, a navigation window occupies the left side of the screen (as shown in Figure 8-6). The Navigation window provides a quick display of the Site Settings page, lists and libraries, workflows, site pages, site assets, content types, site columns, external content types, data sources, master pages, page layouts, site groups, and subsites. In addition, it offers an All Files view that shows you all the files in the site (which is similar to the behavior of SharePoint Designer 2007).

Figure 8-6:
The
SharePoint
Designer
navigation
window.

The page layouts navigational menu is only displayed if the site is a *publishing site* — a site that has the SharePoint Server Publishing Infrastructure feature activated. (For more about the Server Publishing Infrastructure, see Chapter 4.)

The Design section of SharePoint Designer is dynamic — what you're working on provides the context that determines which commands are displayed. For example, the Design section displays everything from the settings screens to the editors to the Workflow Designer.

The top of the Design section includes a navigational component similar to a Web browser. The Design section's navigational component includes a Home button and Forward and Back buttons to move through the history of windows that have been opened. For example, if you've clicked the Settings page, and then opened an editor, and then clicked to a different list altogether, you can hit the Back button to retrace your steps back through the various windows. In addition, a *breadcrumb* component (*Hansel and Gretel,* anyone?) shows the location of the current component in the overall hierarchy of the site. For example, if you're editing the columns in a calendar list, you see a breadcrumb "trail" to show that the location is the site, the List and Libraries galleries, the calendar list, and then the editor. SharePoint Designer allows multiple design windows to be open at the same time — say, an editor, a gallery screen, and/or a settings page. Each window is represented by a tab. The Design section's navigational components are shown in Figure 8-7.

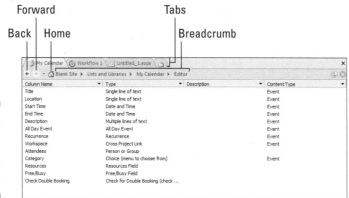

Figure 8-7:
The Design section's navigational component.

You can change the order in which the tabs are displayed across the screen by clicking them and dragging them either left or right. This is helpful when you want to see the tabs in a particular order as you work. For example, you might want to keep the tab that contains your style sheet always to the left of the tab that contains the page editor.

The breadcrumb feature is also a handy way to navigate to a specific window in the same context as the window you're viewing. For example, if you're viewing the settings window for a page, you might want to do a quick click to the editor window for this page without having to move the cursor down to the Edit File link. You can see the available windows that you can move to from the current window by clicking the drop-down arrow on the rightmost breadcrumb, as shown in Figure 8-8.

Figure 8-8:
Using the breadcrumb feature to launch context-specific windows in the location of the current window.

Configuring with Settings windows

A *settings window* provides configuration details and controls for a particular component of SharePoint. Components such as sites, pages, lists, libraries, and workflows all have settings pages associated with them. If you need to configure a list, for example, you don't have to open the list in the browser and then navigate to the settings page. You can view and configure the settings for the list right from SharePoint Designer — in a settings window like the one shown for a Calendar list in Figure 8-9.

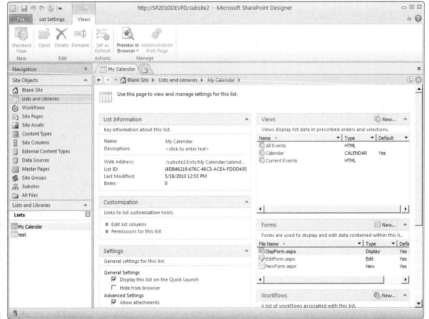

Figure 8-9: The settings window for a Calendar list.

When you first create a site using SharePoint Designer, the initial screen that appears is the settings window for the new site.

Viewing gallery windows

A *gallery* is a grouping of SharePoint artifacts displayed in a window. For example, when you click Lists and Libraries in the navigation window, you're presented all the lists and libraries on the site. Whenever you click any navigation button in the navigation window, SharePoint Designer pulls all the artifacts from the site for that navigation button (for example, Content Types) into one grouping — and displays that group in a gallery window.

You can view a gallery of the following types of SharePoint artifacts by clicking the corresponding navigation item for each one:

- ✔ Lists and Libraries
- ✔ Workflows
- ✔ Site Pages
- ✔ Site Assets
- ✔ Content Types
- ✔ Site Columns
- ✔ External Content Types
- ✔ Data Sources
- ✔ Master Pages
- ✔ Page Layouts
- ✔ Site Groups
- ✔ Subsites

I've introduced most of the items in the preceding list elsewhere in this book (see the index for help). The Site Assets category, on the other hand, may sound unfamiliar; it's like a toolbox where the site stores artifacts that it uses to do its work — such as Cascading Style Sheets (CSS), JavaScript, XML, images, and text files.

Each gallery has a corresponding SharePoint Designer Ribbon tab where you can find the commands specific to that gallery. For example, the Master Page Gallery has a Ribbon tab called Master Pages that offers functionality such as creating, editing, and managing your site's master pages.

Developing in Editor windows

SharePoint Designer contains a number of different editor programs that are used for SharePoint development. For example, when you develop a page, you're using a Page Editor (as shown in Figure 8-10). If you're developing a workflow, you use the Workflow Editor. The tool fits the job.

The following editors are available in SharePoint Designer:

- ✔ **Page Editor:** Use this editor to develop pages. For example, when you want to develop a new content page you will do it using this editor.

- ✔ **Workflow Editor:** This editor is designed to develop workflows. Do you need to create a workflow that sends a new proposal off to your 15 executives for approval and tracks their feedback? This is the editor you will use to do it.

- ✔ **List and Library Editor:** Use this editor to work with Lists and Libraries. When you need to work with the views, forms, workflows and content types that are attached to a list or library, this is the editor you will use.

- ✔ **Content Type Editor:** Developing content types often takes patience as you figure out exactly which columns for metadata you want to include. When you need to develop a content type, however, this editor is the one you will use.

- ✔ **Column Editor:** The column editor lets you develop metadata columns for your SharePoint libraries in a single interface. When you need to configure the columns on your site, this is the editor you will use in SharePoint Designer.

- ✔ **Script Editor:** When you need to develop code such as Cascading Style Sheets (CSS) or HyperText Markup Language (HTML), you will use this editor to get the job done. The editor is actually nothing more than a glorified text editor with some nifty features, such as turning key words different colors, to help you identify key words syntax.

- ✔ **Image Editor:** The image editor is a simply image manipulation program that you can use to modify your images. You can do things such as changing the brightness, contrast, and color or even cropping, rotating, or flipping the image.

- ✔ **Text Editor:** This editor is similar to using WordPad or Notepad but without having to leave the SharePoint Designer application. Need to edit a text file on your SharePoint site? This is the editor you can use.

- ✔ **XML Editor:** The XML editor is similar to the script and text editor but provides some nifty functionality for getting the syntax and formatting of eXtensible Markup Language (XML) documents correct.

- ✔ **External Content Type Editor:** Just like the Content Type editor is used to work with content types, this editor is used to develop content types that are external to your SharePoint environment. An example of an external content type might be a grouping of metadata that is stored in your Line of Business (LOB) system that you want to interact with in SharePoint. The external content type would contain the connection information and the details of the metadata and how it should be used by SharePoint.

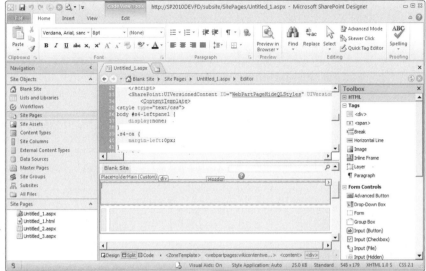

Figure 8-10:
Developing
a page
using the
Page
Editor in
SharePoint
Designer.

Introducing other helpful features

In addition to the Ribbon, navigation, settings, galleries, and editors, a number of other features make life much easier in SharePoint Designer.

Logged In As

As a SharePoint developer, you often log in to different sites as different users. It's easy to get turned around and forget which credentials you used to log in to the site. Confusion, begone: A new feature called Logged In As provides a solution. The Logged In As button sits in the lower-left corner of the screen. When you hover the mouse pointer over this button, it displays the username you're currently using for the site. If you actually click this button you can log in to the same site using *different* credentials. The end result is that you can switch user accounts in a jiffy, without having to close and re-open SharePoint Designer.

Skewer Click

When you're developing a master page or layout, the styling and HTML tags can get confusing. The very nature of Cascading Style Sheets (CSS) is that they *cascade* (well, yeah) in the order the styles were applied. The problem is that it's easy to get confused if you're in a hurry to determine what styles are working where, which tags are nested within other tags on the page, who's on first, and all that. The Skewer Click button allows you to click a point in the page and see all the styles and tags that are involved in that particular point. You can think of the Skewer Button as turning the mouse pointer into a long skewer, like the ones used for shish kebab. When the mouse is clicked at a point on the page, the skewer rams through all the layers of styling and tags on the page, and a popup appears — showing all the tags that were skewered, as shown in Figure 8-11. (Yum.) You can think of the skewer functionality as a mode that turns the mouse into a lethal weapon ready to be stabbed at some portion of the design surface. You activate the skewer weapon (or shall we say *feature*) by clicking a button in the Ribbon called Skewer Click. Once the button is clicked the mouse is ready and waiting to be clicked somewhere on the design surface. Once skewered you can move the mouse pointer over the different tags in the box that pops up at the point where you skewered the design surface and see the styles associated with that particular tag; they show up in the CSS properties pane.

When you're trying to apply a brand to a SharePoint master page, it can be difficult to figure out which piece of the SharePoint page to style in order to get that signature appearance. For example, if you want to change the header image, the normal approach would be to hunt through the HTML tags and CSS style sheets to find the correct tag to style. This approach works, but it involves a lot of trial and error. To identify what part of the page you've just affected, you might want to (say) change a border to bright lime. An easier approach is to use the Skewer Click — simply skewer the image (as shown in Figure 8-11) and you can see all the tags and styles that are currently applied. You'll know instantly where to go to change the look and feel without having to hunt through the code.

CSS Properties pane

Pop-up menu of HTML tags   Skewer Click button

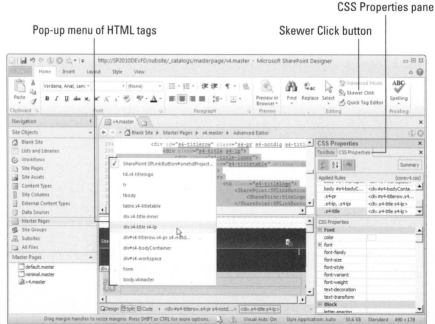

Figure 8-11: Skewer Click displays all HTML tags and CSS styles associated with the specific point of the page that was clicked.

Normal-mode editing versus Advanced-mode editing

One of the challenges of SharePoint Designer is knowing how *not* to mess up how the page works. For example, as you develop a page, it's way too easy to edit a portion of the page that isn't designed to be altered, which can gum up the works accidentally. SharePoint Designer provides a solution to this problem: Normal-mode editing and Advanced-mode editing. When you click the Edit File drop-down menu, you can choose between these editing modes, as shown in Figure 8-12.

✔ **Editing in Normal mode:** This mode restricts portions of the page that shouldn't be edited in order to add content; it's much like editing a page from the browser. In Normal mode you can't edit (and so can't mess up) portions of the page such as global navigation, local navigation, or header and footer information.

✔ **Editing in Advanced mode:** This mode, on the other hand, allows you to edit any portion of the page — it's much like opening an .aspx page in Visual Studio or even Notepad. Advanced mode gives you more flexibility *and* access to all parts of the page — including those not intended for editing — which means you can break the page completely if you make a mistake.

Editing a page in Advanced mode customizes the page and detaches it from its site definition. The customized page then lives in the SQL Server database. This isn't a huge problem but it could affect performance or cause additional work when the site is upgraded. (For more about customized pages. check out the "Ghosts in the database" sidebar in this chapter.)

A SharePoint administrator can restrict the use of Advanced mode in SharePoint Designer, which is a way to exert more control over the functionality available to different users of SharePoint Designer.

Locking down SharePoint Designer

SharePoint Designer is a powerful tool; as such it must be carefully used. It's easy to break an entire site with a seemingly innocuous click of the mouse. In the past, many server-farm administrators have jumped to the conclusion that SharePoint Designer can cause trouble — and have simply barred its use site-wide.

SharePoint Server 2010, however, provides a more flexible scenario; SharePoint Designer capabilities can be governed and restricted by administrators at the levels of the farm and the site collection. For example, a farm administrator can restrict a Web Application and determine what SharePoint Designer features to make available to site-collection administrators. In the same manner, a site-collection administrator can govern the use of SharePoint Designer on a specific site and determine the functionality available to site's owners and designers.

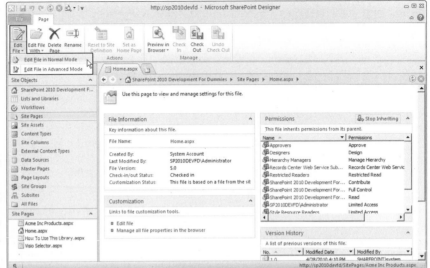

Figure 8-12:
You can edit
a page in
Normal or
Advanced
mode.

You can think of the governance model as a hierarchy — with the farm administrator at the top. If a farm administrator has restricted access to SharePoint Designer at the Web Application level, then site-collection administrators can't turn on any Designer functionality for the site owners and designers. A red warning message tells the site-collection administrator that the server administrator has, in effect, declared SharePoint Designer off limits.

To configure the SharePoint Designer governance settings for the farm, in Central Administration, click General Application Settings and then choose Configure SharePoint Designer Settings. The settings page allows SharePoint Designer to be restricted in four ways, as shown in Figure 8-13.

The site-collection administrator can govern SharePoint Designer for a specific site collection in two stages:

1. Specifying settings by clicking Site Actions⇨Site Settings and then choosing SharePoint Designer Settings (located under the Site Collection Administration grouping).

2. Restricting SharePoint Designer functionality for site owners and designers as shown in Figure 8-14.

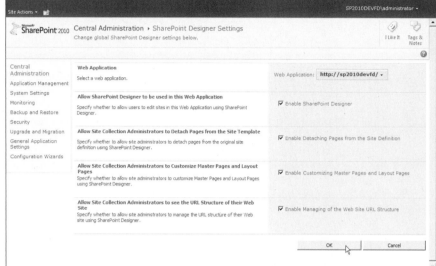

Figure 8-13:
Governing
SharePoint
Designer
for site-
collection
administra-
tors from
Central
Admin-
istration.

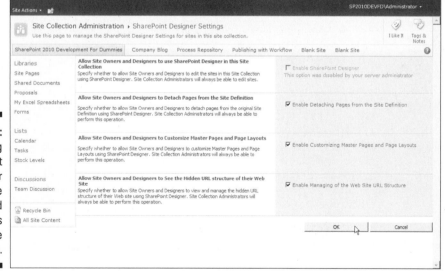

Figure 8-14:
Governing
SharePoint
Designer
for site
owners and
designers
from Site
Settings.

Taking SharePoint Development Beyond the Browser

Many SharePoint development tasks can be accomplished right from the browser — such as developing content pages, adding Web Parts to Web Part pages, publishing content using publishing pages, as well as developing such things as lists, libraries, content types, and site columns. Although the browser is very powerful in the SharePoint world, there comes a time when you have to take your development effort beyond the browser. SharePoint Designer provides much of the same capabilities as working directly in the browser — and then some. Using SharePoint Designer, you can expand your development efforts with such tasks as these:

- ✔ Developing master pages and page layouts
- ✔ Building custom Web Part pages to include customized Web Part zones
- ✔ Customizing Web Parts such as the XSLT List View Web Part (XLV)
- ✔ Developing Cascading Style Sheets (CSS)
- ✔ Developing SharePoint workflows
- ✔ Developing JavaScript functionality

When you get to the point of diving into custom .NET code, the tool of choice is Visual Studio (covered in Chapter 11).

Developing pages

The SharePoint Designer Page Editor is used to develop pages. You can find it in the tabs that make up the Ribbon at the top of the screen.

The Ribbon for developing pages offers different commands depending on the mode in which you're editing a page. If you're editing a page in Normal mode, then only a subset of functionality is available. If you're editing a page in Advanced mode then the Ribbon contains all the commands of Normal mode as well as additional advanced functionality.

The Normal-mode Ribbon offers you these tabs:

- ✔ **File:** This tab is feature common to all Office 2010 products; it provides common commands such as Save, Save As, Close Site, Help. The File tab also contains a quick-open feature for opening sites and pages, and for creating items.

The File tab is also known as the Backstage View. The Backstage View of SharePoint Designer is shown in Figure 8-15.

✔ **Home:** This tab provides basic commands such as font-formatting tools, paragraph formatting tools, find and replace, spelling check, and previewing your page in the browser. The Home tab is shown in Figure 8-16.

✔ **Insert:** Use this tab to insert components such as tables, pictures, links, data views, forms, controls, Web Parts, Web Part zones, and symbols. The Insert tab is shown in Figure 8-16.

✔ **View:** This tab provides a view of the page being edited. You can view the page you're editing in Code view, Design view, or a Split view that's half Code view and half Design view. In addition, you can turn on the various visual aids, task panes, a ruler, and a grid. The View tab is shown in Figure 8-16.

✔ **Code View Tools (Edit):** This tab provides page-editing capabilities such as working with markup tags, bookmarking a point in the page markup, IntelliSense (which offers context-sensitive syntax suggestions), code snippets, code-formatting tools, hyperlink tools, and Code Editor options. The Code View Tools (Edit) tab is shown in Figure 8-16.

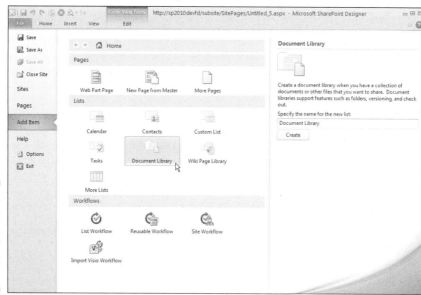

Figure 8-15:
The Backstage View of SharePoint Designer.

Home

Insert

Figure 8-16:
The Home,
Insert, View,
and Edit
tabs on the
SharePoint
Designer
page editing
Ribbon.

View

Code View Tools (Edit)

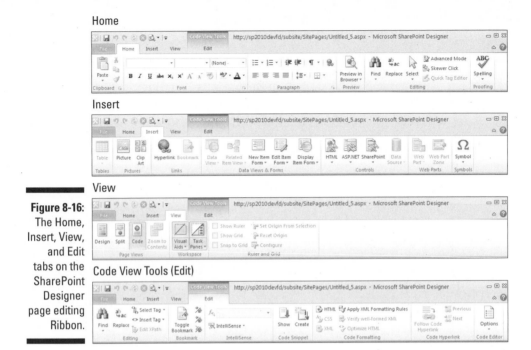

In Advanced mode, the Ribbon contains all the same tabs as the Normal editing mode but also includes the following tabs:

- **Layout:** The Layout tab provides layout functionality for the page such as layers, page size, margins, page element arrangement. The Layout tab is shown in Figure 8-17 (top).

- **Style:** The Style tab is used to manage the style and look of feel of the page. Use this tab for managing and developing master pages and CSS style sheets. The Style tab is shown in Figure 8-17 (bottom).

Figure 8-17:
The Layout
tab (top)
and Style
tab (bottom) on the
SharePoint
Designer
page editing
Ribbon.

As a rule, administrators of server farms and site collections control the use of SharePoint Designer. If you don't have the privileges needed to edit pages in Advanced mode, then your administrator probably hasn't turned on that feature for you. For more about SharePoint Designer governance, check out the "Locking down SharePoint Designer" subsection earlier in this chapter.

In addition to the standard Ribbon tabs, specialized tabs appear on-screen according to the component of a page you're editing. For example, say you've inserted a list view into a Web Part zone on your page. A new grouping of tabs appears, offering the commands you need for using Web Parts and developing list views (as shown in Figure 8-18).

Figure 8-18:
The specialized Web Part Zone Tools and List View Tools tabs in SharePoint Designer Ribbon.

Many different elements have specialized tabs. Which tabs appear in the Ribbon depend on the item selected on the design surface. For example, if you're working with a Web Part contained in a table located in a Web Part zone, then you're offered the specialized tabs called Table Tools, Web Part Tools, and Web Part Zone Tools.

Your SharePoint farm administrator controls whether you can develop master pages and page layouts, and can lock down this capability in a SharePoint site. If you can't view or edit master pages and page layouts (and your work requires those privileges), ask your administrator to turn on these features for you. Also, if master pages and site pages are showing up but you don't see Page Layouts in the navigation window, make sure that the Publishing Infrastructure feature is activated for the site. (For an introduction to master pages and site pages, as well as some more detail about publishing in SharePoint, see Chapter 4.)

If you remove a control from the master page that is required by other pages that inherit properties from the master page, you've got trouble. Doing so can possibly break the entire page. For example, if you remove the calendar control from the master page and then try to add a calendar to a page that inherits from the master page, the page you're modifying won't be able to render the calendar because it's looking for the removed control.

Developing views for lists

A *list* is the fundamental container for storing data in SharePoint. Data doesn't amount to much if you can't view it. Thus a view of a list is a very important piece of SharePoint development. If you've taken a spin around SharePoint, you've viewed a lot of list data — nearly everything in SharePoint is stored in lists. For example, if you add an Announcement to your page, the data is stored in a list and becomes list data, which you embed in your page by using a List View Web Part. If you develop your own SharePoint list — say, of recipes — you display the recipes using a List View Web Part.

Every list — and every library — automatically has a default Web Part available in the Web Part gallery. Adding a standard view of a list to a page is as easy as adding the Web Part associated with that list. For example, the recipe list has a recipe Web Part that you can add to a page by using either the browser or SharePoint Designer.

A library is just a specialized list that associates a file with each list item.

Chapter 4 takes a detailed look at adding a Web Part to a page using the browser. You can also add the List View Web Part to a page by using SharePoint Designer; follow these steps to add (for example) a Recipes list:

1. **Open SharePoint Designer and then connect to the SharePoint site where you want to add the list view Web Part.**

2. **Browse to the page on which you want to add the list view Web Part.**

3. **Click the Edit button located on the Page tab in order to begin editing the page.**

4. **With the page in Edit mode and the cursor in the area where you want to add the list view, click the Insert tab and click the Data View drop-down button.**

5. **Choose the Recipes list from the drop-down menu.**

When you have the List View Web Part on the page, you can customize and develop it further in SharePoint Designer. When you're working with the List view, Designer presents you with a series of specialized tabs in the Ribbon — the List View Tools (refer to Figure 8-18). You can use these specialized tabs to apply conditional formatting, sort your list data, organize the list as multiple pages, add or remove columns, change the look and layout, configure the Web Part, and add or work with tables.

The List View Web Part is actually an XSLT List View (XLV) Web Part. The XLV Web Part uses standard XSLT. You can develop the list view using SharePoint Designer and the List View Tools (sounds like a vocal group, doesn't it?) — but when the time comes to dive into the code, you can rest assured that the Web Part is using standards-based XSLT. (If some of these terms sound like abracadabra, sneak a peek at the next paragraph.)

EXtensible Markup Language (XML) is a standardized method of storing data. To apply styles to XML data, you have to use a different markup language: EXtensible Stylesheet Language (XSL). In order to view data over the Web, yet another markup language must be used: HyperText Markup Language (HTML). Of course, if you have data stored as XML and want to display it on the Web, you have to translate it into the HTML format first. To transform XML data into HTML (which actually turns into XHTML when you follow the rules that govern XML), you need a transformation language — in this case, XSL Transformations (that's XSLT for short). In SharePoint, the List View Web Part uses standard XSL and XSLT — which means you can use it anywhere on the Web. You can find a lot more information on XSL at this link:

```
www.w3schools.com/xsl/
```

SharePoint lists use forms for displaying, editing, and creating items. You can use InfoPath to edit these forms — and launch it right from the Ribbon in SharePoint Designer. To edit a form in InfoPath, browse to the settings page of the list or library whose forms you want to edit; then click the Design Forms in InfoPath button (in the Ribbon on the List Settings tab). Chapter 6 explains how SharePoint is integrated with InfoPath.

Styling your page with CSS

Changing the look and feel of a SharePoint page is accomplished using Cascading Style Sheets (CSS). Using SharePoint Designer you can create new styles, apply existing styles, manage style sheets, and attach style sheets to your page. You can find the style commands (logically enough) on the Style tab, as shown in Figure 8-17.

Creating a new style

To style a page using SharePoint Designer, follow these steps:

1. **Browse to the site that contains the page you want to style, and then click Site Actions⟹Edit in SharePoint Designer.**

2. **Navigate to the gallery containing the page you want (most likely that's Site Pages), and then click the page to open it in a new tab.**

   The initial tab contains the settings for the page.

3. **Click the Edit File drop-down button on the Page tab of the Ribbon and choose Edit File in Advanced Mode (as long as your administrator has made this mode available).**

If this option isn't available flip back to the discussion earlier in the chapter about Normal mode versus Advanced mode and then go hassle your administrator.

4. **Select the Style tab in the Ribbon and click the New Style button.**

The New Style dialog box appears, as shown in Figure 8-19. Here's where you can create a style:

- The top of the New Style dialog box allows for the style to be configured.

- The CSS selector allows you to specify which HTML component will use this style.

- The style can also be defined in the current page only, in a new style sheet, or in an existing style sheet.

- If the current page is selected, then the CSS styling will be embedded right into the page.

5. **Click OK to embed the style in the page.**

SharePoint Designer updates the page automatically to include a new Style element that shows the new style defined.

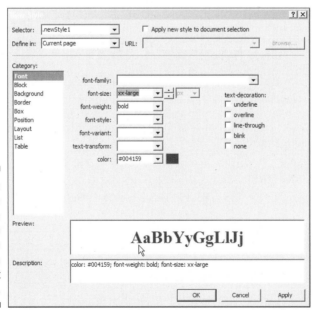

Figure 8-19:
Creating a new style using the New Style dialog box in SharePoint Designer.

Applying existing styles

If you want to apply a style that's already developed, you can do so by using the Attach Style Sheet button located on the Style tab of the Ribbon. You can choose to attach the new style either as a link or as an import. The link method adds an HTML link tag that references the style sheet. The import method uses a CSS import tag to import the styles into the page.

Attaching a style sheet to a page

Styling a page takes a different approach depending on whether you're working with the page in Normal edit mode or Advanced edit mode:

- **In Normal edit mode,** you're limited to creating a customized version of the main `corev4.css` file and storing it in the `styles` directory.

- **In Advanced mode,** you have access to a Style tab that provides the ability to create, apply, attach, and manage style sheets from anywhere in the site as shown in Figure 8-17.

Editing styles in Normal mode still allows you to edit a style but there are some big caveats. When you edit a style in Normal edit mode, a new tab opens that is a copy of the `corev4.css` file. Any edits you make to the styles will be reflected in this copy of `corev4.css`. The customized `corev4.css` style sheet must go in the `styles` directory. Be careful, however; the `styles` directory affects every page in the site. The styles in the `styles` directory are also not capable of changing when the theme is changed. If a style file isn't in the `styles` directory, then you must use the Advanced Mode Editor and the Style tab to attach a style sheet to the page.

Styling with themes

The main style sheet for SharePoint is called `corev4.css` — a Cascading Style Sheet with nearly 7,500 lines of styling information, used throughout the SharePoint environment. Working with styling in Normal Edit mode can be difficult since overriding a style that the rest of the site uses can be accomplished without realizing what has happened. For example, you might change the background color of part of your page to blue — only to discover that the background for *all* list views, throughout the entire site, use the same style and now have a blue background. If the text is also blue, the pages become a blur of blue — unusable.

Creating styling that pulls from a theme gives tremendous flexibility to non-developer administrators. For example, you might pull the color of your fonts from the current site theme. If an administrator of the site changes the theme, the styling in your pages updates automatically to reflect the new font color.

TIP

To get your custom CSS styling to pull from theme styles, first you must place your CSS file in a `Themable` folder; you have these basic options:

- If the Publishing Infrastructure feature is activated, here's the path:

  ```
  http://<Root Site>/Style Library/~language/Themable
  ```

- If the Publishing Infrastructure isn't activated for the site, the path looks like this:

  ```
  http://<Root Site>/Style Library/Themable
  ```

- If the Publishing Infrastructure isn't activated, you can create the `Style Library/Themable` structure manually.

For more about the Publishing Infrastructure in SharePoint, see Chapter 4.

To insert a theme color into your CSS style sheet, you can add comments, but they have to be constructed in a way that the SharePoint theme engine will understand. The theme engine scans the CSS file, recognizes the replacement tokens in the comments, and then inserts the theme color as specified in the comments. The following example illustrates pulling the theme color represented as `Accent1-Lighter` and setting it as the background color. If the default theme is used, then the background color will be specified as `#00FF00`. If a theme is applied then the `#00FF00` theme is replaced with the color defined for `Accent1-Lighter`. Here's what that looks like:

```
/*[ReplaceColor(themeColor:"Accent1-Lighter")]*/ background-color:#00FF00;
```

The SharePoint engine can replace the following CSS items:

- **Colors:** Using the `ReplaceColor` code.
- **Fonts:** Using the `ReplaceFont` code.
- **Images:** Using the `RecolorImage` code.

  `RecolorImage` also contains three methods: `blend`, `tint`, `fill`.

The `corev4.css` file uses these special placeholder words, called *tokens*, for theme replacement and is an excellent reference source for syntax and context. The `corev4.css` file is located on the file system at

```
C:\Program Files\Common Files\Microsoft Shared\Web Server Extensions\14\
        TEMPLATE\LAYOUTS\1033\STYLES\COREV4.CSS
```

The names of the theme colors can be viewed and the colors edited on the settings page for the theme. To access this page, click Site Actions⇨Site Settings and then select the Site Theme link located under the Look and Feel section. Each theme color, such as `Accent1`, has degrees of color associated with it. For example, you can specify how much `Accent1` you want to apply — `Accent1-Lightest`, `Accent1-Lighter`, `Accent1-Medium`, `Accent1-Darker`, and `Accent1-Darkest`.

The theme names are outlined in Table 8-1. Each name offers the following options for degrees of color: Lightest, Lighter, Medium, Darker, and Darkest.

Table 8-1	SharePoint 2010 Theme Names	
Text/Background – Dark 1	Text/Background – Light 1	Text/Background – Dark 2
Text/Background – Light 2	Accent 1	Accent 2
Accent 3	Accent 4	Accent 5
Accent 6	Hyperlink	Followed Hyperlink

SharePoint stores its content and its configuration information in SQL Server databases. Using such a database allows SharePoint to provide an easy interface so users can create and modify content on the fly. The SharePoint user interface then talks to the databases to make changes instead of trying to work with files on the file system. This is a great architecture for simplifying the user interface and making the product robust — but pulling files from the databases all the time can cause a lot of extra work when the system is rendering Web pages. To help reduce this extra load, SharePoint often stores its template pages on the file system and only moves them to the database when the corresponding pages are customized. The template files stored on the file system are known as *site definitions*. When a page is customized, it's copied into the database — which is also known as removing the page from its site definition. (See the "Ghosts in the database" sidebar for a spirited aside on that topic.)

Ghosts in the database

The terminology for pages that live on the file system or that live in the database has changed over the years. Originally the terms "ghosted" and "unghosted" were used. The terminology was from the perspective of the database; a "ghosted" Web page was a page that lived on the file system and appeared as a ghost to the database. Because the database didn't actually "see" the page, it was a ghost. An "unghosted" page, on the other hand, was one that had been customized — which detached it from its site definition and moved a copy into the database. The database could see the page, thus it was considered unghosted. Recently Microsoft has dropped this spooky terminology and made the same distinction with more straightforward terms: *customized* and *uncustomized* pages, respectively. (If you just had a sudden moment of enlightenment, you're not the only one.)

When you work with a page using SharePoint Designer in Advanced edit mode you can modify the template file that is stored in the site definition. When you edit the template file, however, remember that you're *customizing* the page — so you're also doing two more things:

- ✔ Detaching the page from its site definition.
- ✔ Storing the customized page in the database.

When you customize a page, SharePoint Designer warns you that you're about to detach the page from its site definition. If you go ahead and customize the page anyway, a blue icon shows up next to the file in the Gallery view — letting you know the page has been fiddled with (that is, customized). Be careful with customizing pages; it can cause unintended performance and upgrade problems down the road.

If you're an administrator who just doesn't hold with all this tweaking, you can lock down SharePoint Designer and remove the capability to detach pages from their site definitions; all you have to do is restrict the use of Advanced Edit mode. For details, check out "Locking down SharePoint Designer," earlier in the chapter.

Customizing a SharePoint workflow

A SharePoint *workflow* allows you to create a sequence of tasks that are performed in response to specific conditions as the process progresses. Those conditions and tasks are contained in workflow *steps*. For example, the first step in a workflow might involve an approval for new content. When new content has been approved, the second step might be to send an e-mail to notify people that the content is available. Business processes rarely fit into such a tidy box, however, so workflows nearly always have to be customized. You don't want to try to shape your business process to fit a specific workflow tool — that's too limiting — so SharePoint Designer gives you the means to create custom workflows that match your business process.

The SharePoint Designer navigation pane provides a Workflows item that provides an entry point into the site's workflows. When you open the Workflows gallery, you see a listing of all the site's current workflows. The Ribbon also updates to show the Workflows tab (as shown in Figure 8-20).

Each site starts out with standard global workflow items such as the Approval Collect Feedback. These are useful, as far as they go — but they can't cover every situation, so sometimes you have to develop your own custom workflows.

You can create a new workflow in SharePoint Designer in the New section of the Workflows Ribbon (clear labels — gotta love 'em). The Site tab, which is the default Ribbon tab displayed after you open a site, also contains a New section in which you can create a List and Reusable workflow. You can create any of three general types of workflows:

- ✔ **List workflow:** The most common scenario is to create a workflow for a particular list. You can start up such a *list workflow* in several ways: when a new item is added to a list, when a user manually starts the workflow, or when an item in the list is modified. For example, you might want to create a workflow for a Recipes list that requires approval from the head chef before it's posted to the site for everyone to see.

- ✔ **Reusable workflow:** A *reusable workflow* is similar to a list workflow but it can be used on multiple lists because you attach it to a content type rather than to one specific list. When the content type is added to a list, the workflow follows the content type. For example, if you've packaged up the fields for a recipe into a content type, you wouldn't want to create new workflows for every single person who creates a list that contains a recipe. Using a reusable workflow you could still require the chef's approval of the recipes, regardless of what lists they might occupy on the site.

- ✔ **Site workflow:** A *site workflow* isn't attached to a specific list or a particular content type; it's designed to be used more generally throughout the site.

When you're creating a new workflow, you don't have to start from scratch. You can start with the standard SharePoint global workflows and customize them to meet your needs. When you click a global workflow you want to edit, a dialog box appears, informs you that the workflow is read-only, and asks whether you'd like to create a local copy to edit. That's your cue to start customizing.

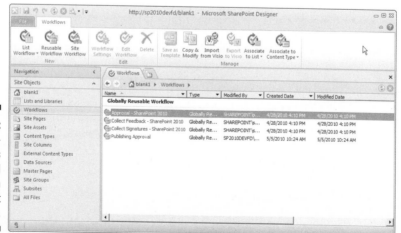

Figure 8-20:
The Work-
flows
gallery and
Ribbon in
SharePoint
Designer.

You build up a workflow by adding steps, conditions, and actions to the Workflow Design window. A *step* is a logical portion of the workflow that contains conditions and actions. You can add multiple steps to a workflow in to match the steps in your business process.

At the core of a workflow is an action. An *action* is the portion of the workflow that actually does some work. (For example, you might have an action to send an e-mail, set a field in a list, or perform a calculation.) You have to tell an action when to perform its task — and that's the purpose of a *condition*. You can, of course, create a workflow with only actions and no conditions. Such a workflow would just perform its logic without checking for any conditions. (Go ahead, if you don't mind tempting fate and Murphy's Law.)

A condition provides logic to the workflow and tells its actions whether to perform the work. For example, you might have a condition that checks to see whether a purchase request is greater than $100. If the purchase request is greater than $100, then an action might be set up to send an e-mail to a manager.

The conditions available in SharePoint Designer 2010 are outlined in Table 8-2.

Table 8-2	SharePoint Designer 2010 Conditions	
Condition	*List Type Availability*	*Category*
If any value equals value	List, Reusable, Site	Common Conditions
If current item field equals value	List, Reusable	Common Conditions
Created by a specific person	List, Reusable	Other Conditions
Created in a specific date span	List, Reusable	Other Conditions
Modified by a specific person	List, Reusable	Other Conditions
Person is a valid SharePoint user	List, Reusable, Site	Other Conditions
Title field contains keywords	List, Reusable	Other Conditions

The actions available in SharePoint Designer 2010 are outlined in Table 8-3.

Table 8-3	SharePoint Designer 2010 Actions	
Action	**Availability**	**Category**
Add a Comment	List, Reusable, Site	Core Actions
Add Time to Date	List, Reusable, Site	Core Actions
Do Calculation	List, Reusable, Site	Core Actions
Log to History List	List, Reusable, Site	Core Actions
Pause for Duration	List, Reusable, Site	Core Actions
Pause until Date	List, Reusable, Site	Core Actions
Send an E-mail	List, Reusable, Site	Core Actions
Set Time Portion of Date/Time Field	List, Reusable, Site	Core Actions
Set Workflow Status	List, Reusable, Site	Core Actions
Set Workflow Variable	List, Reusable, Site	Core Actions
Stop Workflow	List, Reusable, Site	Core Actions
Capture a version of the Document Set	List, Reusable, Site	Document Set Actions
Send Document Set to Repository	List, Reusable, Site	Document Set Actions
Set Content Approval Status for the Document Set	List, Reusable, Site	Document Set Actions
Start Document Set Approval Process	List, Reusable, Site	Document Set Actions
Check In Item	List, Reusable, Site	List Actions
Check Out Item	List, Reusable, Site	List Actions
Copy List Item	List, Reusable, Site	List Actions
Create List Item	List, Reusable, Site	List Actions
Declare Record	List, Reusable	List Actions
Delete Item	List, Reusable, Site	List Actions
Discard Check Out Item	List, Reusable, Site	List Actions
Set Content Approval Status	List, Reusable	List Actions

(continued)

Table 8-3 *(continued)*

Action	Availability	Category
Set Field in Current Item	List, Reusable	List Actions
Undeclare Record	List, Reusable	List Actions
Update List Item	List, Reusable, Site	List Actions
Wait For Field Change in Current Item	List, Reusable	List Actions
Lookup Manager of a User	List, Reusable, Site	Relational Actions
Assign a Form to a Group	List, Reusable, Site	Task Actions
Assign a To-do Item	List, Reusable, Site	Task Actions
Collect Data from a User	List, Reusable, Site	Task Actions
Start Approval Process	List, Reusable, Site	Task Actions
Start Custom Task Process	List, Reusable, Site	Task Actions
Start Feedback Process	List, Reusable, Site	Task Actions
Extract Substring from End of String	List, Reusable, Site	Utility Actions
Extract Substring from Index of String	List, Reusable, Site	Utility Actions
Extract Substring from Start of String	List, Reusable, Site	Utility Actions
Extract Substring of String from Index with Length	List, Reusable, Site	Utility Actions
Find Interval Between Dates	List, Reusable, Site	Utility Actions

An important aspect of building workflows is interacting with process *owners* — the folks who know the business process well enough to help you identify the steps, conditions, and actions you need when you develop the workflow. Without a visual representation, however, it's difficult for a workflow developer to communicate accurately with the process owner. Visio to the rescue! You can export a SharePoint Designer workflow as a Visio Workflow Interchange (VWI) file. Then the person who needs the picture can import the VWI file into Visio — which dutifully creates a picture version of the workflow. (For more about exporting and importing workflows between Visio and SharePoint Designer check out Chapter 7.)

Chapter 9

Developing Reports with Report Builder

Leaders have to act more quickly today. The pressure comes much faster.

— Andy Grove

*B*usiness is busting at the seams with an overload of digital data. In the past, the problem leaders faced was not having enough data. Now, the problem is having too much data flowing in from all corners of the organization — and no pontoons to keep everyone above the flood. So finding a mechanism for turning the raw data into usable information — and putting that info to work — becomes critical. Organizations that can master that trick will succeed; the rest become overwhelmed and overloaded.

As data abounds in the information age, it's not enough to have a few dedicated people cranking out reports. The time for self-service reporting has arrived. Every organization has a wealth of knowledge about the processes and procedures that make the company succeed. The problem: that knowledge is trapped in the minds of the employees. Providing everyone with the capability to tap into the data and create reports *based on their individual knowledge* is a critical step to success. Sharing information — in the form of reports, in a collaborative environment such as SharePoint — benefits the whole organization.

The reporting solution that Microsoft has developed is called Reporting Services, and it's part of SQL Server. Reporting Services can be integrated with SharePoint in order to provide the benefits of a collaborative content management.

In this chapter, you get handle on using Reporting Services to make data connections, retrieve datasets, and build reports. You dissect the components of a report and see how those components can be developed using Report Builder. Finally you attain the vision of delivering reports to end users using a SharePoint Web Part. Enlightenment awaits.

Understanding Reporting Services

SQL Server is often thought of as a database *platform* — a basis for custom programs tailored to specific business needs, not just a database engine that stores configuration data and content. Although SQL Server has a world-class database engine, it also provides other components for business intelligence. Its component that renders reports is a reporting engine called SQL Server Reporting Services (SSRS). Microsoft recognized that a centralized portal platform such as SharePoint was a natural fit with reporting — and began this potent alliance with SQL Server 2005 Service Pack (SP) 2, which integrated the two technologies tightly.

To integrate SharePoint Server 2010 with Reporting Services, you must use SQL Server 2008 R2; earlier versions won't cut the mustard. For more about configuring SharePoint for integration with Reporting Services, point your browser to the following address:

```
msdn.microsoft.com/en-us/library/bb326356.aspx
```

Touring Reporting Services and its reports

A Reporting Services report consists of an eXtensible Markup Language (XML) file defined by using Report Definition Language (RDL), a specific XML Schema Definition (XSD). Even if this alphabet soup sounds complicated, the way it works (thankfully) is actually very simple: An XML file is just a text-based file that follows certain formatting rules. You can write your own XML files using any text editor you want, even time-honored Notepad. For more information about XML, check out the following URL:

```
www.w3schools.com/xml/default.asp
```

For the moment, keep in mind that XML is a set of general rules that dictate how to structure data. Because a report is very specific kind of document, of course, additional information is required: In particular, an XSD file must dictate exactly how to compose the XML to create a Report Services report. The good news is that this trick is straightforward: The XSD file simply defines what tags can be used in the XML document. Microsoft developed a specific type of XSD file for Reporting Services — called Report Definition Language (RDL) — thus every Reporting Services report is a text file with the .rdl extension. Theoretically, you *could* open Notepad and start writing your own Reporting Services reports — which would take a lot of time and be *really* complicated — but why suffer? To make life easier, Microsoft developed Report Builder specifically for creating those special RDL files.

Happily, you can use other tools besides Report Builder to create RDL files. If you're a programmer, chances are you'll be happy to know that one such tool lives in Visual Studio — its Report Designer component (for more information about designing reports using Visual Studio check out *Professional SQL Server Reporting Services* (WROX) which yours truly co-authored). A number of third parties have also developed tools for developing RDL files (reports).

Report Builder provides an intuitive interface very similar to Microsoft Office; non-programmers who use it to develop Reporting Services reports should feel right at home. Report Builder includes a Ribbon across the top of the application window that guides users visually to the reporting commands. The Ribbon, a common on-screen element throughout Microsoft Office, is now part of SharePoint and its tools, offering a familiar look and feel to new users. For example, you might have analysts who use Word and Excel day in and day out. When they move into report development, they won't be shocked with a completely foreign-looking interface. The idea is that even though the tool is different, the look and feel remains the same across Microsoft products.

A report consists of three primary components:

- ✔ A connection to some source of data that will be used in the report.
- ✔ A selection of the available data at the other end of the connection.
- ✔ A display of the selected data.

All three of these components can live in a single report — in other words, in a single RDL file.

You can store data-connection information directly in your report, but a best practice is to store data-connection information externally — and simply reference it in your report. External data connections can be used for multiple reports — which makes life easier for the administrator who has to create a data-connection file that multiple report developers can use while they're building that conquering horde of reports. You can create a shared data connection by adding the Report Data Source content type to a SharePoint library and then creating a new data-source item.

Managing the contents of reports

SharePoint is tightly integrated with Reporting Services. Because reports have their home in SharePoint, they can take advantage of the enterprise-wide content-management features of SharePoint — in particular, these:

- ✔ **Versioning:** This process tracks changes to each new version of a report. When a report is checked out, edited, and checked back in, a new version is created. Be careful though — versioning can be turned on and off for a document library. Make sure it's turned on before you assume that versioning is taking place.

- ✔ **Check-in/check-out:** Much like checking a book in and out of a library, this process locks the report so that only the person who has it checked out can edit it. When that person has completed those changes, he or she checks it back in so others can have a chance to check it out as well.

- ✔ **Security:** Applying document security restricts which users may read or edit reports in a library. This is important for highly confidential reports that should only be seen by (say) the finance people.

- ✔ **Workflow:** Creating SharePoint workflows helps you route documents through a specific business process. For example, you might need to get feedback from just about the entire company and approval from every boss within a 10,000-mile radius. Using the workflow feature, you can let SharePoint do the work of routing that document around and obtaining feedback and approval for you while you grab a coffee.

As if these features weren't enough, end users can launch Report Builder right from SharePoint. (That Microsoft — there they go again, spoiling the users.)

Setting up a library for reports

A library that stores Reporting Services reports must include the Report Builder Report content type. You have various ways to create a library for storing reports built in Reporting Services — so long as that library contains the Report Builder Report content type. To create a new library with the Report Builder Report content type, follow these steps:

1. **Choose Site Actions⇨New Document Library.**

   The New Document Library dialog box opens.

2. **Provide a name and description for the document library.**

   Also note that versioning is turned off by default. If you want to track versions of this document, select Yes under the versioning section.

3. **Choose None for the Document Template.**

   The library won't need one because it'll be used to store Reporting Services reports.

   The final configuration should look similar to Figure 9-1.

4. **Click Create to create the library.**

   The next step is to add the Report Builder Report content type to the library.

5. **Click the Library Settings button (located on the Library tab of the Ribbon).**

   By default, a library won't let you alter content types. To turn on the capability to alter content types, click the Advanced Settings link, and in the Content Types section, select Yes next to the Allow Management of Content Types option.

6. **Click OK to return to the Library Settings page.**

   A Content Type section appears on the settings page.

7. **Click the Add from Existing Site Content Types link.**

   Doing so brings up the Add Content Type dialog box.

8. **Select the Report Server Content Types group to narrow the list of available content types.**

9. **Select the Report Builder Report content type and then click the Add button.**

   Doing so adds this content type to the library.

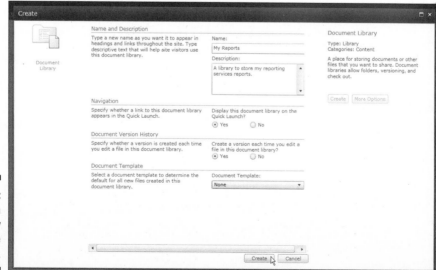

Figure 9-1:
Creating a
new library
to store
reports.

10. **Click OK to return to the library settings page.**

    The New Report option now shows up under the New Document drop-down list, as shown in Figure 9-2. Notice that the default Document content type is still present — and is still the default if an end user clicks the New Document button without selecting the drop-down list.

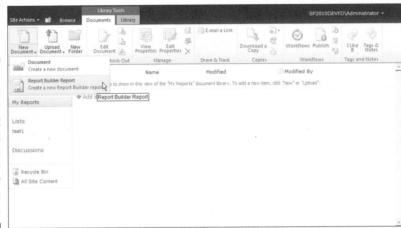

11. **Remove the Document content type by navigating back to the Library Settings page, clicking the Document content type, and then choosing Delete This Content type.**

    The result is that the Report Builder Report is the only option for adding new items to the library.

When a user clicks the New Document button to add a report to a library, SharePoint launches Report Builder automatically. If a user doesn't have Report Builder installed, SharePoint downloads Report Builder automatically and installs it on his or her local machine.

When Report Builder launches, it presents a Getting Started screen (as shown in Figure 9-3). The Getting Started screen provides an intuitive interface for getting started with Report Builder. Here you can create a new report, create a new dataset, open a saved report, or open a recent report. When you're creating a new report, you can choose from a number of different wizards or simply start with a blank report.

Because Report Builder can be launched directly from SharePoint, end users can easily begin creating their own reports right away. The reports can then be stored back in the SharePoint library and shared with other users. The end result is a self-service report development environment. Because

SharePoint is at the center of the self-service environment, IT maintains governance and visibility — and end users can create and share reports without taxing IT's limited resources. The idea is to free up the expertise of IT for more technical and pressing matters.

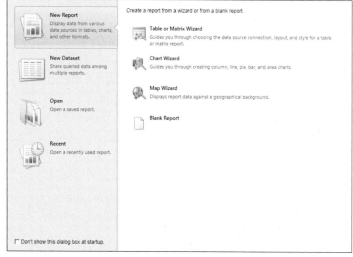

Figure 9-3:
Report
Builder
launches
with an intu-
itive helper
screen.

The connections that reports use can be locked down to use only approved data connections that administrators have created. Report Builder can use these shared data connections, so IT doesn't have to help every single user set up every single data connection to an approved data source.

Taking a Spin around Report Builder

The Report Builder 3.0 application provides a simple and intuitive user interface for Reporting Services development. Report Builder includes the familiar Ribbon across the top of the screen, which contains Home, Insert, and View tabs, in addition to a large round button in the upper-left corner of the screen, right where you'd find the Office button in Microsoft Office programs. This button is the one you use to open new reports, save the current report, publish report parts, and check for updates. Here's a quick tour of the Report Builder Ribbon:

  ✓ **Home:** You use the Home tab to apply standard formatting to fonts, paragraphs, borders, numbers, and the layout of the page. In addition, when you want to see the report rendered you can click the Run button. The Home tab is shown in Figure 9-4.

Figure 9-4:
The Report
Builder
Ribbon
with the
Home tab
selected.

✔ **Insert:** The Insert tab is where you find most of the functionality you use in Report Builder. The Insert tab allows you to insert report items such as tables, charts, gauges, text boxes, and images. The Insert tab is shown in Figure 9-5.

Figure 9-5:
The Report
Builder
Ribbon
with the
Insert tab
selected.

✔ **View:** The View tab allows you to show and hide the functionality windows that show up in Report Builder. For example, you can turn on and off panes such as Report Data, Properties, the Ruler, and Groupings. The View tab is shown in Figure 9-6.

Figure 9-6:
The Report
Builder
Ribbon with
the View tab
selected.

When you work in Report Builder, a series of panes — the Report Data, Properties, Groupings, and Ruler panes, shown in Figure 9-7 — offers additional development tools.

✔ **The Report Data pane** provides a series of folders that organize the report data that can be added to a report. For example, you might want to add data items from the standard folder for built-in fields (such as `Report Name` and `Page Number`) to your report. You could do this by clicking a data field and dragging it onto the report. In addition to the built-in data fields, you'll also see data fields that are pulled back from your data connection. The data connections and datasets can also be accessed from the Report Data pane.

✔ **The Properties pane** displays the properties for the selected component. For example, if you have a Gauge control selected, you see the properties for that specific control.

✔ **The Groupings pane** allows you to group data in a meaningful way. For example, you might want to group employees by manager or by group sales data — month, week, and day.

✔ **The Ruler pane** simply provides a ruler around the report design surface.

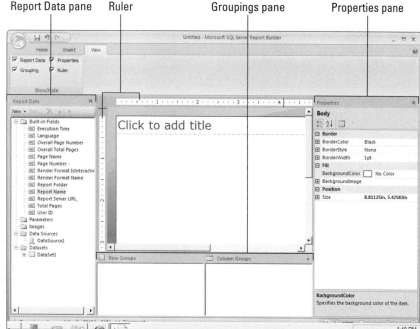

Figure 9-7:
The Report Builder panes that can be turned on and off in the View tab.

Developing a Report

Developing a report in Report Builder takes three basic steps:

1. Obtaining the actual data that you want to report on.

2. Building the report using the available reporting components.

3. Displaying the report to those who need its information.

In business-intelligence-speak, a report is *consumed* when someone receives it, absorbs its contents, and makes use of the information in it. (No bonfires required.)

Microsoft maintains an extensive collection of information about its products on the TechNet site. For more about Report Builder 3.0, visit

```
technet.microsoft.com/en-us/library/ee706623.aspx
```

Scrounging up some data

A report wouldn't be of much value without data. Happily, getting data into a report using Report Builder takes only two steps:

1. Setting up the connection to the data source.

2. Pulling data to use in the report.

Report Builder can create data connections to the following data sources:

- **Microsoft SQL Server:** The Microsoft database product.

- **Microsoft SQL Azure:** The Microsoft "cloud-computing" environment that does its work on the Internet.

- **Microsoft SQL Server Parallel Data Warehouse:** A data warehouse built on top of the SQL Server product.

- **Microsoft SQL Server Analysis Services:** A special type of database known as an OLAP cube that lives within the SQL Server product.

- **Microsoft SharePoint List:** A list of data housed within SharePoint.

- **OLE DB:** A generic data connection designed to pull data from a number of different data sources.

- **ODBC:** A generic data connection designed to pull data from a number of databases which are vendor agnostic. For example, Oracle has its own database and an ODBC connection could be used to pull data from an Oracle based database.

- ✔ **XML:** A file-based data container.

- ✔ **Oracle:** The database product produced by the Oracle Corporation.

- ✔ **SAP NetWeaver BI:** The business-intelligence product produced by the SAP corporation.

- ✔ **Hyperion Essbase:** The database system similar to SQL Server Analysis Services. The Essbase company was acquired by Oracle in 2007.

- ✔ **TERADATA:** A data-warehousing solution offered by the Teradata Corporation.

Setting up a data source connection

A common scenario is to create a report on the data contained in a SharePoint list. You can create a data source that feeds data to a SharePoint list (where you can then report on it) by following these steps:

1. **Right-click the Data Sources folder in the Navigation pane and choose Add Data Source.**

    Note that if the Navigation pane isn't shown, you have to enable it by selecting it on the View tab of the Ribbon.

2. **Provide a name for the new data source and then select Use a Connection Embedded in My Report.**

    The other option is to use a shared data connection that has already been created.

3. **Choose Microsoft SharePoint List from the Data Connection Type drop-down menu.**

4. **Enter the URL to the site in the Connection String box.**

    The URL follows this format:

    ```
    http://<server>/<site>
    ```

    An example is `http://sp2010devfd/reports`.

5. **Click the Credentials tab and enter credentials for the data connection.**

    The most common scenario is to use the current Windows user account.

6. **Click back on the General tab and test the connection.**

    Your completed screen looks similar to Figure 9-8.

7. **Click OK to return to Report Builder.**

    The new connection, named `ListDataSource`, now appears under the Data Sources folder, and you can now use it to obtain data.

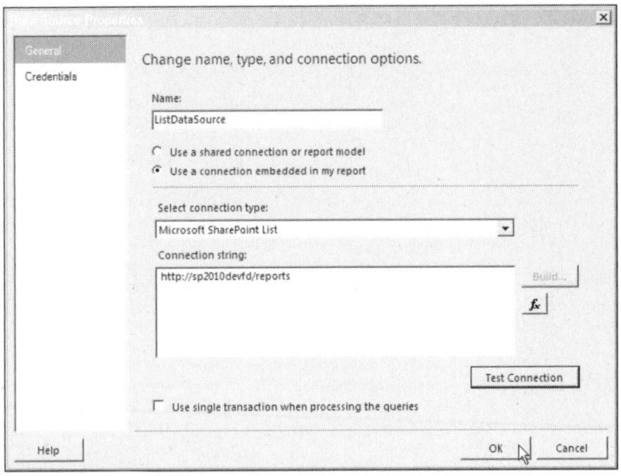

Figure 9-8:
Creating a
data-source
connec-
tion to a
SharePoint
list.

Pulling data for a report

With a data source in place, the next step is to obtain some data. The data you bring back from the data source is called a *dataset.* You can obtain a dataset from a SharePoint list's data source by following these steps:

1. **Right-click the Datasets tab (located in the Navigation pane) and choose Add Dataset.**

   The Dataset Properties dialog box appears.

2. **Select the option to embed the dataset within the report.**

   The other option is to use a shared dataset.

3. **Choose the list data source you've already created; then click the Query Designer button.**

   The Query Designer provides an interface for accessing the lists and libraries contained in the site.

4. **Expand the list that contains the data you want to include in your report.**

   You can select the fields from the list that contain the specific data you need in the report. In this example, I'm reporting on a simple sales list that contains fields for Store, State, and Sales Amount.

5. **When the fields are selected, click OK to return to the Dataset Properties dialog box.**

   The XML created by the Query Designer is now displayed in the query box, as shown in Figure 9-9.

6. **Click OK to return to Report Builder.**

   The fields from the SharePoint list are now available under the newly created dataset, as shown in Figure 9-10.

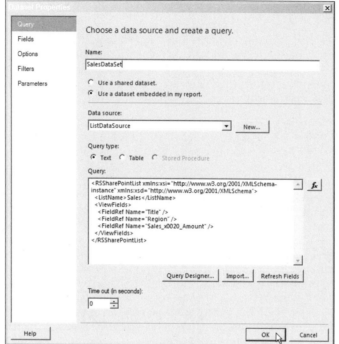

Figure 9-9:
The Dataset
Properties
being used
to create
a query
against a
SharePoint
list.

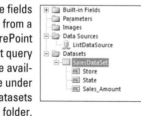

Figure 9-10:
The fields
from a
SharePoint
list query
are avail-
able under
the Datasets
folder.

When you're developing reports, often you'll find yourself creating duplicate
elements for every report. For example, the connection to a SharePoint site or
database might be the same one for 10 different reports; each report needs its
own (duplicated) connection. Creating a connection once and then re-using
it with multiple reports is one of the ways Reporting Services saves time.
Sharable elements include data connections, datasets, and report parts.

Building a report

When you have the data available, you're ready to build a report. A report consists of *reporting components* such as data regions, data visualizations, report items, subreports, report parts, and header and footer information. The following sections introduce you to these building blocks, which you can use to develop the reports your organization needs.

Data regions

The way data is presented in a report is a crucial factor in the success of a report. You could argue that just obtaining the data from the data source is good enough, and that people viewing the report should understand the data and draw their own conclusions. Unfortunately, most people don't want to view the raw data; they want the report to synthesize data for them in some way. As a report developer, your job is to tease and coax the information out of the raw data — and display it in a way that's intuitive and powerful for the consumers of the report. The data regions are the components that provide the framework for laying out the data in your report. The data regions consist of a table, a matrix, and a list.

The *table* data region is a grid that's much like an Excel worksheet — rows and columns that you can use to display data; each column is a *field* and each row is a *record*. For example, a table that displays address information might contain columns for `First Name`, `Last Name`, `Address 1`, `Address 2`, `City`, `State`, and `Zip Code`. Remember, each row represents a record; if you were reporting on 3,000 addresses, then you'd have 3,000 rows in the report. As your dataset increases and more records are added to the report, the table grows vertically.

Using a table enables you to not only display the detailed data represented by each record, but also group the data to form an aggregate. For example, you might want to group the addresses by `State` and then (within each `State` group) group the data again by `City`. The `City` group might then include the individual records for each address. A table using addresses contained in a SharePoint list is shown in Figure 9-11. Click the Run button (in the Ribbon on the Home tab) to render and view the report: Report Builder queries the data source for data and then renders the report, as shown in Figure 9-12.

Notice the words surrounded by brackets in Figure 9-11 such as `[City]`, `[State]`, and `[First Name]`. These are actually very simple *expressions* — Microsoft Visual Basic statements that you use to perform actions such as calculations and formatting a report item. For example, you might want to combine the first name and last name into a single column. If you're working with numeric data, you might want to add the values in two different fields and then subtract the value in a third field. Expressions are beyond the scope of this chapter — but Microsoft provides a wealth of information about expressions on their TechNet site at technet.microsoft.com/en-us/library/dd220516.aspx

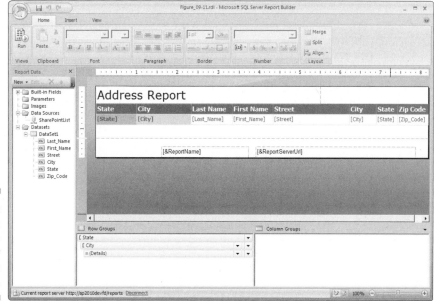

Figure 9-11:
Using a
table to
display
address
records.

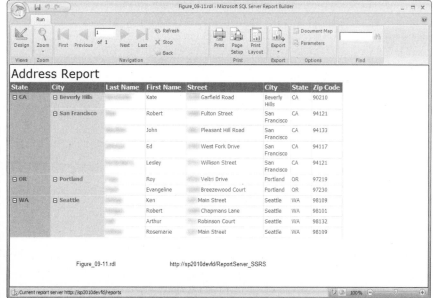

Figure 9-12:
Rendering
a report
in Report
Builder.
Notice the
addresses
are grouped
by State and
then by City.

Matrix data region

A *matrix* is similar to a table but can also grow horizontally in the same manner as a PivotTable in Office Excel. Just like a PivotTable, a Reporting Services matrix displays aggregate values (grouped both horizontally and vertically). Accordingly, a matrix must have an aggregate function associated with every field that has more than one entry. Examples of aggregate functions include Sum, Average, Max, Min, and Count. If the data isn't numeric (an address is a typical example), then you cannot use a numeric function such as Sum on it at all; if you do, you get only an error message for your pains. Instead, you must use a non-numeric function such as Count, which simply counts up the records returned. (Figure 9-13 shows a matrix used to count the addresses in each city-and-state combination.) As you add fields to the row-and-column groupings of the matrix, it expands horizontally and vertically — just like a PivotTable in Excel.

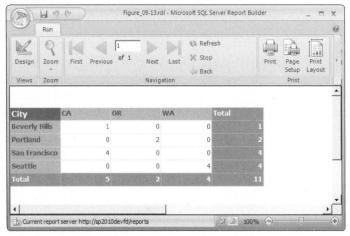

Figure 9-13:
Using a Reporting Services matrix to count the records for every city-and-state combination.

List data region

The remaining type of data region — the *list* — displays free-form data without the constraints of the grid that gives structure to a table or matrix. Using a list, you can add fields anywhere in the report that might be appropriate. You might use a list to develop (for example) a report to print invoices for all the customers who owe you money; you can even use a list with a report to print mailing labels.

Data visualizations

Sure, you have to display any data you put in a report (or what's the point?), but to really bring a report to life, you need visualizations. Report Builder includes *visualizations* you can add to a data region (such as a table) and display for every record in the dataset. For example, you might want to put a Sparkline (tiny graph) or gauge in a designated column of a table so viewers of the report can have the same picture of what the data means, along with the raw data.

The following list describes the visualizations available in Report Builder. You insert a visualization by clicking the appropriate button in the Ribbon on the Insert tab, and can then configure the visualization manually or use a wizard to connect the visualization to the data.

- ✔ **Chart:** Numerous charts are available in Reporting Services, including a column chart, line chart, pie chart, bar chart, and area chart. For a simple column chart, showing the number of people living in each city, see Figure 9-14.

- ✔ **Gauge:** Anyone who's driven a car is familiar with gauges — for speed, gas level, oil temperature, whatever a driver needs to monitor. The Gauge control in Report Builder serves the same purpose, showing a value on a scale to represent an amount of something in need of measuring. For example, you might have a sales gauge showing the current sales figure for the month. Various styles of gauges are available — from a standard gauge that looks like it belongs in a car to a sliding gauge similar to a temperature gauge. Figure 9-15 depicts a series of gauges that show sales by store.

- ✔ **Map:** A map visualizes the distribution of data over a geographic region. For example, you might have sales figures for each store represented by the size of a bubble positioned over each geographic region. You might also have each county in the state highlighted to show the number of employees for each county. Assigning a color (say, green) for the county might mean you have the correct number of people employed; red might mean you're understaffed in that county. The employees in the county could lend additional information to help describe why a particular region is underperforming.

  One nice feature of the Map component in Report Builder is that you can integrate Bing maps and add the road, aerial, or hybrid view to your report.

  Due to ever-shifting global politics, the only map of a country you'll find in Reporting Services is that of the United States. If you need maps of other regions or countries, you can download them or create your own.

- ✔ **Data Bar:** A *data bar* is a small bar chart you can put in each cell of your table report, next to the numbers, to provide a small visualization of the data in the table.

- ✔ **Sparkline:** A *Sparkline* provides a similar function to the data bar however instead of a bar chart, it's a line chart.

- ✔ **Indicator:** As with a data bar or a spark line, you can put this small gauge in a table in a report.

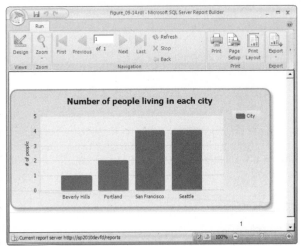

Figure 9-14:
A simple
column
chart in
Report
Builder.

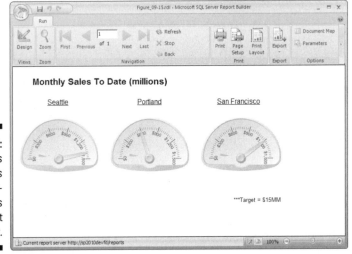

Figure 9-15:
A series
of gauges
show-
ing sales
against
target.

You can manipulate and customize visualizations in a mind-boggling number of ways — to zero in on business details or to fit an established design. For example, you might want to tweak a chart to fit your exact business needs (say, track the number of paisley surfboards your company sold in California in July). You might want the border of a map's legend to have a certain look, particular fonts, and a specific position. You can do all that in Report Builder. Microsoft has assembled a wealth of information about working with Report Builder visualizations on a very handy TechNet site at

technet.microsoft.com/en-us/library/ee706623.aspx

Report items

In addition to data visualizations, Report Builder also provides standard on-screen design items that may be just what you need to refine the look and feel of your report. Report items include a text box, image, line, and rectangle.

Subreports

A *subreport* is a component you can use to display another report inside the report you're developing — and pass parameters to the subreport based on users' interaction with the main report. For example, you might have a report that displays customers. The report might have a subreport section that displays the details of customer interactions embedded in the overall Customers report.

Report parts

A *report part* is simply a piece of a report, usually one you've developed. For example, if you find yourself building a sales graph that must be included in many different types of reports, you could make it into a report part and simply add it to a new report as a whole piece. That way you don't have to go through all the steps of re-creating the same sales-graph section of a report each time you develop a new report that needs the same kind of section.

Header and footer

The header and footer of the report are prime places to include some of the built-in report fields, such as the name of the report, the time the report was rendered, and the page number.

The built-in report fields include the following:

- ✔ **Execution Time:** The date and time the report was executed.

- ✔ **Language:** The (human) language in which the report was written.

- ✔ **Overall Page Number:** The current page number and total number of pages in the report, or section of the report. For example, if the entire report contains 220 pages, you can display the current page number within the total report (say, Page 25 of 220). The alternative is to display the page number within the current grouping. For example, you might have a field that displays page 3 of 5 within a specific category of products but page 25 of 220 for the entire report (which includes all categories).

- ✔ **Overall Total Pages:** The overall total page count of the report.

- ✔ **Page Name:** The name of the current page, if it has one.

- ✔ **Page Number:** The current page number. Note that Reporting Services allows you to reset page numbers within a report and contains an Overall Page Number variable to track pages in the entire report, exclusive of resetting the Page Number variable.

✔ **Render Format Is Interactive:** Returns a True or False value depending on the format in which you've rendered the report. If the report allows interaction, then this value is True; otherwise the value is False.

✔ **Render Format Name:** The format in which you rendered the report (such as PDF, HTML, Image, Excel, or Word).

✔ **Report Folder:** The folder that contains the report.

✔ **Report Name:** The name of the report.

✔ **Report Server URL:** The URL to the report server.

✔ **Total Pages:** The total number of pages contained in the report.

✔ **User ID:** The ID for the user account used to run the report.

Getting started with wizards

Although you can develop complete reports from scratch, it's often easier to use a wizard to create a new report that includes a table, matrix, chart, or map. You launch the New Report wizard from the main Start screen that appears when you first open Report Builder, as shown in Figure 9-16. In addition, you can launch a wizard from the Insert menu by clicking the drop-down menu for a table, matrix, chart, or map.

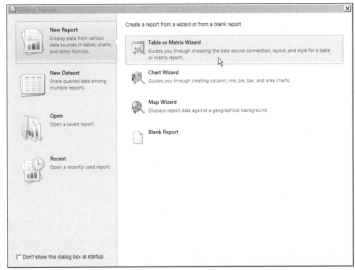

Figure 9-16: A number of wizards are available on the Report Builder Start screen.

Each wizard walks you through the process of choosing data and designing a report. When you've completed the wizard's steps, it displays your report in

Design view. You can then continue developing and tweaking your report or publish it for other users to view.

Of course, if you want to develop a coherent report (which is pretty much the purpose of reporting, isn't it?), you'd be wise to do some planning first. Microsoft has an excellent collection of report-planning information available on their TechNet site at

technet.microsoft.com/en-us/library/dd220520.aspx

Displaying a report in SharePoint

Viewing a Reporting Services report in SharePoint is as easy as clicking the report in the document library. The report opens in the browser, where you can view it as shown in Figure 9-17.

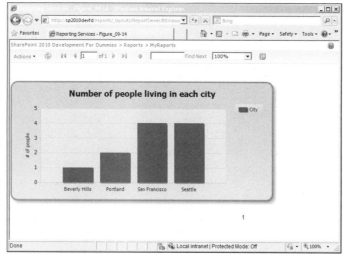

Figure 9-17: A Reporting Services report rendered in the browser.

The other option is embedding a report in a SharePoint page by using the SQL Server Reporting Services Report Viewer Web Part (located under the SQL Server Reporting category in the Web Part gallery). After adding a Web Part to the page, you can point it to a report — and then embed the report within the page so it will render with the page, as shown in Figure 9-18.

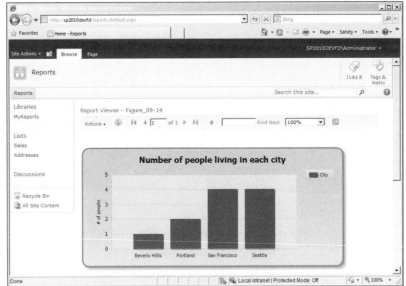

Figure 9-18:
A Reporting
Services
report
embedded in
a SharePoint
page.

Chapter 10

PerformancePoint Development with Dashboard Designer

> *The number-one benefit of information technology is that it empowers people to do what they want to do. It lets people be creative. It lets people be productive. It lets people learn things they didn't think they could learn before, and so in a sense it is all about potential.*
>
> — Steve Ballmer

*T*his chapter zeros in on the SharePoint standalone program whose main mission is to help you develop the tools for business intelligence — PerformancePoint. So first things first: *business intelligence* (BI for short) is an organizational use of information that's analogous to military intelligence: getting timely information about how your business is performing so you can make sound decisions and shape an effective strategy.

BI has become a highly effective (and widespread) way to handle the data that keeps an organization alive. The need to tame that data is enterprise-wide: Decision-makers battle with vast amounts of raw data; other employees, regardless of echelon, must also be able to view information that is accurate, timely, and appropriate to their roles in the organization. A BI system provides

✔ A place to put all that data — typically OnLine Analytical Processing (OLAP) databases for lightning-fast retrieval.

✔ Special tools for interacting with the OLAP databases — delivered as networked services — so everyone can get to the needed information in an efficient, self-serve way.

✔ More tools for turning the raw data into usable information that's (relatively) easy to understand at a glance.

✔ A strange new language of "dimensions," "measures," and "cubes" — okay, sometimes this last characteristic has to be tamed and managed in its own right.

No surprise that understanding the ins and outs of Microsoft BI is a book unto itself (no, really, there is one — *Microsoft Business Intelligence For Dummies* by yours truly, published by Wiley).

Microsoft seems to have understood this crying need for coherence; they've integrated business intelligence into the SharePoint platform from the get-go. SharePoint has been settling into the center of many organizations for some time as a one-stop source for digital content and information — so integrating it with heavy-duty data-crunching systems was a natural fit.

When Microsoft talks about the BI capabilities that come with SharePoint, the term it uses is Insights. SharePoint Insights — almost a distinct product unto itself — is like a toolbox full of features and functionality best suited to BI uses. Among these, the big kahuna is PerformancePoint Services. Other hefty Insights components include Excel Services (see Chapter 5) and Visio Services (see Chapter 7).

This chapter is devoted to PerformancePoint Services. It offers a look at how Microsoft has brought self-serve development (like do-it-yourself, only better) to creating dashboards on the SharePoint platform. You get to know the tool used to build the content that PerformancePoint carries to the users who need it: Dashboard Designer. Then you get to use Dashboard Designer to create data connections and develop specialized BI content such as scorecards, Key Performance Indicators (KPIs), filters, and (well, yeah) dashboards. Finally, you get a handle on deploying all that juicy content to SharePoint so other users can view it, interact with it, and use it to guide where the organization goes next.

Zooming in on PerformancePoint Services

As SharePoint has gained steam in the marketplace, it's pulled in other Microsoft products that used to stand alone; now those Microsoft products are SharePoint components. PerformancePoint is a case in point: Prior to SharePoint 2010, PerformancePoint Server was a standalone product. When BI started to offer a new range of uses, the parts of PerformancePoint Server best suited to those tasks were transplanted to SharePoint 2010.

Now, when you purchase SharePoint Server 2010 Enterprise, you get . . . PerformancePoint Services' greatest hits!

Speaking of greatest hits, one of the most popular tools you can build for use with PerformancePoint Services is a BI dashboard to view in a SharePoint site. This display works much like the dashboard in your car; it serves up critical information about your business systems where you can see it in an easy-to-view format while you're making decisions about where you want your business to go. For example, you might have a gauge similar to a speedometer that shows a different kind of speed: the rate of production (how fast your company makes its product). Is that rate meeting market demand? Do you need to change the rate? Well, first you need a real-time indicator of what's going on. If (like many of us) you're old-school enough that you prefer gauges instead of blinking numbers in your displays, PerformancePoint can accommodate you — not only with gauges, but also a range of other efficient ways to view your critical data, including tables and graphs.

The tool used to develop BI dashboards in SharePoint is Dashboard Designer. When a dashboard is published to a SharePoint site, it takes the form of a normal Web Part (for a refresher on Web Parts, see Chapter 4). Each component of the dashboard is a Web Part on the page; pulling data from various sources and displaying information just as diverse and interconnected as the data on speed, oil pressure, and fuel level you'd see displayed on a car dashboard. The Web Parts are grouped together and displayed on the same page, providing a cohesive view of critical business information.

When you're using Dashboard Designer to build such a view of information, typically you use one or more of these PerformancePoint components (explored throughout this chapter):

- **Key Performance Indicators (KPIs)** to identify and monitor the numbers that most affect your business.

- **Scorecards** to provide snapshots of how well your business did in a particular time period.

- **Reports** to summarize the current state of business processes for decision-makers.

- **Charts** to provide at-a-glance comparisons.

- **Graphs** to show trends.

- **Grids** to organize data and make it easily accessible.

- **Filters** to focus on selected aspects (dimensions) of the data.

- **Dashboards** to give the people in the driver's seat an array of accurate information on the state of the business and where it's going.

Creating a Business Intelligence Center site

SharePoint actually dedicates one of its site templates to business intelligence. The template is called, aptly enough, Business Intelligence Center (BIC for short). The site includes a series of lists and libraries designed to be used for business intelligence — including a Dashboards library and a PerformancePoint Content list. The site even offers an introductory page that describes some of the features of business intelligence in SharePoint, as shown in Figure 10-1.

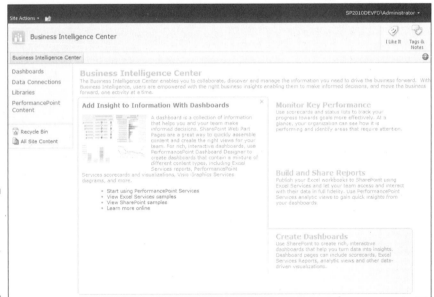

Figure 10-1: A Business Intelligence Center site in SharePoint.

To create a Business Intelligence Center site in SharePoint, follow these steps:

1. **Click Site Actions⇨More Options to open the Create dialog box.**

2. **Select the Site filter and then choose the Business Intelligence Center site template.**

3. **Enter a title for the site and a URL.**

    In addition, you can click the More Options button to configure permissions and navigation.

4. Click the Create button to create the site.

The new Business Intelligence Center site appears in the browser. From there you can develop a dashboard, using the tools and features I explain in "Developing a Dashboard" later in this chapter. If you're new to Dashboard Designer, you might check out "Taking a Spin around Dashboard Designer" before you jump right into your development work.

Before you can see the Business Intelligence Center site show up in the list of available site templates, you must have the Publishing Infrastructure (see Chapter 4) and PerformancePoint Services features activated for the site collection that will become the parent for the new BIC site. You can activate those features for a site collection by clicking Site Actions⇨Site Settings and then choosing Site Collection Features from the Site Collection Administration grouping. (Another way to activate features for a site is to choose Site Actions⇨ Manage Site Features on the settings page.)

Adding PerformancePoint content to a site

Using a nicely packaged site template such as the Business Intelligence Center keeps things simple — but what if you want to add PerformancePoint content to an existing site? No problem: That process is as simple as adding the PerformancePoint content types to an existing list. Make sure it *is* a list, though, and not a library. If you try to add the content types to a library you won't find them available. The PerformancePoint content types hang out under the PerformancePoint grouping; that's where you find them when you're adding content types to a list — and Table 10-1 shows you what to look for. See Chapter 4 for an introduction to working with content types.

Table 10-1	PerformancePoint Content Types	
Content Type	**Type**	**Description**
PerformancePoint Data Source	Library	Adds an XML-based data-source file for PerformancePoint Services to the library using Dashboard Designer. The XML file has an extension of `.ppsdc` (which stands for PerformancePoint Services Data Connection).

(continued)

Table 10-1 *(continued)*

Content Type	Type	Description
PerformancePoint KPI	List	Adds a new Key Performance Indicator (KPI) to the list using Dashboard Designer. A KPI represents a critical piece of data that is monitored to determine the health or status of a given process or metric. For example, you might have a sales KPI that represents the totals sales for a particular product in a given time period. Sales below a certain threshold might show a red icon; sales slightly below target might show a yellow indicator; sales on target or above might show a green indicator.
PerformancePoint Filter	List	Adds a new Filter to the list using Dashboard Designer. A filter reduces a data set to only those items that meet certain criteria. For example, you might have a data set showing sales for all products. You might set up a filter to restrict the sales data to a particular time period or product.
PerformancePoint Indicator	List	Adds a new Indicator to the list, using Dashboard Designer. An *indicator* is a visualization that shows the status of a given data point. For example, you might have a bar indicator showing 10 different levels of visualization based on percentage achieved of a sales goal. The bar might increase to show progress as a growing percentage of the target.
PerformancePoint Dashboard	List	Adds a new dashboard to the list using Dashboard Designer. A *dashboard* is a container for other PerformancePoint components. For example, you might create a dashboard with two columns: a filter in the left column and a series of indicators in the right column.
PerformancePoint Report	List	Adds a new report to the list using Dashboard Designer. As a usable summary of data, a *report* can take the form of output from any of various service applications — for example, Reporting Services (see Chapter 9) or Excel Services (see Chapter 5).

Content Type	Type	Description
PerformancePoint Scorecard	List	Adds a new scorecard to the list using Dashboard Designer. A *scorecard* shows progress toward a given goal. For example, you might have a scorecard that displays the actual amount of product sold versus the target amount. You might have a row in the scorecard for every product and a column showing current sales as a percentage of the target figure. You might also include an indicator showing a red, yellow, or green icon that reflects progress toward the target.

PerformancePoint content often contains other types of PerformancePoint content. For example, a Key Performance Indicator (KPI) contains an indicator, a scorecard contains KPIs, and a dashboard contains the components that make up a cohesive view of your business.

If you don't see the PerformancePoint content types available for a list, then you'd best make sure you have the proper features activated. For a detailed walk-through of activating those proper features, check out this Microsoft step-by-step guide:

`technet.microsoft.com/en-us/library/ee836146.aspx`

Taking a Spin around Dashboard Designer

The Dashboard Designer tool presents the same user interface as other Microsoft products — with the familiar Ribbon across the top — except it's divided into three distinct sections. Left to right, the parts of the Dashboard Designer screen (shown in Figure 10-2) are as follows:

  ✔ The **Workspace Browser** on the left side of the screen is where you find data connections and PerformancePoint content. As you create data connections and add new items of content, the Workspace Browser is where they appear on-screen. The Workspace Browser is also where you select the data connection(s) or content you want to put together or tweak in the Design pane.

✔ The **Design pane** (also known as the *design surface*) takes up the center of the screen — and most of the Dashboard Designer application. The top of the Design pane contains tabs based on the item that is currently opened. For example, if you're designing a dashboard, then you have an Editor tab and Properties tab. You select an item to display on the Design pane by clicking it in the Workspace Browser.

✔ The **Details pane** on the right side of the screen shows you details about the specific PerformancePoint content that's open in the Design pane. For example, if you're designing a dashboard, then the Details pane includes items that you might want to add to the dashboard such as scorecards, reports, and filters.

When you select either Data Connections or PerformancePoint Content in the Workspace Browser, here's the gist of what you see next:

✔ A list of items appears in the Design pane.

✔ The SharePoint tab lists all items located on the SharePoint server.

✔ The Workspace tab lists all items specific to your Dashboard Designer session.

Editor tab   Design pane

Workspace Browser   Properties tab   Details pane

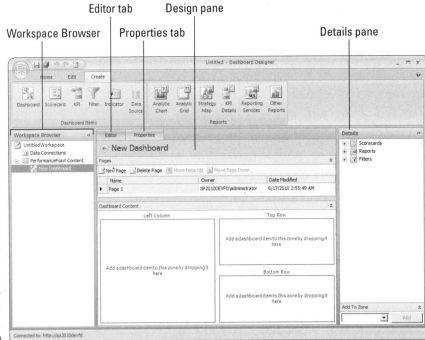

Figure 10-2:
The Dashboard Designer screen, showing a new dashboard open.

If you want to work on a particular component that already exists on the server, you just double-click it and watch it move to the Workspace Browser window under the PerformancePoint Content section. (Pretty slick.) The item *also* shows up under the Workspace tab when you select your PerformancePoint content in the Workspace Browser window. (Say what?)

Having two on-screen images of your content can be confusing at first and take some time to understand. Here's why you have two images: One is a way to say "here's what this looks like" to anyone who's working with PerformancePoint. When you bring the image into your workspace, any changes you make will be only your own changes; they won't change the general image.

You can save a workspace as an XML-based Dashboard Definition Workspace (`.DDWX`) file. This can be useful when you want a copy of the workspace in a simple text based file format. To save a workspace you simply click the big round Office style button in the upper left of the screen and choose Save. PerformancePoint components live in SharePoint lists and libraries; the `.DDWX` file lets the dashboard know where to find each component, how to connect to it, and where it should be laid out on the page.

Of course, no tour of Dashboard Designer would be complete without a quick introduction to the ubiquitous Ribbon. If you've used other Microsoft products then the Ribbon should be familiar. In Dashboard Designer it includes a Home, Edit, and Create tab.

  ✔ **Home:** This tab (shown in Figure 10-3) offers commands that multiple dashboard components have in common — including the PerformancePoint workspace and its associated items.

Figure 10-3: The Home tab in Dashboard Designer.

  ✔ **Edit:** You use this tab to custom-tailor the properties of the PerformancePoint component displayed on the Design pane. For example, if you're designing a scorecard and click the Edit tab, you see sections for the scorecard font, header, view, settings, and comments as shown in Figure 10-4.

Figure 10-4:
The Edit
tab with a
scorecard
opened in
Dashboard
Designer.

✔ **Create:** You use this tab to conjure up brand-new PerformancePoint content. This tab includes buttons to create dashboards, data items, and reports (as shown in Figure 10-5). Clicking a button launches a wizard to guide you through the creation process. (Further details of PerformancePoint components such as dashboards, scorecards, and KPIs crop up throughout this chapter.)

Figure 10-5:
The Create
tab in
Dashboard
Designer.

Developing a Dashboard

Developing a dashboard is fairly straightforward when you're using the Dashboard Designer tool: You launch the tool, obtain your data, develop the PerformancePoint components you want, add those to a dashboard, and then publish the finished dashboard to SharePoint — where any user with appropriate permissions can view it.

Launching Dashboard Designer

If business intelligence still seems a bit newfangled, don't worry: SharePoint's got your back. A site based on the SharePoint Business Intelligence Center template includes information pages that describe business intelligence in SharePoint. The pages describe the various BI components built in to SharePoint — such as Excel Services, PerformancePoint Services, and Reporting Services. On the PerformancePoint page, you find a link that invites you to Start Using PerformancePoint Services. Clicking this link brings up a page that describes PerformancePoint Services in particular. Take a little while to give it a once-over. Then you can click the handy button on the same page that launches Dashboard Designer. The button has a really obvious label — Run Dashboard Designer — as shown in Figure 10-6. If you've never used Dashboard Designer before then clicking the button uses Microsoft ClickOnce technology to download, install, and open the tool on your local computer.

ClickOnce technology is also used for Report Builder (a SharePoint tool detailed in Chapter 9). The idea behind ClickOnce is that all an end user need do is click a button on a SharePoint site to install, update, or open Dashboard Designer — automatically. When a new version of the tool is installed by an administrator on the server, ClickOnce recognizes that change the next time a user launches the tool — and updates the version residing on the user's local computer. With ClickOnce minding the details, the latest version of Dashboard Designer launches automatically whenever you begin to create or edit a piece of PerformancePoint content on a SharePoint site. You also have several other ways to open Dashboard Designer:

- For a new piece of content, you simply click the New Item button to get a list of the PerformancePoint content types.

- For existing content, you click the drop-down context menu for a particular item and choose Edit In Dashboard Designer, as shown in Figure 10-7.

- After Dashboard Designer is installed on your local computer, you can open the tool by using the Start menu (Start➪All Programs➪SharePoint➪ PerformancePoint Dashboard Designer) and get right down to business . . . intelligently.

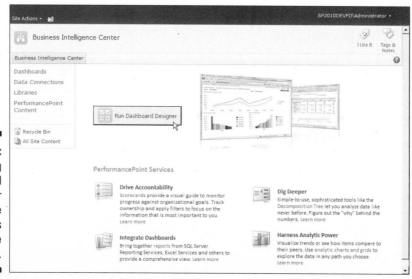

Figure 10-6: Launching Dashboard Designer from the Business Intelligence Center site.

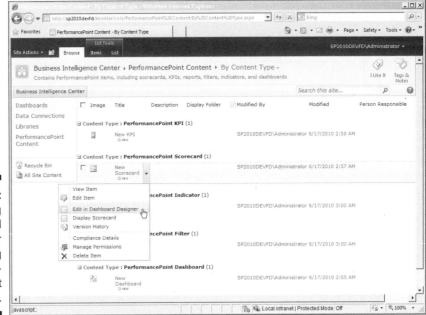

Figure 10-7:
Launching
Dashboard
Designer
by editing
a Perfor-
mancePoint
component.

Show me the data

Of course, a dashboard needs data to display or it's just so much wasted screen space. Not to worry. Dashboard Designer can obtain data from the following sources:

- ✔ SQL Server Analysis Services
- ✔ Excel Services
- ✔ Excel Worksheet
- ✔ SharePoint List
- ✔ SQL Server table

One of the most common scenarios for building dashboards involves data that lives in a SQL Server Analysis Services database (also known as an OLAP cube). To create a data connection to such a data source, follow these steps:

1. **Select Data Connections in the Workspace Browser and then click the Create tab.**

   Notice that the only button not disabled is the Data Source button. Note that Data Connections is the name of a SharePoint document library that hangs out in the same site as the PerformancePoint Data Source content type you've added. This is already set up in the Business Intelligence

Center site template — but if you are working with a blank site, then you'll have to add this document library to get the folder to show up in Dashboard Designer.

2. **Click the Data Source button to launch the Data Source Template dialog box.**

   The dialog box allows you to choose the type of data source you want to create. In this example you use data from a typical SQL Server Analysis Services cube.

3. **Select Analysis Services and then click OK.**

4. **Select authentication type in the Authentication section.**

   If you're working on a development server, then you most likely want Per-User Identity as the authentication type.

5. **Enter the server and instance name in the Data Source Settings section.**

   For example, my development server is SP2010DEVFD and the instance name is SSRS so I enter SP2010DEVFD\SSRS. This is the server that contains the source databases. In the next step — when you select a database from the drop-down list — it will be a database running on the server that you enter in this step.

6. **Select a database from the drop-down list.**

   In this example, I've installed the sample databases — which you can download from the CodePlex site at

   ```
   msftdbprodsamples.codeplex.com
   ```

   In this instance, I chose to connect to Adventure Works DW 2008R2 database.

7. **Select a cube (SQL Server Analysis Services database) from the cube drop-down menu.**

   In this example, I chose the Sales Summary cube. Figure 10-8 shows the completed configuration page for this data connection.

8. **Change the name of the data connection by clicking the Properties tab and providing a name.**

   You can also choose to add a folder that will contain the data connection. Using this approach, you can group data connections in folders under the Data Connections folder in Workspace Browser.

9. **Save the data connection.**

   You have two ways you can save it:

   • Right-click it in the Workspace Browser and choose Save.

   • Click the Save button (located at the top of the application screen).

   The completed data connection now shows up in the Workspace Browser as shown in Figure 10-9.

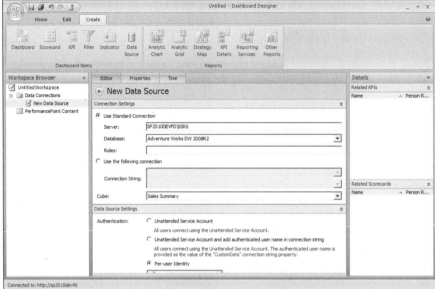

Figure 10-8:
Configuring a typical SQL Server Analysis Services data source in Dashboard Designer.

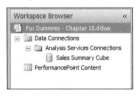

Figure 10-9:
The Analysis Services cube shows up in the Workspace Browser under Data Connections.

This example used a sample OLAP cube provided by Microsoft. If your company uses SQL Server Analysis Services, odds are your IT department has already put some cubes in place and manages them. Check with your IT department for specific connection information.

Understanding dashboard items

When you have a data connection in place, you're ready to start developing PerformancePoint content — in the form of indicators, KPIs, scorecards, and filters. With your PerformancePoint content in hand, you can pull it all together into a nice-looking dashboard and publish it to your SharePoint site.

Indicator

An *indicator* is a visual representation of a piece of data that provides some insight into the status of the data. You come in contact with indicators all the time in your everyday life. For example, a stoplight is an indicator that tells you when to proceed through the intersection, when to slow down, and when to stop. A PerformancePoint indicator does much the same thing for business processes; it takes the form of a small on-screen image.

You can develop your own indicator images or alter the indicators that come with Dashboard Designer.

You can choose any one of various images as your indicator (as shown in Figure 10-10) — but the root purpose is the same, regardless of image: represent the status of a piece of data and provide an insight into the data based on a particular criterion.

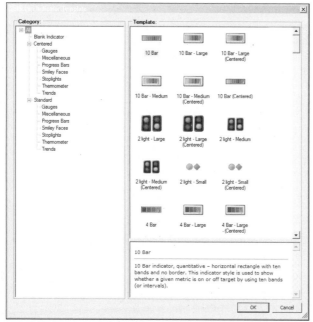

Figure 10-10: Dashboard Designer gives you a choice of ways to visualize indicators.

Key Performance Indicator (KPI)

A *Key Performance Indicator (KPI)* is simply a piece of data that gives you a strong clue to how your business or organization is really doing. A KPI might consist of sales data, manufacturing output figures, or any other piece of information that your organization considers "key" (business-speak for "too important to do without") in the making of critical decisions. A KPI includes the indicator images that were discussed in the Indicator section in order to provide a visualization of the data. When you create a KPI, you choose an indicator image to represent the various states of the data.

You can think of an indicator as the image that shows the various states of a piece of data. You might want to develop your own indicators or customize existing indicators. A KPI is (technically) the status of that item of data that shows up visually in the indicator image (analogous to the speed that shows on a speedometer) so you can assess it at a glance.

Scorecard

A *scorecard* is a collection of KPIs that take a snapshot of the overall health of some specific aspect of your business or organization — usually how near it is to reaching a goal at a specific point in time. For example, you might want to develop a sales scorecard that shows a listing of the sales of all products along with their targets for (say) the first quarter. A visual indicator such as a green, yellow, or red arrow could show how the sales for each product are tracking toward their target.

Another example of a scorecard: inventory levels in a finished-goods warehouse. You might develop the scorecard to keep track of when inventory levels get above or below a certain threshold, and have the icons change to yellow (when levels are getting low) and then red (to warn that you'd better restock *now*).

To create a scorecard that displays data from an Analysis Services cube, follow these steps:

1. **Browse to the Business Intelligence Center site and then click the PerformancePoint content list.**

2. **Click the Items tab in the Ribbon.**

    A drop-down menu appears.

3. **Click the drop-down menu and select PerformancePoint Scorecard, as shown in Figure 10-11.**

    Doing so launches Dashboard Designer and starts the wizard that walks you through the process of creating a new scorecard.

4. **Choose Analysis Services as the template and then click OK.**

5. **Click the SharePoint tab to access the content located on the SharePoint server.**

6. **Select the Analysis Services data connection that you created previously in the chapter (Sales Summary Cube), as shown in Figure 10-12.**

7. **Click Next to continue.**

8. **Choose the option to creates KPIs from the SQL Server Analysis Services measures, and then click Next.**

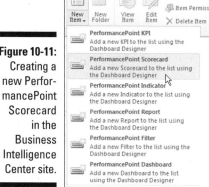

Figure 10-11:
Creating a
new Perfor-
mancePoint
Scorecard
in the
Business
Intelligence
Center site.

Sales Summary Cube

SharePoint Site tab

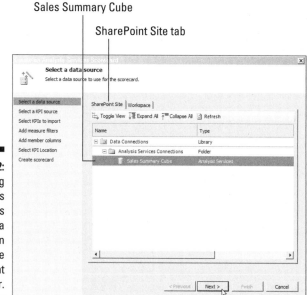

Figure 10-12:
Choosing
an Analysis
Services
data
connection
from the
SharePoint
server.

9. **Click the Add KPI button to add Key Performance Indicators to your dashboard.**

   • You can change the actual and target measures by clicking the drop-down menu for each column, as shown in Figure 10-13.

   • You can change the KPI name by clicking it and typing in a new name.

TIP

Notice that the target value is the same measure as the actual value by default. This makes for a pretty boring scorecard because the actual will always equal the target. You can choose a different measure as a target (or enter a value by hand) by configuring the KPI in Dashboard Designer after you've created the scorecard.

10. **When you've added all the KPIs needed for the scorecard, click Next to continue.**

11. **You can choose to add filters, but for this example (and the time being), click Next to continue without adding any filters.**

12. **You can add members and measures for columns, but for now, click Next to continue and use the default columns.**

13. **Choose the list you want to use for storing your scorecard and KPIs.**

    If you're using the Business Intelligence Center, then the list is named PerformancePoint Content and (surprise!) it's already selected for you.

14. **Click Finish to create the scorecard and display a preview of it in Dashboard Designer.**

15. **Click the Properties tab and provide a name for the scorecard.**

16. **(Optional) Create a folder to group your scorecard content.**

    The final scorecard, as previewed in Dashboard Designer, is shown in Figure 10-14.

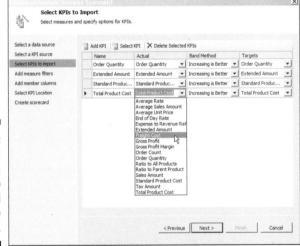

Figure 10-13: Adding and configuring the KPIs to be used in the scorecard.

REMEMBER

Think of a PerformancePoint scorecard as a container for KPIs. You can create KPIs separately and then add them to the scorecard or you can create them in the course of creating the scorecard.

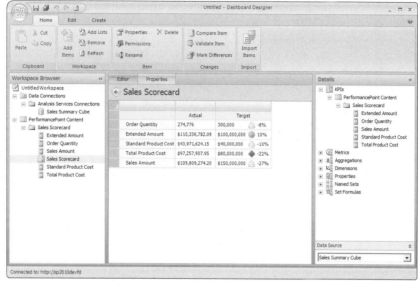

Filter

You can narrow down and manipulate the data you feed into a scorecard or report by using a PerformancePoint Filter. A *filter* allows you to select a specific grouping of data according to one or more criteria that narrow the focus of the scorecard or report. For example, you might have a scorecard that displays Sales for the entire world. To avoid giving someone in the boardroom a splitting headache, let's say you kindly apply filters to narrow the scorecard's scope — say, to sales shown by city, product group, or salesperson. You can embed a filter in your scorecard or set it apart as an interactive component that users can manipulate in real time when they want to see the specific information it offers.

An interactive filter can take any of the following forms:

- **List:** A drop-down list from which a user can select a single value.
- **Tree:** A directory tree from which a user can select a single value.
- **Multi-Select Tree:** A directory tree from which a user can select multiple items.

When you're creating a filter, a wizard walks you through the steps — which include choosing the type of filter you want to use. To create a multi-select tree filter — may as well start out with something fairly impressive, right? — follow these steps:

1. **In Dashboard Designer, select PerformancePoint Content in the Workspace Browser and then click the Create tab.**

2. **Click the Filter button to launch the Filter wizard.**

3. **Choose Member Selection as the filter type and then click OK.**

4. **Choose the data connection you created to the Analysis Services cube (earlier in the chapter, in "Show me the data") and then click Next.**

5. **Click the Select Dimensions button to choose which options you want to be available in the multi-select tree.**

   A dialog box appears, showing all the dimensions available for the data connection. Choose `Product.Product Categories` (as shown in Figure 10-15).

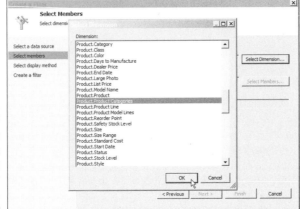

Figure 10-15: Choosing a dimension to use for the filter.

6. **Click the Select Members button to choose which members of the dimension should show up in the multi-select tree.**

   In this usage, a *member* is a fact or piece of data — for example, the month or year — in included in a particular dimension. In this example, you select all four members as shown in Figure 10-16.

7. **Click Next to continue.**

8. **Choose the Multi-Select Tree as the display method for the filter, and then click Finish to create the filter, as shown in Figure 10-17.**

   The filter appears in the Workspace Browser in Dashboard Designer.

9. **Provide a descriptive name for the filter (such as Product Categories).**

You might also want to move the filter into the Sales folder with the other PerformancePoint components associated with Sales information. You select the folder that the filter appears in by selecting the filter in Workspace Browser and then clicking the Properties tab and choosing the folder's location.

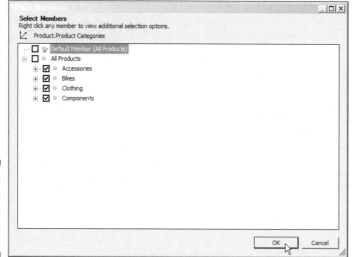

Figure 10-16:
Choosing members to use for the filter.

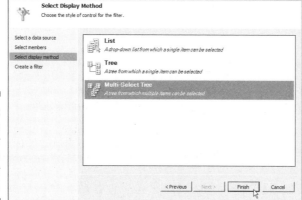

Figure 10-17:
Choosing the filter type in the New Filter wizard.

Dashboard

A *dashboard* is a container that displays various PerformancePoint components in a cohesive, at-a-glance view of some aspect of your business. For example, you might have scorecards, filters, and reports pertaining to (say) sales all on the same dashboard. Each component represents a unique piece of content; the dashboard simply pulls them together on the same page (or series of pages).

A dashboard can include PerformancePoint content but you can also include other SharePoint components — such as a Reporting Services report or Excel Services worksheet — on the same dashboard.

Creating a dashboard is as simple as clicking the Dashboard button on the Create tab and then dragging components onto the different zones of the dashboard. Creating and publishing a dashboard is equally straightforward; just follow these steps:

1. **Select PerformancePoint Content in the Workspace Browser and then click the Dashboard button on the Create tab.**

2. **Choose a template for the layout of the dashboard and then click OK.**

   For this example, choose the two-column layout and watch the new dashboard appear in Dashboard Designer with (presto!) a two-column layout, as shown in Figure 10-18.

3. **Expand the scorecard and filter trees (located in the Details pane on the right side of the screen) to view the scorecard and filter you created earlier in the chapter.**

4. **Drag the scorecard to the right column and the filter to the left column, as shown in Figure 10-18.**

5. **Click the down arrow in the upper-right corner of the filter in the left column and then choose Create Connection.**

   The Connection dialog box allows you to send connection information from the filter to the scorecard. Note that the filter is already selected in the Get Values From field.

6. **Select the scorecard in the Send Values To field.**

   The filter is now linked with the scorecard.

7. **Click the Values tab in the same Connection dialog box.**

   The Values tab allows you to choose and configure a field to receive the source values and the field values sent from the filter.

8. **Choose Row for the Connect To field.**

   Doing so ensures that selected product categories show up as a row in the scorecard.

9. **Choose Display Value for the Source Value.**

   You want the displayed product category to be sent to the scorecard.

   The completed connection dialog box is shown in Figure 10-19.

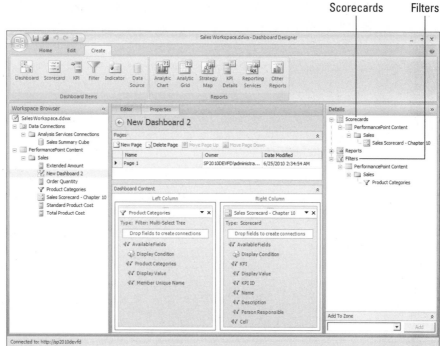

Figure 10-18:
A two-column PerformancePoint dashboard containing a scorecard and filter.

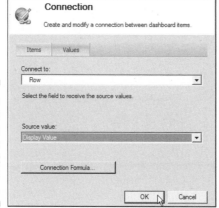

Figure 10-19:
Using the Connection dialog box to connect a filter to a scorecard.

10. **Click OK to complete the Connection dialog box and return to Dashboard Designer.**

The dashboard is now complete and ready to be published.

11. **Right-click the dashboard in the Workspace Browser and select Deploy To SharePoint.**

TIP

Choose the library where the dashboard should be deployed.

If you're using the Business Intelligence Center site, then you see a Dashboards library selected by default.

The completed dashboard, complete with scorecard and filter, is shown in Figure 10-20. When a user selects a series of product categories from the tree and clicks Apply, the scorecard updates to reflect only the selected product categories. (Very slick indeed.)

Filters   Filters applied to Sales Scorecard

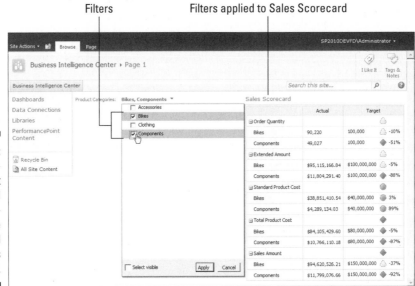

Figure 10-20:
A PerformancePoint dashboard with a multi-select tree filter and sales scorecard.

A dashboard is actually a Web Part page. Each PerformancePoint component is stored in a SharePoint list and displayed on the SharePoint Web Part page.

Other reports

In addition to the standard PerformancePoint components, you can also add other reports to your dashboard. In particular, you can add the following:

✔ **Analytic chart or grid:** This type of report uses SQL Server Analysis Services (SSAS) as a data source.

✔ **Strategy map:** This type of report includes visual components that reflect the interdependencies of your organization's various objectives. It uses a scorecard as its data source and a Microsoft Visio diagram as its visual component.

✔ **KPI details:** This type of report shows details about a particular KPI contained in a scorecard. When a user clicks a particular KPI in the scorecard, the KPI details component updates to show the details of that KPI.

✔ **Reporting Services report:** This type of report allows you to add a Reporting Services report to a dashboard. For more about Reporting Services reports, see Chapter 9.

✔ **Excel Services worksheet:** This type of report allows you to add an Excel worksheet to your dashboard.

For more about Excel Services, see Chapter 5.

Scorecards, dashboards, KPIs — what?

The terminology of SharePoint can be confusing at times. For example, if you've been working through this chapter and the topic of a *scorecard* comes up, you'll know instantly what it is — a component that contains KPIs and that can be added to a dashboard. Right? Well, someone who just read a book about a business methodology called *Balanced Scorecard* may be thinking about something utterly different. Same word, different meanings (those depend on context).

Always keep context in mind when you're thinking about or discussing scorecards, dashboards, and KPIs. If you're talking to businesspeople, they might be thinking about a different set of similar-sounding terms that have specialized meanings in business-speak. If (on the other hand) you're talking to a developer who's been working with Dashboard Designer, then already you have some SharePoint concepts in common — especially if you're discussing that particular tool.

Even though the terminology is the same, the connotations can be different. You might be thinking of a *scorecard* as a PerformancePoint component that contains *KPIs* (another PerformancePoint component) and is displayed in a *dashboard.* A businessperson might be thinking of the business theory behind a "balanced scorecard." Jargon springs eternal; be ready to clarify as needed. Even in my professional career as a consultant, I constantly have to remind myself to keep the terminology I use *in context.*

Part IV
Unleashing the Programmer Within

The 5th Wave · By Rich Tennant

"Our automated response policy to a large company-wide data crash is to notify management, back up existing data and sell 90% of my shares in the company."

In this part . . .

This part introduces you to some of the programming aspects of SharePoint development. In particular, you explore Visual Studio — the primary tool used in Microsoft programming. You get the lowdown on how to use Visual Studio and (especially) the SharePoint object model — for SharePoint development. You get a look at developing one of the primary components of SharePoint — the Web Part. Finally you behold the secret of building PowerShell scripts for SharePoint — and so gain the power to interact with the platform in ways you never dreamed possible. (White lab coat and insulated gloves optional.)

Chapter 11

SharePoint Development with Visual Studio

Increasingly, people seem to misinterpret complexity as sophistication, which is baffling — the incomprehensible should cause suspicion rather than admiration.

— Niklaus Wirth

*W*hat SharePoint 2010 has done is redefine the term *developer.* No longer do you need to be a programmer to develop business solutions. Using the tools covered throughout the book you can build solutions on the SharePoint platform without ever having to write a line of code.

At some point, however, a time may come when you need something so specific that you can build it only by writing code. For example, you might require a Web Part that provides a very specific proprietary algorithm that can only be developed using code. Or you might want to develop a Web Part that can be packaged up and deployed to other organizations that run their own farms so users can simply add it to their pages without having to build their own Web Parts. When you've determined that you need to write code to get the job done, then it's time to crack open a tool called Visual Studio.

In this chapter you get an overview of Visual Studio — the primary programming tool for Microsoft platform development, including (of course) programming SharePoint. You get a look at the SharePoint Software Developer Kit (SDK), which provides a wealth of information and sample code to use when you're developing your own programs. You figure out how to tell apart the different types of SharePoint programming and what it means to develop a SharePoint feature using a Visual Studio project. Finally, you get a shot at a gold star for playing nicely in your own SharePoint sandbox using Sandboxed Solutions.

Introducing Visual Studio

The Microsoft products use a programming platform known as .NET. The terminology can be confusing because .net is also the name of a top level domain. You might have seen a domain such as www.mycompany.net which ends in .net. The Microsoft .NET however has nothing at all to do with the .net in domain names.

Visual Studio is the primary tool you will use to write code for the Microsoft platform and thus a tool to write .NET code. Visual Studio is known as an Integrated Development Environment (IDE).

Getting into an Integrated Development Environment (IDE)

An IDE is a tool specifically designed for writing code. Just like you would use a word processing tool such as Microsoft Word to write letters or an e-mail program such as Microsoft Outlook to write e-mail, you would use Visual Studio to write .NET code for SharePoint.

The nice thing about Visual Studio is that it combines all the tools you need to develop code such as compilers and debuggers as well as a plethora of other goodies. You could of course write code using any text editor and then compile it using the .NET compiler program and then use a different program to debug it and then manually link the various libraries you will use, but that would be a lot of work.

Okay, I know more than one of my hard-core programmer friends still love doing it the manual way. Some of them even use an old-school text editor called vi, which provides a *command prompt* (a couple of characters on a line, a colon, and then a lot of blank space — similar to what you'd see in DOS) instead of a Graphical User Interface (GUI) like the one for Word (or even Notepad). Note that vi has different command-line modes for either input or sending commands to the program. If you're in the command mode, then typing a letter on the keyboard such as J means to move the cursor down one line and K means to move the cursor up one line. Need to delete a character on the screen? That's the H key. Some say that after you master the vi commands, working in vi is faster than a modern GUI interface, but I think you're fine just sticking with a modern text editor that uses the arrow keys to move up and down and the Delete key to delete characters.

Telling the Visual Studio editions apart

The Visual Studio tool comes in many different editions that span everything from free starter editions to a complete team system. Here's a quick introduction to each one:

- ✔ **Express Editions:** The Express Editions are free to download and are geared toward specific languages. The Express editions include Visual Basic, Visual C#, Visual C++, and Visual Web Developer. These editions can get you up and running quickly and are great for hobbyists.

- ✔ **Professional Edition:** The Professional edition of Visual Studio includes the bulk of the functionality that's required for .NET development and is designed for individual developers and small teams.

- ✔ **Test Professional Edition:** The Test Professional edition is geared toward quality assurance and testing teams with tools for testing impact analysis and Microsoft Test Manager.

- ✔ **Premium Edition:** The Premium edition expands on the Professional edition by adding advanced features around debugging, remote server exploration, unit testing, architecture modeling, and Office and Mobile device development.

- ✔ **Ultimate Edition:** The Ultimate edition includes advanced features such as lab management, Web performance testing tools, and load testing.

- ✔ **Team Foundation Server:** The Visual Studio Team Foundation Server is a complete solution that includes features such as version control, work item tracking, project management, build automation, and reporting.

Examining the .NET Framework

The .NET Framework is at the root of nearly all Microsoft application development, integrated into everything from SQL Server to SharePoint, and it helps to have a basic understanding of what it is and how it works.

The .NET Framework is essentially a storehouse of code — a resource that Microsoft makes available to help programmers write code more efficiently — and all the code it contains runs on (of course) the Windows operating system. To help you get a handle on what the .NET Framework is and how it works, here's a quick overview of how programming languages work — and why they're necessary tools for building software:

- **A language only a computer chip could love:** If time and money were no object (instead of the same thing, which is usually an obstacle), then every software program could be developed by writing code in a language that the CPU chip could understand. But the language that the CPU *does* understand is made up of 0s and 1s; to do even the simplest interaction means feeding tens of thousands of strings of 0 and 1 codes into the CPU. Because this is theoretically possible — but not realistic for people to do — programming languages were developed. A *programming language* uses English type syntax that's easier for humans to understand and write. The English-style programming code is then fed into a software application called a *compiler* that converts it into the 0s and 1s that the CPU knows and loves.

- **Intermediate Language (IL):** Programming languages and compilers have made writing computer code very efficient; unfortunately, not all CPUs understand the *same* 0 and 1 codes. For example, if you write a program and compile it for a CPU made by one company and then move the program to a computer with a CPU made by another company, the program will break. The reason: The second CPU won't understand what to do with the 0s and 1s of the program. To get around this problem, computer scientists came up with a very smart idea: Instead of having the compiler translate a computer program from the English syntax to 0s and 1s, they have the compiler translate the English syntax to a language that various CPUs can translate into the languages *they* understand. This intermediate language is called, aptly enough, *Intermediate Language (IL).* (It's sort of like naming your dog "Dog.") How it's translated into 0s and 1s for the CPU is the topic of the next bullet.

- **The Common Language Runtime (CLR):** Another computer program called the *Common Language Runtime (CLR)* actually translates the Intermediate Language into the 0s and 1s that the CPU can understand. Thus a developer can write a piece of software code, compile it once into Intermediate Language, and then run it on any computer that has the CLR software already installed. This entire process — including the English-syntax computer languages, Intermediate Language (IL), and the Common Language Runtime (CLR) — is called *.NET* (pronounced "DOT-net"); nobody's quite sure why — maybe it just sounded cool.

A number of English-syntax computer languages are available in the .NET environment — in particular, Visual Basic, C# (pronounced "C-sharp"), F#, and C++, among many others. All these languages compile the English-syntax code into Intermediate Language (IL) that can be understood by the Common Language Runtime (CLR). As with spoken languages, however, each language has its own subtleties and nuances. Some people prefer the C# language over Visual Basic as a programming tool. Others have been writing code in languages such as C++ for many years, and changing to a completely new language can be a painful experience. Whatever their quirks, however, all these languages can be used to write software code that can be compiled into IL code and understood by the CLR. You can see the option to install these languages on the installation screen (shown in the upcoming Figure 11-1).

Reusing code is another standard part of the programming scene. After all, people have been writing code for decades, and a lot of it is very well written — so why make every developer write all the code needed for a software program from scratch? Life is short. So Microsoft developed a vast library of pre-built code that developers can use to write software programs. Put together enough of this ready-made code, and you have a solid frame for the rest of your program — which (I suspect) is why this library of code is called the .NET Framework.

Installing the SharePoint Tools

Unlike most of the other SharePoint tools, Visual Studio is a product that must be purchased separate from SharePoint. Before you go out and buy the product, however, ask your Microsoft representative whether your licensing agreement already includes Visual Studio and other products.

A number of tools and products are bundled with Visual Studio to make your development efforts less burdensome. One of these components is the package of tools needed for SharePoint development. When you're installing Visual Studio 2010, you can select the Microsoft SharePoint Developer Tools (as shown in Figure 11-1). The installation instructions are beyond the scope of this book, so for information about installing Visual Studio 2010, check out this Web address:

```
msdn.microsoft.com/en-us/library/e2h7fzkw.aspx
```

Also notice in the screenshot that you can install SQL Server Express — the free version of SQL Server — if you want to develop database applications using Visual Studio. Because installing SharePoint in a development environment also installs SQL Server, you don't need to install it again on your local machine.

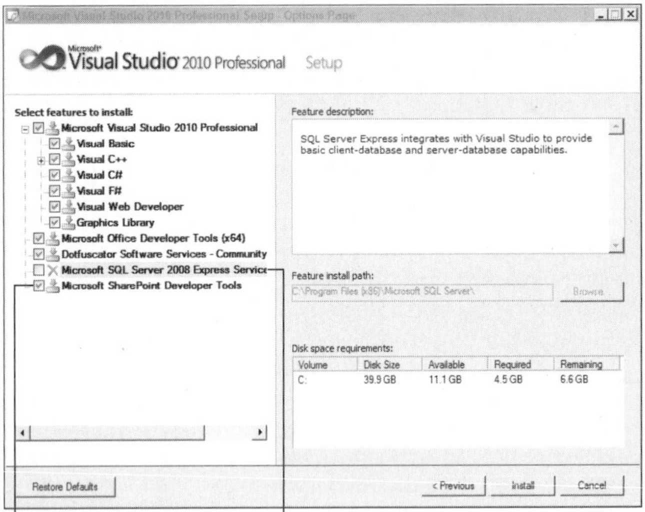

Figure 11-1:
Installing
the
Microsoft
SharePoint
Developer
Tools for
Visual
Studio.

SharePoint Developer tools

Not installing SQL Server Express

Taking a Spin around Visual Studio

The Visual Studio application is divided into six primary zones that are common to most types of programming, as shown in Figure 11-2.

These zones consist of the Toolbar across the top, the Toolbox on the left side of the screen, the Programming and Design Surface in the middle of the screen, the Output Window at the bottom of the screen, the Solution Explorer window at the upper right of the screen, and the Properties window at the lower right of the screen.

- **Toolbar:** The toolbar consists of the standard operations you use for creating a new project, saving a project, configuring settings, building the project, debugging, and deploying among many other functions.

- **Toolbox:** This window contains all the canned components you might want to use in your project. For example, if you're developing a Web Part, then you have a list of components that you might want to use in the Web Part such as textboxes, labels, panels, and buttons.

- **Programming and Design Surface:** The center window of Visual Studio is used to write code or design the user interface using the design surface. You can switch between the code window and the design window, or even choose a split screen.

✔ **Output Window:** The output window provides you feedback when deploying, debugging, or testing your code. For example, when you build and deploy your solution, you see the status as Visual Studio moves through the various steps needed to complete the operations.

✔ **Solution Explorer Window:** This window shows a tree structure of all the components that make up your solution. For example, if you're developing a Visual Web Part, then you see a file for the project as well as folders for the various files that make up the project.

✔ **Properties Window:** This window shows which specific properties are available for the currently selected component. For example, if you've selected a button on the design surface then the properties window will reflect the properties for that specific button.

The windows that make up the Visual Studio environment can be organized and shuffled around so that you can create the environment that feels most comfortable to you. The layout described in this section is simply the out of the box layout.

Toolbox

Toolbar   Programming and design surface   Solution Explorer window

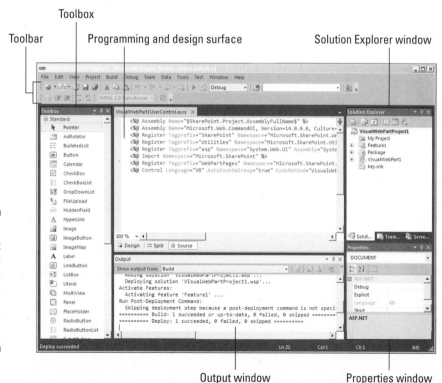

Figure 11-2:
The default windows that make up the Visual Studio application.

Output window   Properties window

Checking out SharePoint projects in Visual Studio

A Visual Studio project is simply a collection of code and configuration files that are geared toward a particular type of development. For example, you might create a Windows application project if you wanted to create a stand-alone program that you can run on your local computer. You might create a Web application if you want to create a Web site. Because we are talking about SharePoint, you want to create a SharePoint project, as shown in Figure 11-3.

The first thing to notice when you create a Visual Studio project is that you can create the project in any of the programming languages that you chose to install when you installed Visual Studio. If you're more comfortable in Visual Basic, use that language. If you just went through a C++ course, you can use that language instead.

The navigational tree on the left hand side of the project selection screen acts like a filter. For example, notice that you can expand and collapse the tree for each language type. Within each language type, you can expand the SharePoint folder. Within the SharePoint folder, you can select between the 2007 version and the 2010 version of SharePoint. Each time you drill down into the tree, you're narrowing down the project types to a more specific scenario.

When programming a SharePoint solution, you choose from a number of project templates, as shown in Figure 11-3. The following list outlines the project types and how they fit into the SharePoint landscape:

- **Empty SharePoint Project:** An empty SharePoint project that allows you to start from nothing and build the solution as you best see fit.

- **Visual Web Part:** Chapter 4 explains how to develop pages by adding Web Parts, which are reusable Web components. A number of Web Parts are available out of the box with SharePoint, but you can also create your own custom Web Part using this project template. Developing Web Parts is covered in Chapter 12.

- **Sequential Workflow and State Machine Workflow:** You can create SharePoint workflows using SharePoint Designer (Chapter 8) but sometimes you need a highly customized workflow. When your workflow requirements are beyond the capabilities of SharePoint Designer, you can crack open Visual Studio and use this project to create a workflow at the code level with limitless possibilities.

  A Sequential Workflow, as the name implies, performs a sequence of the events. There can be decisions along the way but the decisions are internal to the workflow. For example, the workflow might perform one set of events if the value of a reimbursement field in the list is greater than $500 and perform a different set of events if the value is less than $500.

A State Machine Workflow, on the other hand, defines a number of possible paths that the workflow can take, but the actual path taken is the result of external events. For example, you might create a State Machine Workflow for tracking and processing manufacturing orders. The states of the workflow might represent all the possible states of the manufacturing process, including accepted or rejected orders. The states might perform custom logic such as updating other systems or sending notifications. The key is that the logic for the workflow stems from external events. In this case, from the manufacturing process itself.

The workflow engine that SharePoint uses is called Windows Workflow Foundation (that's WF, not WWF); it's part of the .NET framework, so you can use it in many types of development besides SharePoint projects.

✔ **Business Data Connectivity Model:** When you need to integrate with Line Of Business (LOB) systems, the SharePoint technology to use is called Business Connectivity Services (BCS). When you need to program the connectivity components that BCS uses, the Visual Studio project to use is the Business Data Connectivity Model. Using this model, you can develop connections to backend systems such as SAP, Oracle, or even custom databases to integrate those LOB systems with your Intranet portal.

Available languages

SharePoint folder

Figure 11-3:
Create a
new project
in Visual
Studio.

✔ **Event Receiver:** When users interact with SharePoint, they are creating events. These events all have receivers that Microsoft has developed. For example, if you add a new item to a list, doing so fires (launches) an event. Using the Event Receiver project, you can create your own custom events that do anything you want. For example, when a new item is added to a list, you might capture that event and send off a number of tracking e-mails, or synchronize external systems with the data being added in SharePoint. Among the plethora of events in SharePoint that you can capture: events that fire when files are moved, events that fire when a new site is created, and nearly endless possibilities with custom events.

✔ **List Definition:** If you've worked with SharePoint, then you're familiar with the concept of a List. A SharePoint List is simply a list of data that you can develop using tools such as the Web browser or SharePoint Designer. Every list starts with a definition; Microsoft includes a number of ready-made list definitions with SharePoint that you can access by clicking Site Settings➪More Options and then clicking the List filter on the Create screen. For example, when you create a Contacts List, you're using the list definition that Microsoft created for contacts. When it comes time to create your own custom list that includes things such as a custom Event Receiver, you can use the List Definition project type.

✔ **Content Type:** Just as you can create a list definition in Visual Studio, you can also create a SharePoint Content Type. When you're including a custom content type in your SharePoint application, you can use this project type to do the job.

✔ **Module:** When you want to add files to your SharePoint application, you can also add a module to store them. For example, you might want to deploy text files for documentation. Adding the Module project type includes a `sample.txt` file as an example.

✔ **Site Definition:** Whenever you create a new site using your Web browser, you're using the site definitions that Microsoft has provided; one such example is when you create a new team site. When you need a custom site definition that people can also use to create sites, you can use this Site Definition project type.

✔ **Import Reusable Workflow:** The Import Reusable Workflow project type is for creating new projects based on an existing reusable workflow. For example, you might have created a workflow using SharePoint Designer and now want to customize it and incorporate it into your SharePoint application. You can use this project type to import the workflow and then customize it.

✔ **Import SharePoint Solution Package:** When you need to import an existing SharePoint Web Solution Package (WSP), you can use this project type.

Peering into SharePoint

When developing a SharePoint solution using Visual Studio, you often want to peer into the SharePoint farm and look at items such as the lists, libraries, content types, and sites. Using a feature of Visual Studio called Server Explorer, you can browse not only the SharePoint farm, but also important components of a server (such as the services running or the event logs). You can view Server Explorer by clicking the View⇨Server Explorer. Figure 11-4 shows Server Explorer in action.

Figure 11-4:
Browsing key components of a server and SharePoint farm using Server Explorer in Visual Studio.

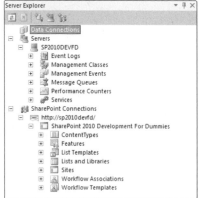

Organizing Your Visual Studio Solutions

When you start creating Visual Studio projects for SharePoint, the number of files, folders, and containers can be daunting. To make matters worse, you hear people talk about SharePoint "features," "packages," and "solutions." How these pieces fit together is very simple when you understand how it all works — but getting to that point can be frustrating and time-consuming.

Adding projects to solutions

When you create a new Visual Studio project, you're actually creating a Visual Studio solution *and* a Visual Studio project. You can, of course, create an empty Visual Studio solution and then add projects to it later — but if you just create a SharePoint project from scratch — based on one of the templates described in the earlier section, "Checking out SharePoint projects in Visual Studio" — then Visual Studio creates the solution for you automatically.

✔ You can create an empty Visual Studio solution by selecting the Blank Solution project type — which you access by selecting the Other Project Types and then Visual Studio Solutions filter when you're creating a new project.

✔ You can add projects to the solution by right-clicking the solution and then selecting Add New Project, as shown in Figure 11-5.

Figure 11-5:
Adding a
project to
a Visual
Studio
solution.

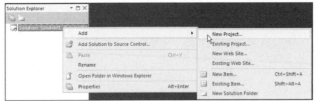

Think of a Visual Studio solution as a container for Visual Studio projects. This solutions-and-project approach is consistent for any type of development you do using Visual Studio — and not just in SharePoint. If you're using Visual Studio, then your files are organized into projects — which are contained in solutions.

Bundling projects into features

The SharePoint world has its own terminology for chunks of functionality called *features*. If you've ever had to administer a SharePoint site, then you're probably familiar with the concept of a feature. As you develop your SharePoint projects in Visual Studio, you need a way to tie it all together for the people administering the SharePoint sites that use your code. For example, you might have a Web Part project that relies on a Content Type project. You wouldn't want the SharePoint site administrators to install one without the other, so you'd add both of them to a SharePoint feature. Then, when a user activates your feature, doing so activates both of these projects you've developed.

You can see all the features available on your SharePoint sites on the site's settings page.

Packaging files into a Web Solution Package

As you begin developing more and more functionality for SharePoint, you might have a number of different features you want to bundle together. You can package all those features in a package known as a Web Solution Package (WSP). The WSP can then be deployed to a SharePoint environment, where site administrators can then activate each of the features in the package.

Chapter 12 walks you through developing a Web Part, adding it to a feature, adding the feature to a package, deploying the package to SharePoint, activating the feature for a site, and then adding the new Web Part to a page. After you've walked through the entire end-to-end process, the terminology will begin to become less confusing.

One of the difficult parts in any type of development is packaging your hard work to be moved to a different system such as a production system. You have to figure out how to get all the code files, text files, help files, images, configuration files, and other pieces that make up your project into a package that someone else can take and install. The SharePoint 2010 platform has created an easy solution to this challenge: It uses Web Solution Packages (WSPs) throughout the platform.

WSP files are actually nothing more than a zipped group of files — but instead of having a `.zip` file extension they have a `.wsp` file extension. Some special files within the zipped file describe the solution. When Visual Studio imports a WSP file, it's simply unzipping the files and looking for those special descriptive files.

WSP files are used throughout SharePoint and not just for Visual Studio projects. Whenever you use your browser to save a site, library, or list as a template, the result is a WSP file.

The WSP standard makes it easy to work with many different tools, depending on the type of development you're doing. For example, you might be developing a site using SharePoint Designer and realize that you need to switch to Visual Studio. You can do so by exporting the solution from SharePoint Designer into a WSP file and then importing it into Visual Studio. All your files and work will now be in Visual Studio — where you can continue your development efforts. Later on, when you're ready to move the site to a production SharePoint environment, you can package the whole shebang as a WSP and then import it into SharePoint.

A Web Solution Package (WSP) is standardized regardless of whether you're using your Web browser, SharePoint Designer, or Visual Studio to develop your solution. Result: It doesn't matter what development tool you're using; the resulting WSP file is the same regardless.

Discover the SharePoint Software Development Kit

You can get help from various places when tackling the task of writing code within the SharePoint environment. In particular, you can download and install the Microsoft SharePoint 2010 Software Development Kit (SDK).

The SharePoint SDK contains a wealth of information regarding programming on the SharePoint platform. The kit includes overviews of programming tasks, sample code, documentation, step-by-step examples, and much more.

You can download the SharePoint 2010 Software Development Kit at

```
msdn.microsoft.com/en-us/library/ee557253.aspx
```

Using the SharePoint Developer Dashboard

The SharePoint Developer Dashboard allows you to see all the calls and resource requests that are going on when a SharePoint page loads. This is vital in understanding how the code is running and, if a problem crops up, what the culprit might be.

When the Developer Dashboard is turned on, you'll see a new section at the bottom of every page that outlines essential information about the code and the database calls that went into loading the page, as shown in Figure 11-6.

Check out Chapter 15 for more about the Developer Dashboard — as well as information about how to turn it on.

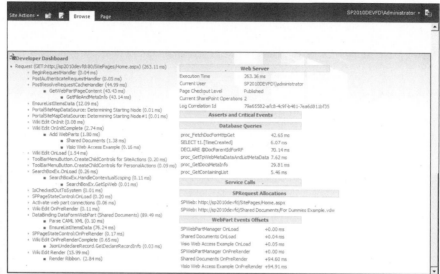

Figure 11-6:
The
SharePoint
Developer
Dashboard.

Playing Nicely in Your Sandbox

In the past, a big issue with adding custom code to a SharePoint site was that you needed administrator level access to the server running SharePoint before you could get your code to work correctly. This caused a lot of problems; administrators didn't want to give developers the required access. An administrator could always install the custom code, of course, but would then have to worry about how well the code was developed — and whether it would cause problems with other parts of the SharePoint platform. Requiring this high level of access just to tweak the code caused pains-in-the-virtual-anatomy for everyone involved.

A solution to this problem emerged in SharePoint 2010: Sandboxed Solutions, which allows a developer's code to run in isolation on SharePoint without affecting other portions of the platform. If something goes wrong with the code, the only sites affected are those running the custom code. SharePoint accomplishes this by isolating the code in areas called *sandboxes.* It's a playground metaphor: The developer can only play in his or her sandbox; should something go wrong, the other sandboxes are not affected. For example, a Web Part that someone has developed might have a bug that attempts to copy each file millions of times. This would be a huge resource drain — and in past versions of SharePoint, such a bug could cause the entire platform to grind to a halt. (That would only have to happen once to make administrators leery of whatever comes to them from the developers.)

With Sandboxed Solutions, the idea is to contain the code in its own sandbox area — and the platform throttles down the resources made available to that sandbox. If a Web Part, or any other code, starts spinning out of control, the rest of the farm will be unaffected. This isolation makes SharePoint administrators happy because

- ✔ The only users yelling about lousy performance are the ones using the custom code.

- ✔ The rest of the SharePoint countryside is safe from the ravages of custom-code-gone-monstrous, so no torchlight parade is needed.

- ✔ The administrators can refer the angry users to the developers instead of fielding complaints from the entire SharePoint user base.

You can target a project as a Sandboxed Solution when you create it in Visual Studio. Creating a new SharePoint project in Visual Studio is covered in Chapter 12.

Chapter 12

Commanding SharePoint through Code

> *Words have allowed the communication of ideas, enabling human beings to work together to build the impossible. Mankind's greatest achievements have come about by talking and communicating, and its greatest failures by not communicating. It doesn't have to be like this. Our greatest hopes could become reality in the future. With technology at our disposal, the possibilities are unbounded. All we need to do is make sure we keep communicating and collaborating.*
>
> — Stephen Hawking

There are different levels, as well as types, of SharePoint development. You can spend most of your time developing SharePoint components such as sites, pages, lists, and libraries — using nothing more than your local browser. When you need to dive deeper down the rabbit hole, you can crack open SharePoint Designer and begin building custom workflows, forms, and styling. When you get to the point that you need a customized solution that's very specific to your needs, then you're ready to delve into writing code and taking full advantage of the SharePoint Object Model.

This chapter covers using the SharePoint Object Model to work with the SharePoint environment through code. It talks about the differences between the SharePoint Object Model and the SharePoint Client Object Model (trust me, they exist) — and when you can, and should, use each. It also walks you through building a simple console application that interacts with the SharePoint Object Model to print the sites and lists in a site collection. Next you explore the SharePoint Web Services and find out what it means to be RESTful (sorry, it doesn't mean a vacation in Aruba, at least not now). Finally, this chapter introduces the client tools Silverlight and JavaScript — and offers pointers on when to use them to enhance your SharePoint sites.

Understanding SharePoint Programming

Long ago, in an office far, far, away, when I was working as a Unix system administrator, the idea of "code" was foreign to me. Oh, sure, I'd written plenty of Unix scripts, but those were essentially bunches of Unix commands that ran in the order I had entered them in my text file. My job was to make sure that the Unix servers were always working properly. A whole other team was responsible for writing any programming code. In my mind, they were doing something deeply technical that bordered on wizardry. I just couldn't get my mind around what it meant to "code."

Then the manager of the programmer team mentioned a problem they were having with two different software systems. He said that one of his programmers was able to weave together some code to bridge the gap between the two systems and solve the problem. I was awestruck. (What was this "weaving together code" and "bridging the gap between systems" of which he spoke?) I wanted to learn how to be a programmer too!

I ended up going back to school, and eventually completed a master's degree in computer science. After my first year, the magic was gone; programming was as straightforward as anything else. Fortunately, the magic wasn't needed; when you understand the basics of programming, you can make a software system — in this case, SharePoint — do just about anything you'd ever want it to do. The only requirements are practice, patience, and research.

When you first learn to program, you usually start with very simple self-contained programs. You might write one that calculates gas mileage (or performs some other sort of arithmetic), accepts input, or writes output to a file. The point of these simple programs is to get you comfortable with the syntax of programming — and with how beasties such as compilers and debuggers work.

When you're writing code for software systems, you have to understand how to move from writing code for your self-contained programs to interacting with an external system. In the case of SharePoint, you can interact with all its wonders through code in two primary ways: the SharePoint Object Model or SharePoint Web Services. Using these two methods you can weave together your own applications that pick and pull and manipulate SharePoint depending on exactly what you're trying to do. The key is that using these methods, you have everything SharePoint has to offer right at your fingertips and can command it as you see fit. As a SharePoint programmer, you become the wizard and SharePoint becomes the wonderful world of Oz.

Introducing Object-Oriented Programming

An Object Model (OM) can often be a difficult concept to wrap your head around. There are many prerequisites to master before you can get an Object Model to do your bidding; fortunately, you don't need most of them to start writing SharePoint code. For example, you should already understand the concepts behind object-oriented programming (nicknamed OOP — or OO if you don't want to sound like you just dropped something), but you don't have to be an expert.

Object-oriented programming is a way to break apart the pieces of a program you're developing into the functional "objects" that each piece represents. For example, if you're creating a simple gas mileage program, then you might develop a piece of code that represents a car. In the code that represents a car, you might have variables for the amount of gas it can hold, the current level of fuel, the speed, and the distance traveled. This piece of code that represents a car is called an object; object-oriented programming creates, manipulates, and arranges such logical objects.

When you're programming your application, you don't need to think about all the components of a car as you build your program. You just *instantiate* (create a new instance of) a car object when you need it — and then work with the components of that car object throughout the program. For example, if you create two cars in your program and then assign a value to a variable to represent the gas level for each car, you might easily get confused which variable goes with which car. Instead you can simply know that car A has a variable that can be accessed as a property of that car object — code such as `carA.fuel = 100` might reference the fuel tank within the car A object. This simple example explains the very basics of how object-oriented programming works. Complete volumes of books and complete college degrees cover the subject, so if you don't feel like an expert, don't worry. You can still get by just understanding the basics and learning about the SharePoint Object Model as you go.

Discovering the SharePoint Object Model

The easiest way to understand the SharePoint Object Model is to imagine taking an entire SharePoint installation and breaking it down into small functional pieces. Some of the functional pieces, or objects, you might have include site collections, sites/sub-sites, lists, libraries, and fields, as shown in

Figure 12-1. Each functional component has a logical object that represents it in code and you can access the object in your own program.

Because SharePoint is a platform, the number of objects is different depending on the way you've developed your implementation. For example, you might have a small implementation with a single site collection or a large implementation with hundreds of site collections. The way the object model is structured never changes. The only thing that changes is how many objects, of which types, your implementation contains. Be careful, though: If you write code that looks for a specifically named object, your code will break if it doesn't find that object.

A group of very smart programmers has already divided SharePoint into its functional objects and created a way for programmers to interact with them through code. All the SharePoint objects taken together represent what is called the SharePoint Object Model.

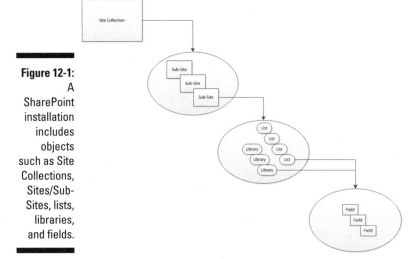

Figure 12-1:
A
SharePoint
installation
includes
objects
such as Site
Collections,
Sites/Sub-
Sites, lists,
libraries,
and fields.

Distinguishing server OM from client OM

As a software architecture, SharePoint is a version of the client-server model: The server runs on a server computer in a data center somewhere, and the users connect to this server using their Web browsers running on their local computers (clients). In the past, any code using the SharePoint Object Model had to run on the same server that was running SharePoint — which was due to the technical difficulty of interacting with the SharePoint server over the network. For Web Parts, this requirement wasn't a problem, because the server running SharePoint is where the Web Part code runs. But if you tried to get SharePoint to work with a program that wasn't intended to run on the same server as SharePoint, you ran into hassles pretty quickly. For example, if you wanted to write a stand-alone Windows application that users could run from their local computers, that program would have to run on a different computer from the one running SharePoint — which meant you couldn't use the SharePoint Object Model. You could, of course, use the SharePoint Web Services to work around that headache, but this was no trivial task.

In SharePoint 2010, Microsoft includes a special subset of the SharePoint Object Model called the SharePoint *Client* Object Model; the idea is to give you a way to work with at least part of the SharePoint Object Model on a client computer. Using the Client Object Model, you can (for example) write your own Windows application for users to install locally, and still develop functionality in your program that interacts with SharePoint — even though SharePoint itself is running on some server way over yonder.

When you're writing your code, be sure you understand where your code will be running. If you write code that will run on the server itself, then you can assume your code will have access to the entire SharePoint Object Model. If you're writing code that won't be running on the same computer that runs SharePoint, be sure to use the SharePoint Client Object Model.

Using the SharePoint Client Object Model, you can design applications that interact with SharePoint but run locally on client computers. For example, you might have a custom application that managers use for tracking inventory. Using the SharePoint Client Object Model, you can integrate this application with your SharePoint implementation by pulling content into the company portal (which runs on SharePoint) from the standalone application — or pushing information from the portal to the application.

A Web Part runs on the server, where it can access the entire SharePoint Object Model. This might seem confusing — after all, users interact with a Web Part when they browse to a SharePoint page using a browser that runs on client machines. The Web Part logic, however, runs on the server; the results are simply sent back to the client using HTML.

Listing your lists

What better way to get a handle on the SharePoint Object Model than to jump right in and build your first application? In this section, I walk you through the creation of two different example applications that help you get started with the basics of writing code for both the SharePoint Object Model and the SharePoint Client Object model. Just keep in mind . . .

- If your application will run on the same server that's running SharePoint, use the full SharePoint Object Model.

- If your application will be running on a computer that isn't running SharePoint, use the SharePoint Client Object Model.

Using the SharePoint Object Model

The following example builds a console-based application that uses the SharePoint Object Model to make a single list of all the sites and lists in a given site collection. When you're doing SharePoint programming, the tool of choice is Visual Studio.

1. **Fire up Visual Studio by clicking Start⇨All Programs⇨Microsoft Visual Studio 2010⇨Microsoft Visual Studio 2010.**

2. **Click the New Project link to create a new Visual Studio project, as shown in Figure 12-2.**

   When you create a new Visual Studio project, you're also creating a Visual Studio solution; a project lives within a solution.

3. **Expand the Visual C# node and then select the Windows project types.**

4. **Select Console Application from the list of available project templates, and then click OK.**

   Visual Studio creates your new project and displays it on-screen.

   Make sure you target the .NET Framework version (3.5) instead of the default version 4.0, as shown in Figure 12-3.

   • The list of available project templates also contains a node for SharePoint project types. SharePoint-specific projects are geared toward developing specific components such as visual Web Parts.

   • Any project type can use the SharePoint Object Model; thus we use the Console Application here for simplicity. Also notice that when Visual Studio creates the project, the code for the console application is already stubbed out.

Figure 12-2: Creating a new project in Visual Studio.

Figure 12-3:
Selecting
the Console
Application
project
type when
creating a
new Visual
Studio
project.

5. **Right-click the project in Solution Explorer, select Properties, and then select Any CPU from the Platform drop-down list on the Build tab (as shown in Figure 12-4).**

   Doing so switches the target platform from the default 32-bit (x86) platform to accommodate the 64-bit platform.

Selecting a 64-bit target platform

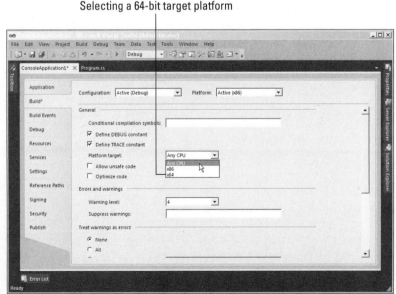

Figure 12-4:
Selecting a
64-bit target
platform
for the
application.

6. **Add a reference to the SharePoint library. Right-click the References node located in the Solution Explorer window, and then click Add Reference, as shown in Figure 12-5.**

   The SharePoint library gives your application access to all the objects, methods, and properties that make up the SharePoint Object Model.

   For more information about the Solution Explorer window and the other windows that make up Visual Studio, check out Chapter 11.

7. **On the .NET tab, scroll down and select the** Microsoft.SharePoint **reference and then click OK button, as shown in Figure 12-6.**

Choosing the Add Reference option

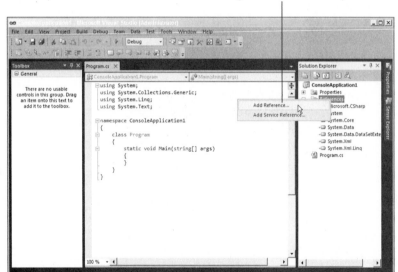

Figure 12-5:
Adding a
reference
to the Visual
Studio
project.

Figure 12-6:
Selecting
the refer-
ence to the
SharePoint
library.

8. **Add a reference to the library by adding a using statement that references the** `Microsoft.SharePoint` **namespace.**

   Add this statement to the top of the code, along with the other `using` statements, as follows:

   ```
   using Microsoft.SharePoint;
   ```

9. **Add the code to the Main method that will instantiate an instance of an** `SPSite` **(site collection) object and then loop through all the sites and lists within each site in the given site collection.**

   The result of running the application is a listing of all sites (even internal hidden sites), as well as the lists contained within each site, as shown in Figure 12-7.

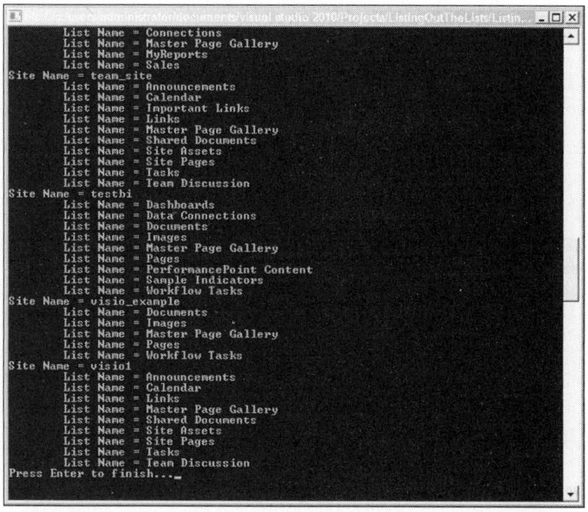

Figure 12-7: A console application using the SharePoint Object Model to list all sites (and lists within each site) for a site collection.

The complete code for the console application is as follows. Note that you will need to change the URL of the server since this code is pointing to my development environment located at `http://sp2010devfd`.

```
using System;
using System.Collections.Generic;
using System.Linq;
using System.Text;
using Microsoft.SharePoint;

namespace ListingOutTheLists
{
 class Program
 {
   static void Main(string[] args)
   {
```

```
    // Instantiate an SPSite object
    // to represent the parent site.
    SPSite mySiteCollection =
        new SPSite("http://sp2010devfd");

    // Loop through all of the sites in the
    // site collection.
    foreach (SPWeb aSite in mySiteCollection.AllWebs)
    {
      SPListCollection myLists = aSite.Lists;
      Console.WriteLine("Site Name = " + aSite.Name);

      // Loop through all of the lists in the
      // current site.
      foreach (SPList aList in myLists)
      {
        // Add a tab for readability '\t'
        Console.WriteLine("\tList Name = "
          + aList.Title);
      }
    }

    // Dispose of the SPSite object.
    mySiteCollection.Dispose();

    Console.Write("Press Enter to finish . . .");
    Console.ReadLine();
    }
  }
}
```

The console application you built will run only on the server computer where SharePoint is running.

Using the SharePoint Client Object Model

It bears repeating: When you use the SharePoint Object Model, your application must run on the same server that's running the SharePoint instance you're working with in your code. If you need your application to run on a server different from the one running SharePoint, you have to use the SharePoint Client Object Model. So here's where you get a crack at the Client Object Model.

The following example builds the same console-based application that you built previously — this time using the SharePoint Client Object Model, which allows you to run the application on any computer (yeah, you *could* run it on the server that's running SharePoint — but that isn't what the Client Object Model is for, so please don't, okay?). The application has the same logic as before — it shows all the sites and lists in a given site collection as items in one list. Here's the hauntingly familiar drill, this time with the Client Object Model:

1. **Fire up Visual Studio: Click Start⇨All Programs⇨Microsoft Visual Studio 2010⇨Microsoft Visual Studio 2010.**

2. **Click the New Project link to create a new Visual Studio project, as shown in Figure 12-2.**

   Note that when you create a new Visual Studio project, you're also creating a Visual Studio solution, even when you use the Client Object Model. Say it with me: *A project lives within a solution.*

3. **Expand the Visual C# node and then select the Windows project types. Select Console Application from the list of available project templates.**

   Be sure to target the .NET Framework version (3.5) instead of the default 4.0, as shown in Figure 12-3.

4. **Click OK to create the project and its corresponding solution.**

   The list of available project templates also contains a node for SharePoint project types. SharePoint-specific projects are geared toward developing specific components such as visual Web Parts.

   That déjà vu you're feeling is because this is the same step done with the SharePoint Object Model in the previous subsection. Any project type can use the SharePoint Object Model, so we use the Console Application here (too) for simplicity — and to emphasize that what you do with the Client Object Model is eerily similar to what you do with the full SharePoint Object Model. Also notice that when Visual Studio creates the project, the code for the console application is already stubbed out.

5. **Right-click the project in Solution Explorer, select Properties, and then select Any CPU from the Platform drop-down list on the Build tab (as shown in Figure 12-4).**

   Doing so switches the target platform from the default 32-bit (x86) platform to accommodate the 64-bit platform.

6. **Right-click the References node in the Solution Explorer window and click Add Reference, as shown in Figure 12-5.**

   Doing so adds references to the SharePoint Client library and runtime, which in turn give your application access to all the objects, methods, and properties that make up the SharePoint Client Object Model.

   For more about the Solution Explorer window and the other windows that make up Visual Studio, refer to Chapter 11.

7. **On the .NET tab, scroll down and select the Microsoft.SharePoint. Client and Microsoft.SharePoint.Client.Runtime references, and then click OK button, as shown in Figure 12-8.**

Figure 12-8:
Selecting
the refer-
ence to the
SharePoint
Client library
and runtime.

Component Name	Version	Runtime ▲
Microsoft.Office.SharePoint.ClientExtensions	14.0.0.0	v2.0.507
Microsoft Office 2010 component	14.0.0.0	v2.0.507
Microsoft Office Server DLC component	14.0.0.0	v2.0.507
Microsoft Office Server DLC task utility	14.0.0.0	v2.0.507
Microsoft.SharePoint.Client	14.0.0.0	v2.0.507
Microsoft.SharePoint.Client.Runtime	14.0.0.0	v2.0.507
Microsoft.SharePoint	14.0.0.0	v2.0.507
Microsoft.SharePoint.Linq	14.0.0.0	v2.0.507
Microsoft® SharePoint® Server component	14.0.0.0	v2.0.507
Microsoft.SharePoint.Publishing	14.0.0.0	v2.0.507
Microsoft® SharePoint® Foundation Search	14.0.0.0	v2.0.507
Microsoft FAST Search Server 2010 for SharePoint	14.0.0.0	v2.0.507

.NET | COM | Projects | Browse | Recent |
Filtered to: .NET Framework 3.5

OK   Cancel

TIP

Because you're using the Client Object Model, you don't have to develop this program on the computer that's running SharePoint — so you might not see the required libraries displayed on the .NET tab. In such a case, you have to copy the libraries you need from the computer that's running SharePoint to the computer where you're doing this development. The files you want are `Microsoft.SharePoint.Client.dll` and `Microsoft.SharePoint.Client.Runtime.dll` — and they're located in this directory on the SharePoint server computer:

```
C:\Program Files\Common Files\Microsoft Shared\Web Server Extensions\14\
        ISAPI
```

When you've copied them to your local computer, you can browse to them by selecting the Browse tab on the Add Reference dialog box and then navigating to the location where you placed the copied files.

8. **Add a reference to the required libraries by adding a** `using` **statement that references the** `Microsoft.SharePoint.Client` **namespace.**

Put the statement the top of the code, along with the other `using` statements, as follows:

```
using Microsoft.SharePoint.Client;
```

Add the code to the Main method so you can query the SharePoint server and loop through the sites and lists.

Note that the logic when using the SharePoint Client Object Model is different from using the standard SharePoint Object Model because (we're assuming that) the code is running on a computer other than the one that's running SharePoint. The result is that your application does not have instant access to all the information running in SharePoint — and has to query the SharePoint server to get the information. Because it would overburden the network and your application to try to get every-thing from SharePoint at once, you use special syntax to load only the portions of the SharePoint Object Model that you need in the application.

The result of running the application is a listing of all sites (even internal hidden sites) and the lists contained within each site, as shown in Figure 12-9.

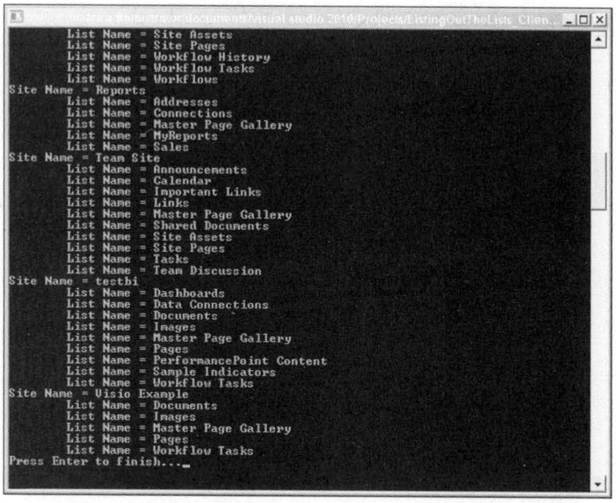

Figure 12-9:
A console application using the SharePoint Client Object Model to list out the sites and lists within each site for a given site collection.

The complete code for the Console Application — this time using the SharePoint Client Object Model — is as follows. Note that you will need to change the URL of the server since this code is pointing to my development environment located at `http://sp2010devfd`.

```
using System;
using System.Collections.Generic;
using System.Linq;
using System.Text;
using Microsoft.SharePoint.Client;

namespace ListingOutTheLists_ClientOM
{
 class Program
 {
   static void Main(string[] args)
   {
     // Create a context reference to the client
     // SharePoint site.
     ClientContext myClientContext =
       new ClientContext("http://sp2010devfd");

     // Instantiate a Web (site collection) object.
     Web mySiteCollection = myClientContext.Web;

     // Set up the query to the server to tell it
     // we want to retrieve the Webs collection
     // from the site collection.
```

```
myClientContext.Load(mySiteCollection.Webs);

// Send the request to the server.
myClientContext.ExecuteQuery();

// Now that we have the Webs collection back
// we will loop through it and print the site
// titles.
foreach (Web aSite in mySiteCollection.Webs)
{
  // Print out the name of the site.
  Console.WriteLine("Site Name = " + aSite.Title);

  // While we are still in the current site we
  // will loop through and print out all of the
  // lists within this site.
  // Instantiate a ListCollection to hold
  // all of the lists.
  ListCollection myList = aSite.Lists;

  // Set up the query to the server to tell it we
  // want to retrieve the Lists from the site.
  myClientContext.Load(aSite.Lists);

  // Send the request to the server.
  myClientContext.ExecuteQuery();

  // Now that we have the Lists collection back
  // we will loop through it and print the list
  // titles.
  foreach (List aList in aSite.Lists)
  {
    // Add a tab for readability '\t'
    Console.WriteLine("\tList Name = "
      + aList.Title);
  }
}

// Dispose of the context reference to the
// server.
myClientContext.Dispose();

Console.Write("Press Enter to finish . . .");
Console.ReadLine();

      }
    }
  }
```

Because this console application is using the Client Object Model it can be copied and run on any Windows computer that has a network connection to the SharePoint site.

Making SharePoint Accessible with Web Services

A Web Service is simply a way to interact with a remote computer system over a network. For example, you might have a computer sitting in your home office that has a special program on it that you developed. Let's say it's your gas-mileage calculation program, and you spent a lot of hard work getting it just right. You might want to let your friends use the logic that you created that takes into account all types of things such as wind speed, road smoothness, and even insect impacts. So how do you let your friends use your program? You could let them come over and use your computer, but that might zap their wallets in gas costs if they live far away. One solution would be to develop a Web Service so they could write their own programs that call out to your program to use its logic. This exact scenario is what Microsoft has already done with SharePoint. With SharePoint running on a server in a data center somewhere, other software applications must connect to it in order to access its functionality and content — so they access the SharePoint Web Services over the network.

Prior to SharePoint 2010, the Web Services were the only way to access SharePoint functionality remotely using code. In SharePoint 2010, however, the SharePoint Client Object Model provides another mechanism for access by remote applications.

Show me the services

Which Web Services are available for SharePoint depend on the edition you've installed. If you're using SharePoint Foundation, then you have a certain list of Web Services available. If you're using the full-featured version of SharePoint Server, then you have another horde of Web Services that support the additional capabilities you get with SharePoint Server.

The following list describes the SharePoint Foundation Web Services that Microsoft provides:

 ✔ **WebSvcAdmin:** Provides methods for managing a deployment of SharePoint Foundation, such as for creating or deleting sites.

- **WebSvcAlerts:** Provides methods for working with alerts for list items in a SharePoint Foundation site.

- **WebSvcAuthentication:** Provides classes for logging on to a SharePoint Foundation site that's using forms-based authentication.

- **WebSvcBdcAdminService:** Provides methods that can be used to import and export Business Data Connectivity Services (BDC) models.

- **WebSvcCellStorage:** Enables client computers to synchronize changes made to shared files that are stored on a server.

- **WebSvcCopy:** Provides methods for copying items between locations in SharePoint Foundation.

- **WebSvcdiagnostics:** Enables client computers to submit diagnostic reports that describe application errors that occur on the client computer.

- **WebSvcDspSts:** Provides a method for performing queries against lists in SharePoint Foundation.

- **WebSvcDWS:** Provides methods for managing Document Workspace sites and the data they contain.

- **WebSvcForms:** Provides methods for returning forms used in the user interface when working with the contents of a list.

- **WebSvcImaging:** Provides methods that enable you to create and manage picture libraries.

- **WebSvcLists:** Provides methods for working with lists and list data.

- **WebSvcMeetings:** Provides methods that enable you to create and manage Meeting Workspace sites.

- **WebSvcPeople:** Provides methods for working with security groups.

- **WebSvcPermissions:** Provides methods for working with the permissions for a site or list.

- **WebSvcSharedAccess:** Provides a method that determines whether a document is being coauthored.

- **WebSvcsharepointemailws:** Provides methods for managing distribution groups remotely.

- **WebSvcSiteData:** Provides methods that return metadata or list data from sites or lists in SharePoint Foundation.

- **WebSvcsites:** Provides methods for working with Web sites.

- **WebSvcspsearch:** Provides methods for performing remote searches within a SharePoint Foundation deployment.

- **WebSvcUserGroup:** Provides methods for working with users and groups.

- **WebSvcVersions:** Provides methods for managing file versions.

- ✔ **WebSvcviews:** Provides methods for working with list views.

- ✔ **WebSvcwebpartpages:** Provides methods to send and retrieve Web Part information to and from Web Services.

- ✔ **WebSvcWebs:** Provides methods for working with Web sites and content types.

The Web Services available for SharePoint Server include all those available for SharePoint Foundation plus some additions, described in the following list:

- ✔ **WebSvcOrganizationProfileService:** Provides an interface for remote clients to read and create organization profiles.

- ✔ **WebSvcPublishedLinksService:** Provides a published links interface for remote clients to read and create published links.

- ✔ **WebSvcSearch:** Provides methods that can be used to remotely query SharePoint Server search.

- ✔ **WebSvcSocialDataService:** Provides an interface for remote clients to read, create, and manipulate social data.

- ✔ **WebSvcUserProfileChangeService:** Provides a user profile interface for remote clients to read and create user profiles.

- ✔ **WebSvcUserProfileService:** Provides a user profile interface for remote clients to read and create user profiles.

Okay, the names of the Web Services might throw you a bit at first. For example, Microsoft adds the prefix WebSvc to the beginning of the name but the *actual* Web Service doesn't have the same prefix. If you're looking for the WebSvcAlerts Web Service, what you find is the service itself, sporting the name Alerts without the WebSvc prefix.

These SharePoint Web Services come in two flavors, each one identified by a distinctive file extension: a traditional ASP.NET Web Service and the newer Windows Communication Foundation (WCF) Web Service.

You can view the SharePoint Web Services by browsing to them on the server, following these steps:

1. **Click Start⇨Administrative Tools⇨Internet Information Services (IIS) Manager.**

2. **Expand the server node as denoted by the name of the server, the Sites node, and finally the specific site node you're using for SharePoint, as shown in Figure 12-10.**

3. **Right-click the _vti_bin folder and then click Explore to view all the files in the directory.**

Notice that you can sort the files by type and can see the different ASP.NET Web Service files and the WCF Web Service files, as shown in Figure 12-11.

Figure 12-10:
Viewing a SharePoint site in IIS Manager.

ASP.NET Web service types

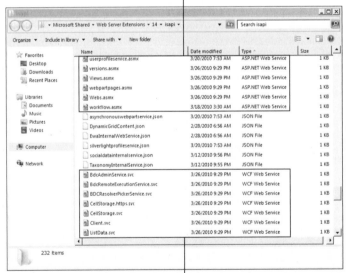

Figure 12-11:
Using Windows Explorer to browse the actual files for the SharePoint Web Services.

WCF Web service types

You can view the actual Web Service pages by browsing to them on your SharePoint site. Their location is in the following form

```
http://<servername>/<sitename>/_vti_bin/
              <webservice>.<extension>
```

For example, when I browse the Lists Web Service and my server name is sp2010devfd, which contains the top level site, then here's what I'd type into my browser, as shown in Figure 12-12:

```
http://sp2010devfd/_vti_bin/Lists.asmx
```

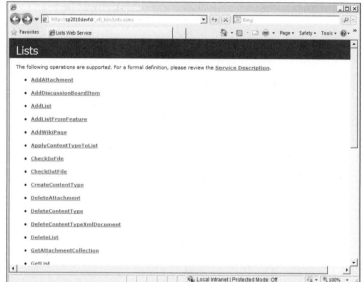

Figure 12-12:
Viewing the Web-SvcLists Web Service in the browser.

REST-based Web Services

No, we're not encouraging slothful programming habits here. REST stands for Representational State Transfer; it's a specification for developers to use when they build Web Services such as the REST-based Excel Web Services mentioned in Chapter 5. You can rest assured, no pun intended, that SharePoint also has REST-based Web Services for working with lists, libraries, sites, and many other parts of SharePoint. The REST-based Web Services are located in the same directory; each was designed specifically to meet the REST specification.

The basic idea of REST is that you can interact with a Web Service using simple HTTP. What does this mean for you? Well, for openers, you can interact with a REST-based Web Service using nothing more than your Web browser. For example, if you want to use a REST-based Web Service to view all the lists in your site, then you can simply point your browser at the URL of the Web Service. The REST-based Web Service for lists is called `ListData.svc` — so you'd type this command into your browser:

```
http://<servername>/<sitename>/_vti_bin/ListData.svc
```

Then all you do is press Enter to get a nicely formed XML list of all the lists in your site, as shown in Figure 12-13.

Figure 12-13:
Using the REST-based ListData Web Service to return the lists in a site.

Notice in the XML output in the screenshot that the feed type is ATOM. A Web browser will render XML output differently depending on the browser settings. Each browser is different — but you can usually change the way your browser renders XML by tweaking those browser settings. Here's how to change the way XML data is viewed in Internet Explorer:

1. **Navigate to Tools➪Internet Options.**

2. **Click the Settings button located under the Feeds and Web Slices section on the Content tab.**

   A Settings screen appears, displaying a check box (labeled *Turn on feed reading view*) that indicates which view is currently set for Internet Explorer.

3. **Depending on whether you want to keep or change the current way IE views XML, clear (or click to put a check in) the check box.**

Lighting Up Your Site with Silverlight

Silverlight technology provides a rich user experience by allowing the Web browser to run a subset of the .NET framework right on the local computer where Internet Explorer is running. You can think of Silverlight as a programming language that requires an add-on to Internet Explorer in order to run the Silverlight programs. If you are familiar with a similar product called Flash that is put out by Adobe, then you are familiar with Microsoft's implementation of the same principle, which they call Silverlight. SharePoint 2010 includes Silverlight technology throughout — so developers can also host their Silverlight applications in the SharePoint environment as a standard feature.

Understanding the need for Silverlight

One of the biggest problems with Web applications such as SharePoint is that the protocols they use were never designed to do much to enhance the user experience per se. The Web started out as a simple way to make information available on the network and connect it with links: HyperText Markup Language (HTML) files were sent over the network using (well, yeah) the HyperText Transfer Protocol — the now-familiar HTTP.

Those parts of a Web address have never changed — and are still the beginning (and usually the end) of every current Web address. Here's a familiar example:

```
www.microsoft.com/default.html
```

The `http` at the beginning of the address tells your Web browser that the address you've entered uses the HyperText Markup Language (HTML) for displaying information. When you enter the Web address and press Enter, your computer queries a special computer on the Internet to find out which computer it has to talk to in order to get information back. In this case, the appropriate computer hangs out in Microsoft-land.

When your computer knows which computer to query, it sends off a request to the Microsoft computer — and the Microsoft computer responds with the information contained on the main Microsoft.com Web site. This type of computer communication is called *client-server architecture:* Your computer is the client and the Microsoft computer is serving up the information you're requesting. This architecture works great for requesting information but it's a no-frills arrangement; it starts to break down when you want to have an inter-active experience. For example, now that you've loaded the main Microsoft.com page, you might want to click something on the page. Your computer now has to send an entirely new message to Microsoft to let the server computer know that you clicked something.

Every time you interact with the page, the entire process has to continually repeat itself. The result is that you see the *page refresh,* or reload, in your browser every time you interact with the information. (And if you think that's slow, just be glad you're not a computer; if you were, every refresh would seem to take centuries.)

In order to remedy the round-trip behavior of the entire Web page each time you interact with it, Microsoft developed a program called Silverlight. When you browse to a page containing Silverlight, the page downloads just as you would expect — but the Silverlight portion of the page downloads and runs *on your local computer.* You can interact with the Silverlight portion of the content without having to request the entire page. Because the Silverlight portion is actually running on your local computer, the information doesn't have as far to travel, so the refresh is faster. Result: a much more responsive and rich experience. No need to wait for the round-trip request and response from the server computer.

Exploring Silverlight development

Typically you build and develop applications to take advantage of Silverlight by using a Microsoft product called Expression Web — an Integrated Development Environment (IDE) similar to Visual Studio, but geared more toward application designers who eat, drink, and breathe *the user experience.* Using Expression Web, designers can build beautiful user interfaces based on the Silverlight platform. Backend programmers can then take those Expression Web projects, open them in Visual Studio, and make them functional — in effect, drop the motor into that shiny body. When the Silverlight application is complete it can be integrated into a SharePoint site by simply adding the out of the box Silverlight Web Part to a page and then configuring it to point at the new Silverlight application.

When you're building Silverlight applications, however, the client-server model of the Web runs into an issue: The Silverlight application is actually running on the local user's computer and not on the Web server that's running SharePoint; there's no way for the user's computer to interact with the SharePoint Object Model. Solution: the very SharePoint Client Object Model described earlier in this chapter. Using the SharePoint Client Object Model, you can develop rich Silverlight applications anywhere you want — and embed them later on in your SharePoint pages, using the extremely handy Silverlight Web Part. Result: Your users get as rich and interactive an experience as they've come to expect (without knowing how much programming blood, sweat, and magic goes into it), right on your SharePoint-based portal.

Microsoft uses Silverlight throughout SharePoint to provide a dazzling user experience. For example, the Create page that you use to filter information between sites, lists, and libraries is all based on Silverlight, as shown in Figure 12-14.

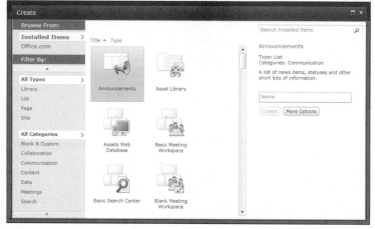

Figure 12-14: The Create screen in SharePoint uses Silverlight.

Enhancing Your Portal with JavaScript

JavaScript is a scripting language designed to give programmers a way to make changes to a Web page after it's already loaded into the user's Web browser. For example, if you load your favorite Web page into your browser, you're getting that content from the server that hosts the content. Your computer is requesting the page and the server is sending you the content over the network. When your computer receives the information, the computer displays what it gets by showing it in the Web browser. As we discussed earlier, the problem arises when you want to interact with that content somehow — as when you click a button or an option in a drop-down list. Your computer has to send that interaction back to the server, which has to reprocess the page according to your interaction.

JavaScript allows a developer to interact with the page without having to send information on this round-trip. For example, a piece of JavaScript might be connected to a button with the logic contained in the JavaScript code. When you click a button on the page, the button simply references the JavaScript code (which was already loaded onto your computer when the page first loaded), and the page can change or update or otherwise react to your interaction in a lot less time. Adding such logic to a static page without having to constantly contact the server to ask what the page should do in response to your interaction is a very powerful concept. No wonder JavaScript is so widely adopted.

SharePoint, too, enables you to make good use of JavaScript. Microsoft has made the SharePoint Client Object Model available so JavaScript logic can interact with the components of SharePoint just like Silverlight. Cagey. Smart. The users would be cheering if they knew what was going on here.

Because JavaScript, like Silverlight, runs on the client computer and not the server running SharePoint, it must use the Client Object Model in order to interact with your SharePoint components.

Microsoft already uses JavaScript throughout the standard SharePoint experience, as seen in the dialog-box framework. For example, whenever you add a new item to a list, you'll notice that a dialog box appears in front of everything and the rest of the site becomes grayed out, as shown in Figure 12-15.

You can use the SharePoint dialog-box framework to write your own dialog boxes — all using JavaScript. I was recently working with one of my clients to use the dialog-box framework as an emergency-notification system. The client was a major energy company; when a storm was approaching, they wanted all their users to know of the potential consequences right away, and to have emergency preparedness at the forefront of their thinking. When a storm was approaching, the dialog box would appear to all customers who accessed the site; people would be forced to see the message before closing the dialog box and continuing with bill-paying (or whatever else they were doing on the site). This is how the organization helped ensure that all their customers were well prepared when a large storm that was likely to cause damage was approaching. And that's where programming gets very practical.

Figure 12-15:
The SharePoint dialog box framework appears when the user enters new items into a list.

Chapter 13

Developing Web Parts

When to use iterative development? You should use iterative development only on projects that you want to succeed.

— Martin Fowler

Okay, regardless of whether you've been jumping around in the book or reading right through, you've probably encountered some of the characteristics of Web Parts. Part II, in particular, talks about developing a SharePoint site using the browser — which includes creating Web Part pages and adding Web Parts *to* the SharePoint pages you're developing. SharePoint comes with a number of very useful Web Parts, but even they can't address all needs. At some point you might need a Web Part that's so specialized and unique that the only option is to create it from scratch. That's why, in SharePoint 2010, Microsoft paid particular attention to the programmer crowd and invested a lot of resources in providing the tools for developing your own Web Parts with minimal effort.

This chapter gets down to the brass tacks of how Web Parts work and how they fit into the SharePoint landscape. You get a look at how to develop a Web Part, package it up, and deploy it to a SharePoint environment.

Understanding Web Parts

When most of us think of a Web site, we imagine a page of information displayed in the Web browser. If you want to change a page like that one, then common sense would tell you that you have to open the file that represents the page and make changes to the portion of the file that needs attention. The problem with this traditional model, however, involves reusability. Imagine you've developed a chunk of ASP.NET code that calculates gas mileage. You can make your code available to everyone — and if some of those folks are programmers (or extra technically inclined), they can take your code and integrate it into their existing Web pages. Alas, copying and pasting chunks of code into pages throughout a site, one at a time, quickly becomes a burden. A drag. Tedious. You get the idea.

To resolve this issue, Microsoft developed the concept of a *Web Part*: a chunk of code that's like a packaged and reusable container that's also a building block. Now, when you develop a Web page, you decide what areas of the page you want to have chunks of content. The areas of the page that can contain the chunks of content are called *Web Part zones*; the chunks of content that live in those zones are (yep) the Web Parts. Web Parts are not new; they've been around for some time. They're not even specific to SharePoint; Web Parts were developed as part of ASP.NET (a feature of the .NET Framework, about which you can find out more in Chapter 11). The Microsoft developers who created SharePoint simply used that handy feature of ASP. NET to create a superb end-user experience for SharePoint Web pages.

Discovering How SharePoint Uses Web Parts

A number of Web Parts come with SharePoint; in fact, a big difference between the SharePoint editions is which Web Parts are available from one to the next. Take, for example, the Chart Web Part that connects to a SharePoint list and displays information graphically in various types of charts. You can configure the Chart Web Part to use a vast number of graph types to display list data — but it's only available with the SharePoint Server Enterprise Edition. If you're using SharePoint Foundation, you don't have the Chart Web Part; to get it, you upgrade to the Enterprise Edition.

As you climb the ladder of SharePoint editions (shelling out the bucks as you go), you get access to additional Web Parts. For example, moving from SharePoint Foundation to SharePoint Server gives you a platoon of additional Web Parts for developing SharePoint sites. Adding Fast Search Server for SharePoint to the mix brings in a plethora of additional search-related Web Parts.

In addition to the Web Parts that come with the different editions of SharePoint, you can create your own Web Parts using Visual Studio. Then you can add your custom Web Parts to the list that users see when they're choosing Web Parts to add to a SharePoint page.

Visualizing Your Web Part

One of the problems that programmers used to run into when developing Web Parts was the design experience. The user interface of a Web Part had to be programmed manually; if (for example) you wanted to add a button to a page, you had to write code to do it. You couldn't just drag a prefab button over from a Toolbox window onto a Design Surface.

Peering into a visual Web Part

A visual Web Part is simply a construct based on Microsoft's newest Web-based programming technology called Active Server Pages (ASP). The newest version of ASP uses the .NET framework and is thus called ASP.NET. A Web page is actually nothing more than a file. A file that contains only HyperText Markup Language (HTML) has the extension .html whereas a Web page file that's based on Microsoft ASP platform has the file extension .asp. The newest version of ASP, called ASP. NET, is Extensible Markup Language (XML) compatible, so Microsoft tacked an X onto the file extension to distinguish it from earlier versions of ASP. Therefore an ASP.NET file, which is XML compliant, has an extension of .aspx.

The SharePoint platform is built on top of the ASP.NET platform and thus if you can program ASP.NET applications, you can move straight into programming SharePoint applications. If you look at a SharePoint page, notice that it often has the .aspx extension. For example, the Web address for my development environment for this book is the following:

```
http://sp2010devfd/SitePages/
    Home.aspx
```

The Web address is telling us that the server name is sp2010devfd and that the page we are viewing is called Home.aspx. Because the file extension for the page ends in .aspx we know that this is an ASP.NET page. You might also see pages in SharePoint that end in .html. These pages are strictly HyperText Markup Language (HTML)-based pages and don't need any special attention from the Microsoft Web server because they don't contain any ASP.NET code. SharePoint has no problem hosting these simple HTML pages as well though.

One component of ASP.NET is called an Active Server Control (ASC), and following in the tradition of the new technology, an X is tacked on the end of its file extension. An ASC file is simply a collection of HTML markup and ASP. NET that represents a functional group. ASP. NET programmers use these ASC files as chunks of reusable code so that they don't have to develop the same functionality over and over again. An ASC file based on the newest version of Microsoft Active Server Pages (ASP) technology, called ASP.NET, has an .ascx extension.

The new visual Web Part is simply an ASC component that's hosted within an ASP.NET Web Part. Many programmers would build Web Parts this way in the past so that they could simply drag components from the Toolbox onto the Design Surface. The problem however became packaging the .ascx file within a Web Part and then deploying that to SharePoint. The process was tedious and fraught with pitfalls that could cause a number of different cryptic errors. Microsoft has formalized the process of using an ascx control to build a Web Part and built tools into Visual Studio and SharePoint that streamline the deployment process. The result is the Visual Web Part project in Visual Studio.

The benefit of the visual Web Part is that you can drag and drop visual components onto a design canvas for a What You See Is What You Get (WYSIWYG) result. A standard ASP.NET Web Part, on the other hand, is much more difficult to design because you have to use code to build up the user interface. Result: You spend a lot of time writing code for the user interface, flipping over to run the Web Part to see what it looks like, and then going back to tweak the code — a time-intensive back-and-forth that's not exactly the picture of efficiency. With the visual Web Part, you drag the components onto the Design Surface and there they are: You can see instantly how the user interface will look and feel to users.

Building a Visual Web Part

Using the Web Parts available in SharePoint is a great way to understand Web Parts — but when it's time to develop your own custom Web Part, there's no substitute for jumping into the fray and building one. So, in this section, you get a crack at building a simple gas-mileage Web Part using Visual Studio. Then comes packaging the new Web Part for deployment to a SharePoint environment, where others can add it to their pages as needed.

Because Web Parts are built on the Microsoft ASP.NET framework, you *could* program a Web Part using nothing more than a simple text editor such as Notepad. But why use that cumbersome approach when you have a tool like Visual Studio available? Let's see . . . struggling along in a text editor versus starting up an Integrated Development Environment (IDE) that already has all the tools and features needed for developing a custom SharePoint Web Part . . . can ya say "no-brainer," folks? (For a refresher on Visual Studio, flip to Chapter 11.)

This example uses Visual Studio to develop a simple visual Web Part that calculates gas mileage. I walk you through this process to give you an idea of how you might go about creating your own Web Parts. The steps look like this:

1. **Fire up Visual Studio by clicking Start⇨All Programs⇨Microsoft Visual Studio 2010⇨Microsoft Visual Studio 2010.**

2. **Click the New Project link to create a new Visual Studio project, as shown in Figure 13-1.**

   Note that when you create a new Visual Studio project, you're also creating a Visual Studio solution; that's because a project lives within a solution. Chapter 11 introduces this terminology, in case you need a refresher.

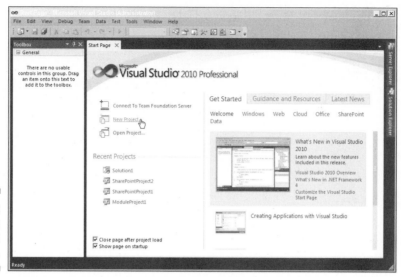

Figure 13-1:
Starting
Visual
Studio 2010.

3. **Expand the Visual C# node and then select SharePoint and the 2010 project types, as shown in Figure 13-2.**

   A wizard dialog box appears, asking which site you want to use for debugging. If you've installed everything on the same server (as I have), then the wizard fills in the site for you automatically, as shown in Figure 13-3.

Figure 13-2:
Choosing
the
SharePoint
2010 Visual
Web Part
project.

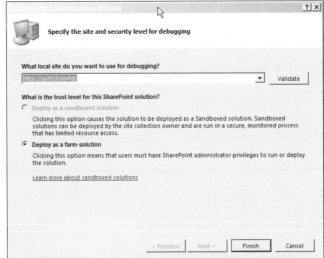

Figure 13-3:
Setting the
SharePoint
server for a
Visual Web
Part project.

Note that the Sandboxed Solution option is grayed out; the only available option for selecting a trust level is to deploy as a farm solution. Visual Studio is context-aware and realizes that you can't deploy a visual Web Part as a sandboxed solution, so it grays out that option. Thus the next step develops a Web Part as a sandboxed solution:

4. **Choose the Empty SharePoint Project template, select Sandboxed Solution, and then add a Web Part by right-clicking the solution in the Solution Explorer window and selecting Add➪New Item.**

   Visual Studio creates the project.

5. **Drag components from the Toolbox onto the Design Surface.**

   For the gas-mileage application, you'd drag these over: an HTML table, 4 labels, 4 text boxes, and a button, as shown in Figure 13-4.

   Notice that you can change the view of the Design Surface to Code view, Split view, or Design view. Dragging a control onto the Design Surface updates the code for the file automatically. This is a nice feature; dragging a control from the Toolbox and instantly seeing the code generated for the control — in real time — can make you feel like a wizard yourself.

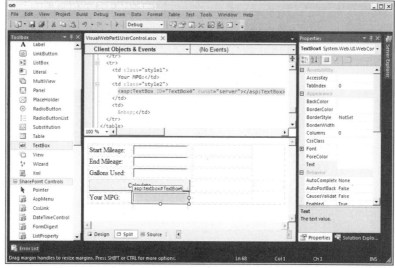

Figure 13-4:
Designing a
Gas Mileage
Web
Part for
SharePoint.

6. **Add the logic to your code to calculate the gas mileage when the Calculate button is clicked:**

   a. *Click the button in the Design Surface and then click the lightning-bolt icon in the Properties window to view the events associated with the button.*

   b. *Double-click the Click event to bring up the code behind file and create a button clicked event.*

   c. *To get your code to calculate gas mileage, have it subtract the starting mileage from the end mileage and then divide by the number of gallons used, as shown in the following code:*

```
using System;
using System.Web.UI;
using System.Web.UI.WebControls;
using System.Web.UI.WebControls.WebParts;
using Microsoft.SharePoint;

namespace GasMileage.VisualWebPart1
{
  public partial class
    VisualWebPart1UserControl : UserControl
  {
    protected void
      Button1_Click(object sender, EventArgs e)
    {
      // Clear any previous error message.
```

```
    this.errorMessage.Text = "";

    // A string to hold our error message.
    String errorText
      = "An error has occurred! Is your input correct?";

    try
    {
      // Obtain the values and cast them.
      Single startMileage
        = Convert.ToInt32(this.startMileageTB.Text);
      Single endMileage
        = Convert.ToInt32(this.endMileageTB.Text);
      Single gallonsUsed
        = Convert.ToInt32(this.gallonsUsedTB.Text);

      // Calculate the miles per gallon.
      Single MPG
        = (endMileage - startMileage) / gallonsUsed;

      // Set the result in the MPG textbox.
      this.yourMPG.Text = MPG.ToString();
    }
    catch
    {
      // An error has occurred.
      // Give a simple message.
      this.errorMessage.Text
        = errorText;
    }
  }

  protected void
    Page_Load(object sender, EventArgs e)
  {
  }
}
}
```

7. **Press Control+F5 to build, package and deploy your new Web Part to your SharePoint site.**

   Your SharePoint site opens; you can browse to a Web Part page and add the newly created Web Part. You can find the new Web Part in the Custom folder of the Web Part directory, as shown in Figure 13-5.

   The completed Web Part is now embedded in the page and ready to calculate gas mileage, as shown in Figure 13-6.

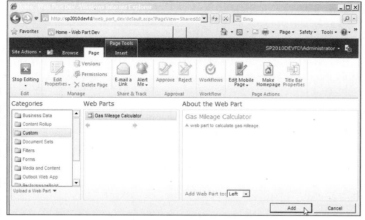

Figure 13-5: Adding the Gas Mileage Web Part to a SharePoint page.

Figure 13-6: The completed Gas Mileage Web Part embedded in a SharePoint page.

Creating Features, Packages, and Solutions

When you're using Visual Studio to develop a SharePoint project, you can simply press Control+F5 to deploy and debug your code. When you've finished developing your code, your next step is to package it for deployment to a SharePoint site.

In SharePoint, a *feature* is simply some combined pieces of SharePoint (functionality, settings, and such) that you want administrators to be able to turn on or off as a single group. For example, you might have a Web Part that relies on a specific SharePoint content type that you've developed. You don't want an administrator to make the Web Part available without that special content type, so you bundle everything into a single feature. When the feature is activated, both the custom content type and the Web Part are made available to the users of the site. As you might expect, the Microsoft developers have already created a slew of standard SharePoint features. You can see a site's available features listed on the site's settings page.

When you're developing SharePoint solutions in Visual Studio, you might have a number of different features that you want administrators to be able to activate and deactivate independently of each other. For this reason a feature is deployed to SharePoint in a construct called a Web Solution Package (WSP). A WSP is thus a container that contains features and a feature is a container that contains SharePoint items such as a Web Part. You can find a more detailed introduction to WSP in Chapter 11.

Solution packages and features contain the files required for installation and configuration on the SharePoint site. To assist you in developing those solution packages and features, Visual Studio offers two tools: Feature Designer and Package Designer.

Exploring Feature Designer

A SharePoint feature has to include a number of installation and configuration files. Sure, you can develop a feature manually, but keeping track of all the different files can be tedious and time-consuming. The Feature Designer tool in Visual Studio saves you some time by giving you a single graphical interface where you can build SharePoint features quickly. Here's a quick look at it:

- ✔ You can launch Feature Designer by right-clicking the Features node in the Solution Explorer window and selecting Add Feature.

- ✔ To open Feature Designer for an existing feature, you right-click the feature and select View Designer.

- ✔ In Feature Designer, you can set the title, description, and scope for your feature, and add items such as the vitally important manifest file (about which more in a minute), as shown in Figure 13-7.

When you use Feature Designer to manipulate a feature's properties, you're actually building the manifest file *behind the scenes*. Notice in Figure 13-7 that you can select the button at the bottom left of the Feature Designer screen to view the manifest file from within the tool.

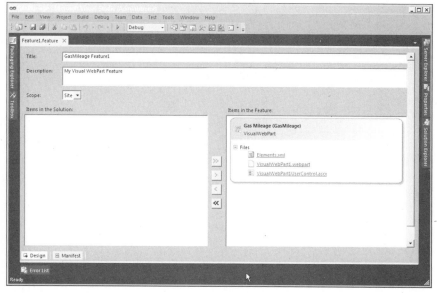

Figure 13-7:
Working
with Feature
Designer
in Visual
Studio.

The Scope property of a feature allows you to set the extent to which the feature will be available in SharePoint. The following list describes the scope settings you can specify:

- **Farm:** Activates the feature for the entire SharePoint farm — which includes all Web applications and site collections.

- **Web Application:** Activates the feature for all site collections within a Web application.

- **Site:** Activates the feature for all sites within a site collection.

- **Web:** Activates the feature for a single site within a site collection.

While you were creating the Gas Mileage visual Web Part earlier in the chapter, Visual Studio was busy creating a feature automatically. The feature contains a single SharePoint item — namely, the visual Web Part you developed. To view this feature in Feature Designer, open the Features node (located in the Solution Explorer window) and then right-click the feature and choose View Designer. Alternatively, you can just double-click the feature to open it in Feature Designer as well.

Wrapping your work in Package Designer

When you've developed your SharePoint items and created your features, you're ready to tuck your hard work into a SharePoint Web Solution Package (WSP) file and send it to an administrator to be deployed to a SharePoint environment. Visual Studio includes a tool called Package Designer that you use to build the WSP file.

Package Designer gives you a great deal of control over the deployment process. For example, you might need to reset the Internet Information Systems (IIS) Web server's processes after the package is deployed on the server. Using Package Designer, you can build this behavior right into your packages.

To open Package Designer, right-click the Package node (located in the Solution Explorer window) and select View Designer. The Package Designer tool opens; behold — you can begin configuring the package, as shown in Figure 13-8.

Items in the Solution

Name property   Reset Web Server check box   Items in the Package

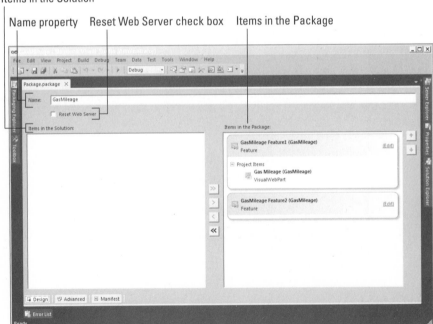

Figure 13-8:
Working with Package Designer in Visual Studio.

Package Designer provides a visual interface to configure the components and properties of a package, as outlined in the following list:

- ✔ **Name:** You can set a name for the package. The name is set to the name of the project by default but can be changed using this property.
- ✔ **Reset Web Server:** Provides the option of resetting the IIS Web server after the package is installed.
- ✔ **Items in the Solution:** The list of the items and features that your Visual Studio solution contains. You can choose which ones you want to add to the package, using the arrows between the windows.
- ✔ **Items in the Package:** Just what the name says: The list of items and features that have been added to the package. Use the arrows between the two windows to add or remove items.

In addition to the Design Surface, there are windows for advanced configuration and for viewing the main manifest file. The buttons for navigating to these other windows are in the bottom-left corner of the screen. The manifest file for a very simple WSP package is shown in Figure 13-9.

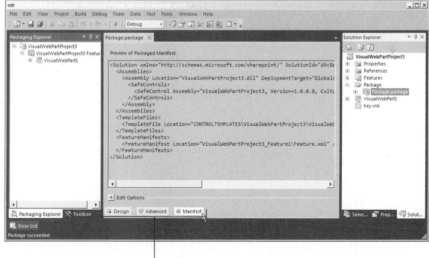

Figure 13-9: Viewing the manifest file for a SharePoint Web Solution Package (WSP).

Click to switch among the views

When you've completed your WSP design you're ready to create the SharePoint Web Solution Package (WSP) file. To create the package, select Package from the Build menu bar, as shown in Figure 13-10.

Figure 13-10:
Packing
up a
SharePoint
Web
Solution
Package
(WSP)
using Visual
Studio.

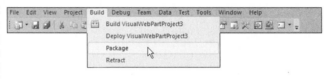

When the packaging process is complete, the WSP file is created in a folder at the end of the following path:

```
SolutionFolder/ProjectFolder/bin/BuildConfiguration
```

For example, if you're developing a Visual Studio solution with the name `CalculatorWebParts` that contains a project named `GasMileage` and have the configuration set to `Debug`, then your WSP file is located in the solution folder under the `CalculatorWebParts/GasMileage/bin/Debug` directory, as shown in Figure 13-11.

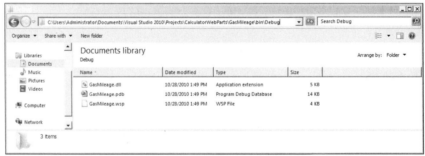

Figure 13-11:
Accessing
the WSP file
once it
has been
packaged.

In addition to Feature Designer and Package Designer, Visual Studio provides a tool called Packaging Explorer to assist you. Packaging Explorer presents itself as a window in the Designer windows; you use it to move or tweak your package. For example, you can

✔ Drag and drop files between features and packages

✔ Add new features

✔ Open features

✔ Validate features

Moving Your Hard Work to SharePoint

When you've completed building the SharePoint Web Solution Package (WSP), you're ready to ship it off to a SharePoint administrator for installation. After the SharePoint administrator has installed the solution, the users can activate it for their sites and start putting the fruits of your labor to work. For example, your solution might contain a feature that contains a Web Part. When the solution is installed, the site administrators can activate that feature. When the feature is activated, the Web Part shows up in the Web Part gallery and users can begin adding it to their SharePoint pages.

Installing a package

You can choose between two different procedures for installing a WSP file. Which one you use depends on whether you want the solution created and installed as Sandboxed or farm-wide. (Chapter 11 introduces Sandboxed Solutions; farm-wide means the solution is installed and available throughout the entire SharePoint environment.) Here's the distinction:

- To install a Sandboxed Solution, the site collection's administrator uses the site collection's settings page at the site-collection level.

- To install a farm-wide solution, a farm administrator uses Central Administration at the farm level.

To install a Sandboxed Solution, follow these steps:

1. **Open the Site Collection Settings page by clicking Site Actions⇨ Site Settings.**

2. **To make sure you're on the site settings page for the site collection, look at the category for Site Collection Administration.**

    - If you see links in the section, then you're on the site collection's site settings page.

    - If you're on the site settings page for a sub-site, you see a link under the Site Collection Administration section to take you to the site settings page for the whole site collection.

3. **Under the Galleries section, click the Solutions link.**

4. **Click the Solutions tab in the Ribbon at the top of the page to activate the Solutions Ribbon and then select Upload Solution.**

5. **Browse to the WSP file and upload it to the solution gallery.**

    When the file has been uploaded, you can activate the solution from the confirmation page, as shown in Figure 13-12.

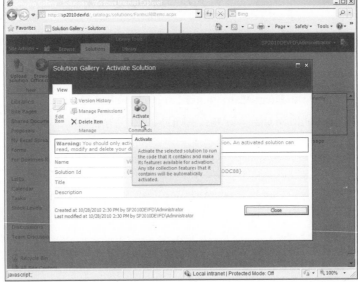

Figure 13-12:
Activating a
Sandboxed
Solution
after it's
uploaded
to the site
collection's
solution
gallery.

To add a farm-wide solution to SharePoint, follow these steps:

1. **Open the Management Shell by clicking Start⇨All Programs⇨ Microsoft SharePoint 2010 Products⇨SharePoint 2010 Management Shell.**

   The only way to add a farm-wide Web Solution Package (WSP) to a farm is to use the PowerShell-based SharePoint 2010 Management Shell. (More about that in the next section, "Deploying a solution.")

2. **Use the following syntax to type the Add-SPSolution PowerShell cmdlet at the command prompt, and then press Enter:**

   ```
   Add-SPSolution –LiteralPath <solution_path>
   ```

   For example, if the path to your WSP file is located at

   ```
   C:\wsp_files\MyFarmSolution.wsp
   ```

   then you would type the command as shown in Figure 13-13. Doing so adds the solution to the SharePoint farm.

Deploying a solution

Adding a solution to the farm is a good start, but it has to be deployed if anyone's going to use it. You can deploy a farm solution by using either Central Administration or the SharePoint 2010 Management Shell.

To deploy a farm solution using Central Administration, follow these steps:

1. **Open the Central Administration Web application by clicking Start⇨All Programs⇨Microsoft SharePoint 2010 Products⇨SharePoint 2010 Central Administration.**

2. **Select the System Settings page from the left hand navigation.**

3. **Under the Farm Management section, select Manage Farm Solutions.**

   The solution that was just added to the farm should be listed as Not Deployed.

4. **Deploy the solution by selecting it: Click its name and then click Deploy Solution, as shown in Figure 13-14.**

   The deployment screen appears, where you can set a specific time to deploy the solution and specify which Web application the solution should be deployed against. For example, you might have a maintenance window from 2:00 a.m. to 3:00 a.m. (you people *are* busy, aren't you?) and choose to deploy the solution during that time and only to the Web application for the Engineering Department.

5. **When you've configured the deployment, choose OK to deploy the solution.**

   • After the solution is deployed, it's available for the target Web application; its status shows up on the Manage Farm Solutions page, designated as deployed.

   • Site Collection Administrators can activate the deployed solution's feature by using the site settings page for the site collection.

   • If the feature contains a Web Part, users can then add it to their pages using the Web Part gallery just as they would any other Web Part in the gallery.

Figure 13-13:
Adding a farm solution using the PowerShell-based SharePoint 2010 Management Shell.

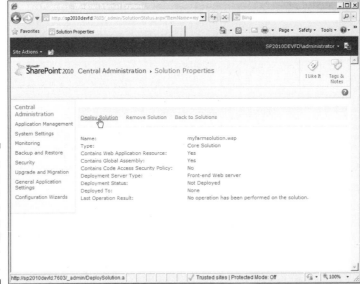

Figure 13-14:
Deploying a
farm wide
solution
using
Central
Administr-
ation.

The SharePoint 2010 Management Shell is actually nothing more than PowerShell with the SharePoint-specific commands already referenced and available in the shell. For more PowerShell details, check out Chapter 14.

Chapter 14

Working from the PowerShell Command Line

The first rule of any technology used in a business is that automation applied to an efficient operation will magnify the efficiency. The second is that automation applied to an inefficient operation will magnify the inefficiency.

— Bill Gates

This chapter covers the powerful, new command-line interface for Microsoft products known as PowerShell. PowerShell is, in effect, DOS-on-steroids — for interacting with Microsoft applications such as SharePoint at the no-nonsense level of the command line. The power of a command-line interface is that you can save a series of commands in a text file (known as a *script*), run them all in a single batch triggered by a single command, and schedule your scripts to run at specific points in time by configuring a timer service.

Scripts can be used for everything from a quick peek at a particular piece of SharePoint configuration to a complete backup solution. Writing your own scripts for common SharePoint scenarios takes the hassle out of clicking though the same repetitive screens every time you want to perform a series of tasks.

This chapter explores PowerShell — in particular, how to use PowerShell with SharePoint. You get a look at what a PowerShell cmdlet (pronounced *command-let*) is all about, how to write scripts that use the SharePoint cmdlets, and how to write your own cmdlets.

Getting Your Head around PowerShell

Working with a command-line interface, often called a *shell*, can be a daunting task. If you grew up working with DOS or a Unix-based system, you'll feel right at home with PowerShell. If you're used to a computer that always presents you with a Graphical User Interface (GUI), then typing your commands into PowerShell may seem like going backward in time. After you become familiar with a command-line user interface, however, don't be surprised if you get fond of the speed, flexibility, and robustness you find there; you may get hooked. In fact, I have many good friends who only work with Unix-based operating systems simply because they prefer working with the command line.

Although PowerShell is relatively new to the Microsoft operating systems, it has come on in force; every product Microsoft develops can now be administered using PowerShell. You can do everything with its PowerShell command-line interface that you can with the point-and-click interface. The reverse, however, is not always true; you can't necessarily do everything with the point-and-click interface that you can with the PowerShell command line.

Although you can access the PowerShell interface in a couple of ways (more about that later in the chapter), here's the standard trick: Start⇨All Programs⇨Accessories⇨Windows PowerShell. And *voilà* — you're staring back into time: The PowerShell interface looks very similar to a DOS-based interface, as shown in Figure 14-1.

A PowerShell command is called a cmdlet.

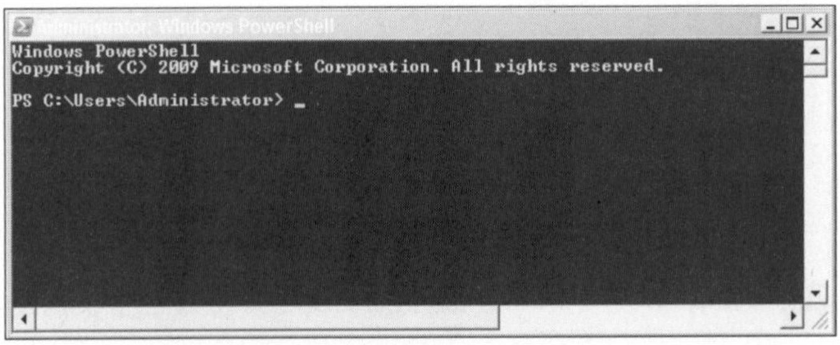

Figure 14-1:
The
Windows
PowerShell
interface.

```
Windows PowerShell
Copyright (C) 2009 Microsoft Corporation. All rights reserved.

PS C:\Users\Administrator> _
```

The line starts with PS — which lets you know you're working with PowerShell and not some other command-line interface such as DOS. The next portion lists the current directory. Finally, you get to the character with the blinking prompt that's waiting for you to type in a cmdlet. For example, to see a listing of all the files in the current directory, type the command

```
get-childitem
```

and then press Enter. A listing of every file in the directory appears on-screen, as shown in Figure 14-2.

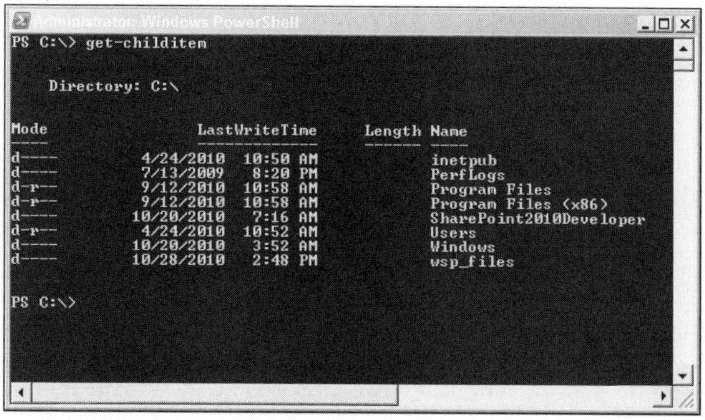

Figure 14-2:
Listing all
the items
in a
directory
using
PowerShell.

Listing all the items in a directory is something you may have done using the DOS command prompt as well. The DOS command used to list the items in a directory is simply dir. If you're a Unix guru, then you know that the Unix command to list the items in a directory is ls. To make life simple, PowerShell also has the ability to alias commands and the folks that developed PowerShell have taken the liberty of aliasing the most common commands. If you type the dir command and press Enter, you get the same result. Likewise, if you enter the ls command, which stems from Unix, you also get a listing of the items in the directory.

For an excellent Web site listing the available PowerShell cmdlets in an easy to read and sortable view, check out the following URL: www.bing.com/visualsearch?g=powershell_cmdlets

PowerShell and SharePoint

For Windows in general, a plethora of cmdlets is available, but to access the cmdlets specific to SharePoint, you have to do a little more work.

When you install SharePoint, you also install the cmdlets that Microsoft has already developed specifically for SharePoint. To actually work with these cmdlets, you have to let PowerShell know how to find them. You could add the SharePoint cmdlets to a standard PowerShell instance but it becomes cumbersome to remember each time you open PowerShell. Instead you can open a PowerShell instance that already has the SharePoint commands referenced. When you installed SharePoint you installed a tool called SharePoint 2010 Management Shell. This tool is actually nothing more than PowerShell but it is much easier open this tool rather than opening up PowerShell separately and then adding the SharePoint reference.

The SharePoint 2010 Management Shell can be accessed by clicking Start⇨All Programs⇨Microsoft SharePoint 2010 Products⇨SharePoint 2010 Management Shell. Remember however that this tool is only available on a computer that has SharePoint installed.

Entering cmdlets into PowerShell

A cmdlet, pronounced "command-let", is a PowerShell command that you type at the command prompt. A cmdlet takes the form of a verb followed by a dash followed by a noun. For example, the cmdlet for obtaining help is called Get-Help. Notice Get, the verb, followed by a dash and then Help, a noun. Typing Get-Help at the PowerShell command prompt will result in a help screen that describes the Get-Help command. Another example of a cmdlet is Get-Process, which is used to list all the processes running on the computer. Notice the cmdlet takes the same form with the Get verb followed by the dash followed by the noun, Process.

A cmdlet by itself is useful, but to fine tune the output, you can provide parameters. A parameter is text that you type after the cmdlet that is used as input. For example, the Get-Help cmdlet can also be used to get help for a specific cmdlet. If you type Get-Help and then a space and then Get-Process you see a help screen for the Get-Process cmdlet as shown in Figure 14-3.

Putting SharePoint cmdlets to work

The power of PowerShell comes with the extraordinary number of cmdlets that are available right out of the box for SharePoint. Among the more than 500 cmdlets for SharePoint, you will find ones that do things such as stopping and starting services, getting and setting properties, and backing up and restoring content. For example, to see a list of all the databases that SharePoint is using, type the Get-SPDatabase command as shown in Figure 14-4.

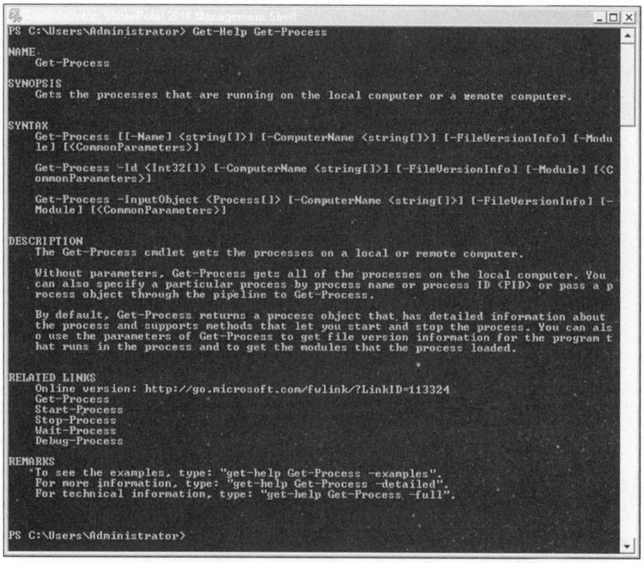

Figure 14-3: An example of using parameters to obtain help for the Get-Process cmdlet.

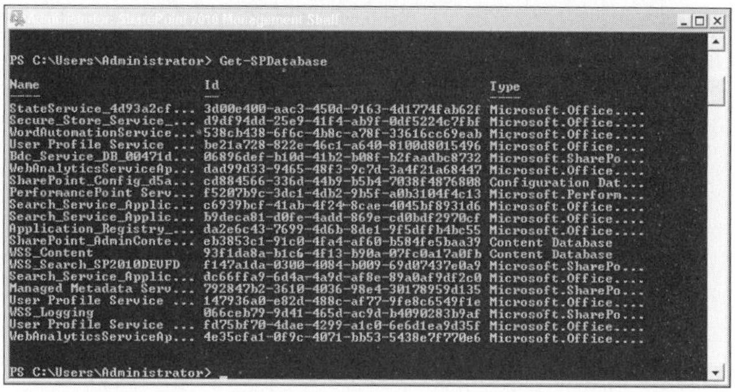

Figure 14-4: Using PowerShell to view all of the SharePoint databases.

Notice that the database names are truncated in the output window. You can use the vertical bar character | to pipe the output of one cmdlet into another cmdlet. To refine the Get-SPDatabase output, you can pipe the results to the Format-Wide cmdlet which allows you to customize the view using parameters as shown in Figure 14-5.

Notice that the Format-Wide command only displays a single property. For the Get-SPDatabase results, the default property is Name. The results are still truncated however because the database names are very long and the output is in two columns. To specify a single column display, you can use a parameter to the Format-Wide cmdlet called column. Setting the column parameter to 1 results in the output we are looking for as shown in Figure 14-6.

Figure 14-5:
Using the
PowerShell
pipe char-
acter to
send output
to another
cmdlet for
formatting.

Figure 14-6:
Using the
PowerShell
format-wide
cmdlet with
the column
parameter
to set the
output of
the Get-
SPDatabase
cmdlet.

A more interesting format however might be to dump the output to a Comma Separated Value (CSV) file that can then be opened with Office Excel. You can achieve this by piping the output to the Export-CSV cmdlet. For example, typing

```
Get-SPDatabase | Export-CSV c:\SharePointDatabases.csv
```

at the command prompt results in a CSV file being created with the output. You can then open this file with Excel in a spreadsheet format.

Finding SharePoint cmdlets

To see a list of all available commands for SharePoint, you can use the Get-Command cmdlet. Make sure you're in the SharePoint 2010 Management Shell and type Get-Command at the command prompt and press Enter. The result is a listing of all available commands. In addition you can use a star character as a wildcard to narrow the display. For example, typing

```
Get-Command Get-SP*
```

gives you a list of every command that has the verb Get and whose noun begins with SP. Typing Get-Command *-SP* (note the two asterisks) returns all verbs and all nouns that begin with SP.

Another method for finding the nouns that begin with SP is to tell the Get-Command cmdlet that you want to search only on the noun portion of the available cmdlets. To do this you would use the –noun parameter as follows:

```
vGet-Command -noun SP*
```

Asking PowerShell for cmdlet help

As you can imagine, remembering the usage syntax for cmdlets and parameters can become quite complicated. To make life easier (for the poor abused aspirin bottle, anyway), PowerShell includes a cmdlet designed specifically for providing help on other cmdlets. This kindly cmdlet follows the verb-noun format and is called Get-Help. Typing Get-Help at the command prompt produces the help file for the Get-Help cmdlet. If you follow the Get-Help cmdlet with the name of another cmdlet, you receive the help file specific to that command.

You can see examples for a particular command by including the –examples parameter. For example, to see the help file for the Get-SPSite cmdlet — and to see examples of the command in action — you'd type

```
Get-Help Get-SPSite -examples
```

at the PowerShell command prompt.

The sheer number of cmdlets that are available can be overwhelming. Thus the Get-Help cmdlet becomes one of your best friends when you're working with PowerShell.

In the Unix world, the help command is Man and in the DOS world the help command is Help. These commands have been aliased to the PowerShell Get-Help command to make life easier on those familiar with other command-based interfaces. Typing Man Get-Process or Help Get-Process at the command prompt calls up the same help file you'd get if you typed Get-Help Get-Process.

Moving Beyond Simple cmdlets

Working with PowerShell commands (cmdlets) can be very powerful but a time comes when you need to do more complex feats that are much like (dare we say it) programming. Relax: PowerShell is built on top of the .NET Framework; thus you have access to a tremendous amount of programming functionality. For example, you can store values in variables, use looping to loop through collections of objects, add logic with if/else statements, and get some specialized functions to do your bidding.

If you've worked with a command-line environment before (such as DOS or Unix) then you're familiar with entering commands and getting output back in the form of text that appears on-screen. Well, that's what seems to be going on here, but there's a twist: PowerShell does return text for you to look at — but that output is really a .NET object. PowerShell simply decides which part of the object makes the most sense to show to you on-screen as text.

Saving a value with variables

A *variable* is a place for you to store some value so you can revisit it later. For example, you might create a variable for storing a SharePoint site in the form of an SPWeb object. Later you might want to use that particular SPWeb object but don't want to type the entire command string for obtaining it. You could simply use the variable.

All variables that you create begin with the dollar sign character $. To assign an object to a variable, you use the equal = symbol. For example, to assign the words Hello World to a variable named $my_first_variable, you would type the following at the command prompt:

```
$my_first_variable = "Hello World"
```

The result is that a new String object is created that contains the characters "Hello World". Remember that PowerShell is object-based and thus variables are objects. You can see the type of object by invoking the GetType() method of the object as shown in Figure 14-7.

In the output for the GetType command, you can see that the base object type is System.Object and the name of the object type is String. You can see a listing of all the methods and properties of the variable — which is (as you know) really a String object — by piping the output to the Get-Member cmdlet, as shown in Figure 14-8.

Figure 14-7:
Creating
a String
variable in
PowerShell
and then
getting the
object type.

```
PS C:\Users\Administrator> $my_first_variable = "Hello World"
PS C:\Users\Administrator> $my_first_variable.GetType()

IsPublic IsSerial Name                                     BaseType
True     True     String                                   System.Object

PS C:\Users\Administrator> _
```

Figure 14-8:
Using
the Get-
Member
cmdlet to
view all
methods
and proper-
ties of a
variable that
is a String
object.

```
PS C:\Users\Administrator> $my_first_variable | Get-Member


   TypeName: System.String

Name             MemberType            Definition
----             ----------            ----------
Clone            Method                System.Object Clone()
CompareTo        Method                int CompareTo(System.Object value), int CompareTo(string strB)
Contains         Method                bool Contains(string value)
CopyTo           Method                System.Void CopyTo(int sourceIndex, char[] destination, int destinationIndex,...
EndsWith         Method                bool EndsWith(string value), bool EndsWith(string value, System.StringCompari...
Equals           Method                bool Equals(System.Object obj), bool Equals(string value), bool Equals(string...
GetEnumerator    Method                System.CharEnumerator GetEnumerator()
GetHashCode      Method                int GetHashCode()
GetType          Method                type GetType()
GetTypeCode      Method                System.TypeCode GetTypeCode()
IndexOf          Method                int IndexOf(char value), int IndexOf(char value, int startIndex), int IndexOf...
IndexOfAny       Method                int IndexOfAny(char[] anyOf), int IndexOfAny(char[] anyOf, int startIndex), i...
Insert           Method                string Insert(int startIndex, string value)
IsNormalized     Method                bool IsNormalized(), bool IsNormalized(System.Text.NormalizationForm normaliz...
LastIndexOf      Method                int LastIndexOf(char value), int LastIndexOf(char value, int startIndex), int...
LastIndexOfAny   Method                int LastIndexOfAny(char[] anyOf), int LastIndexOfAny(char[] anyOf, int startI...
Normalize        Method                string Normalize(), string Normalize(System.Text.NormalizationForm normalizat...
PadLeft          Method                string PadLeft(int totalWidth), string PadLeft(int totalWidth, char paddingCh...
PadRight         Method                string PadRight(int totalWidth), string PadRight(int totalWidth, char padding...
Remove           Method                string Remove(int startIndex), string Remove(int startIndex, int count)
Replace          Method                string Replace(char oldChar, char newChar), string Replace(string oldValue, s...
Split            Method                string[] Split(Params char[] separator), string[] Split(char[] separator, int...
StartsWith       Method                bool StartsWith(string value), bool StartsWith(string value, System.StringCon...
Substring        Method                string Substring(int startIndex), string Substring(int startIndex, int length)
ToCharArray      Method                char[] ToCharArray(), char[] ToCharArray(int startIndex, int length)
ToLower          Method                string ToLower(), string ToLower(System.Globalization.CultureInfo culture)
ToLowerInvariant Method                string ToLowerInvariant()
ToString         Method                string ToString(), string ToString(System.IFormatProvider provider)
ToUpper          Method                string ToUpper(), string ToUpper(System.Globalization.CultureInfo culture)
ToUpperInvariant Method                string ToUpperInvariant()
Trim             Method                string Trim(Params char[] trimChars), string Trim()
TrimEnd          Method                string TrimEnd(Params char[] trimChars)
TrimStart        Method                string TrimStart(Params char[] trimChars)
Chars            ParameterizedProperty char Chars(int index) {get;}
Length           Property              System.Int32 Length {get;}

PS C:\Users\Administrator>
```

TIP

PowerShell has a number of built-in variables. To see a listing of all variables, type Get-Variable at the command prompt and press Enter. Any variables that you've defined in your session also appear in the list.

If you set a variable to save the result of a cmdlet that saves more than one object, then the objects are stored in an array. For example, the Get-SPWeb cmdlet returns all the SharePoint sites listed under the site collection that you specify using the Site parameter. If you save the output to a variable, however, you're actually saving each of the sites as its own SPWeb object — and all of them are stored in an array. Figure 14-9 illustrates the difference between saving all the sites in the site collection as an array of objects versus saving a single site as an SPWeb object.

Figure 14-9:
Saving an
array of
SPWeb
objects
versus sav-
ing a single
SPWeb
object.

```
PS C:\Users\Administrator> $my_SPWebs = Get-SPWeb -Site http://sp2010devfd
PS C:\Users\Administrator> $my_SPWebs.GetType()

IsPublic IsSerial Name                                     BaseType
True     True     Object[]                                 System.Array


PS C:\Users\Administrator> $my_SPWeb = Get-SPWeb -Site http://sp2010devfd -Identity team_site
PS C:\Users\Administrator> $my_SPWeb.GetType()

IsPublic IsSerial Name                                     BaseType
True     False    SPWeb                                    Microsoft.SharePoint.SPSecurableObject

PS C:\Users\Administrator>
```

In the SharePoint object model, an SPSite object represents a site collection, and an SPWeb object represents a SharePoint site. This distinction stems from the origins of SharePoint before the terms *site collection* and *site* were used. The way I like to remember these is that an SPSite has the word *site* in it, site collection *begins* with the word Site, and an SPWeb has the word *Web* in it and the Web is where you normally look to find a site.

If you're familiar with Object Oriented programming — also known as OOP — then these concepts will feel like a homecoming. The OO nature of PowerShell is one of the reasons for its tremendous popularity.

Looping

When you're working with variables that contain more than one object in an array, don't be surprised if you get an itch to loop through all the objects in one fell swoop. To loop through an entire array, you can use a cmdlet named ForEach-Object. For example, as previously mentioned, you can save all the sites in a variable (which is actually an array). You can also use the ForEach-Object to loop through each site and then print its Title property. Figure 14-10 shows saving all the SharePoint sites located under the http://sp2010devfd site collection into a variable — and then looping through each of them with the ForEach-Object cmdlet and printing the Title property.

The line of PowerShell shown in Figure 14-10 uses the pipe character | to send the variable representing an array of SPWeb objects called $my_SPWebs to the ForEach-Object cmdlet. The ForEach-Object cmdlet uses a concept known as a *code block*, a designated body of code that follows the ForEach-Object cmdlet and is surrounded by curly braces { }. Everything within those curly braces is part of the code block that the ForEach-Object command will operate on. In this case, I use the Write-Host cmdlet to write output to the screen. The dollar sign followed by an underscore symbol looks like $_ and is a variable that represents the current object as I loop through each object in the array. To access a particular property of the current object, you simply type a period followed immediately by the name of the property — in this case, the Title property of the current object, which looks like this:

```
$_.Title
```

Each time the ForEach-Object cmdlet loops through an object in the array, it sends the static string Site Title: to the console window, followed by the Title property of the current object. A *static string* is just text that has been hard coded into the code and never changes. *Console window* is another term for the PowerShell window that you use to type in commands and view results.

The percentage symbol % is an alias for the ForEach-Object cmdlet. An *alias* is a kind of command that simply replaces a designated symbol, or series of characters, (usually shorter than an actual command) with the cmdlet you want to run. For example, PowerShell sees the % alias and replaces it with the ForEach-Object command — it sees these two commands as identical:

```
$my_SPWebs | ForEach-Object { Write-Host "Site Title:" $_.Title }

$my_SPWebs | % { Write-Host "Site Title:" $_.Title }
```

You can use aliases to save yourself the time and effort of typing cmdlets that you use frequently. If you want to see all the aliases that PowerShell has mapped to specific cmdlets, use the Get-Alias cmdlet.

Figure 14-10:
Saving all
SharePoint
sites in the
collection
into a
variable
and then
looping
through
them
with the
ForEach-
Object
cmdlet.

```
PS C:\Users\Administrator> $my_SPWebs = Get-SPWeb -Site http://sp2010devfd
PS C:\Users\Administrator> $my_SPWebs | ForEach-Object { Write-Host "Site Title:" $_.Title }
Site Title: SharePoint 2010 Development For Dummies
Site Title: All Features
Site Title: Business Intelligence Center
Site Title: Human Resources
Site Title: blank1
Site Title: test2
Site Title: Company Blog
Site Title: data
Site Title: Process Repository
Site Title: pub1
Site Title: Publishing with Workflow
Site Title: Reports
Site Title: Team Site
Site Title: testbi
Site Title: Visio Example
Site Title: Visio Example
Site Title: Web Part Dev
PS C:\Users\Administrator>
```

Adding logic

Using variables to store values and looping through arrays is exciting, but at some point, you'll want to add logic. For example, you might loop through a large array of objects looking for a particular property. If the property is located, you might want to then do something with that particular object. Logic is what enables you to do something at a specific point in the program.

Okay, working at the PowerShell command prompt can be a bit cumbersome if you try to place everything on a single line and then hit the Enter key. Fortunately, PowerShell is smart enough to know when a command is not complete — so it allows you to press the Enter key and continue entering the rest of the command on a new line. The new line begins with two greater-than signs: >> (which PowerShell adds for you automatically to let you know you are on a new line). When you've completed the entire command, *then* you press the Enter key *twice* — and PowerShell executes the entire multi-line code block.

To expand the `ForEach-Object` example from the previous section, here's where you add logic to check whether the `Title` property of the `SPWeb` object matches a title you seek. If the title does match, then you want to print the names of the users for that site. The result is shown in Figure 14-11.

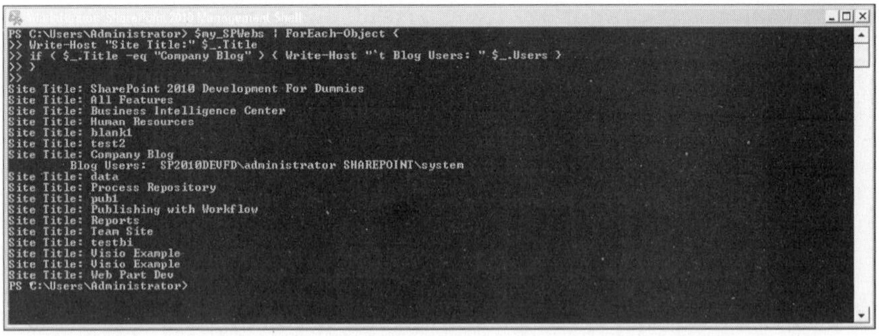

Figure 14-11:
Using an If statement to check for a particular Title property in an SPWeb object.

```
PS C:\Users\Administrator> $my_SPWebs | ForEach-Object {
>> Write-Host "Site Title:" $_.Title
>> if ( $_.Title -eq "Company Blog" ) { Write-Host "`t Blog Users: " $_.Users }
>> }
Site Title: SharePoint 2010 Development For Dummies
Site Title: All Features
Site Title: Business Intelligence Center
Site Title: Human Resources
Site Title: blank1
Site Title: test2
Site Title: Company Blog
          Blog Users:  SP2010DEUFD\administrator SHAREPOINT\system
Site Title: data
Site Title: Process Repository
Site Title: pub1
Site Title: Publishing with Workflow
Site Title: Reports
Site Title: Team Site
Site Title: test1
Site Title: Visio Example
Site Title: Visio Example
Site Title: Web Part Dev
PS C:\Users\Administrator>
```

The comparison operators that you can use in an operation like this one are listed in Table 14-1.

Table 14-1	PowerShell Comparison Operators
Operator	*Description*
`-eq`	Returns `true` if two values are Equal.
`-ne`	Returns `true` if two values are Not Equal.

Operator	Description
-gt	Returns true if the value on the left is Greater Than the value on the right.
-ge	Returns true if the value on the left is Greater than or Equal To the value on the right.
-lt	Returns true if the value on the left is Less Than the value on the right.
-le	Returns true if the value on the left is Less Than or Equal To the value on the right.
-like	Returns true if the value on the right is Like the value on the right. To use this operator, you use a wildcard. For example, the command sample123, written as –like "*23", would return true.
-notlike	Returns true if the value on the right is not like the value on the right. This operator uses a wildcard in the same manner as the –like operator.
-match	Returns true when the value on the left matches the value on the right using a regular expression. For example, "sample123" –match "amp" would return true.
-notmatch	Returns true when the value on the left does not match the value on the right using a regular expression. This is the opposite of the –match operator.
-contains	Determines whether a single value is contained in a series of values. For example, "dog", "cat", "turtle" –contains "turtle" would return true.
-notcontains	Returns true if a single value is not contained in a series of values. This is the opposite of the –contains operator.
-replace	Replaces a portion of the input with the given output. For example, "MyCat" –replace "Cat", "Dog" would result in the output of "MyDog".

Beyond the If/ElseIf/Else statements, PowerShell also supports other conditional logic statements such as While and Switch. If you've worked with code in the past, then the While and Switch statements are familiar to you. If not, rest assured that when you need such statements, they are there. The While statement says that the code block should continuing doing something "while" a condition is true. The Switch statement is an abbreviated version of the If/ElseIf/Else statement.

Working with PowerShell functions

If you're familiar with programming basics, then you're familiar with functions. A *function* is nothing more than a named block of code that has one consistent purpose. For example, you might create code to loop through all SharePoint sites in a site collection and print the site names, as I explain in the previous section. Instead of typing the `ForEach-Object` and `If/Else` statements each time, you could give this code a descriptive name — say `GetSiteTitles`. The named block of code that does this task is now a function; instead of writing the code needed to list the site titles, you can simply call the function.

To create a function, you use the `Function` keyword, followed by the name of the function and the code block. For example, the following PowerShell line creates a function named `ListRootDrive` that simply lists the folders and files in the root `c:\` directory:

```
Function ListRootDrive { Get-ChildItem –Path c:\ }
```

After you've created the function, you can call it — although (sorry) "Here, Function! Here, boy!" won't work. You call a function by typing it at the command prompt. The result is a listing of the c:\ drive as shown in Figure 14-12.

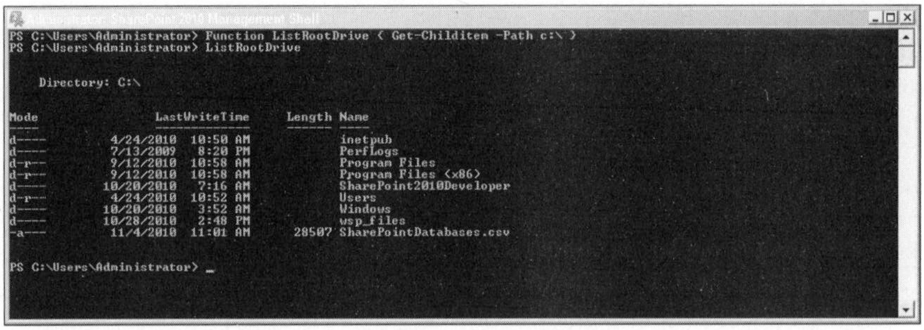

Figure 14-12:
Creating a
new
function to
list out the
files and
folders on
the
c:\ drive.

A function can also take input in the form of an argument. For example, the simple `ListRootDrive` function simply lists the contents of the root drive — but let's say you want to be able to pass in a value for the drive to list. The value that you pass into the function is called an *argument*. An argument is nothing more than a variable that is being passed into the function. There's an example back in the section of this chapter that talks about variables: In PowerShell, all variables begin with the dollar sign character `$`. You define the arguments for a function by listing them in parentheses after the name of the function. For example, to include an argument named

DriveLetter in the ListRootDrive function and then use it in the code block, you would enter the following command:

```
Function ListRootDrive($DriveLetter)
        { Get-ChildItem -Path $DriveLetter }
```

Figure 14-13 shows entering this function and then using it to list the contents of the root drive.

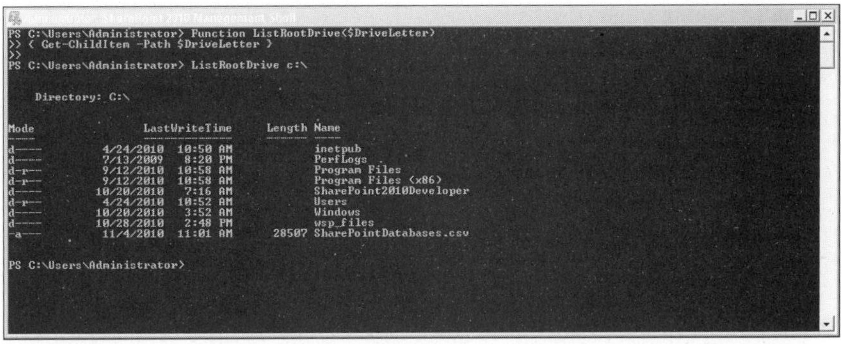

Figure 14-13: Creating a function with arguments for listing a root drive.

When you use functions, a built in variable stores the arguments by default. The variable is called $Args and it contains an array of input arguments that the user has specified. You can use this array to pull arguments instead of explicitly defining a variable name. If you have more than one input argument, then you have to specify which argument you're using at each point in your code block. Because the $Args variable is an array, you specify the position in the array by using an indexer. An indexer is a variable that contains a number that provides a certain position within the array. For example, the first index of the array is specified as $Args[0], the second as $Args[1], and on and on. To illustrate the point, the following three commands all create an identical function — but one names the input argument $DriveLetter, one uses the $Args variable without an indexer (because there is only one argument), and the last uses the first variable in the $Args array by specifying an indexer. Here's what the three commands look like:

```
Function ListRootDrive($DriveLetter)
        { Get-ChildItem -Path $DriveLetter }

Function ListRootDrive
        { Get-ChildItem -Path $Args }

Function ListRootDrive
        { Get-ChildItem -Path $Args[0] }
```

Always concerned for your welfare (just kidding), PowerShell tries to make your life easier by letting you write your commands on multiple lines. You can press the Enter key when you run out of space on the first line and nothing will explode; instead, PowerShell will present you with the continuation prompt >>. When you've completely entered the code block and closed with the } character, you press Enter twice to let PowerShell know it's okay to go ahead and execute the command.

A PowerShell function can be as simple as a single cmdlet — but it can also include as much logic as you want to shoehorn into it. For example, when you typed in the lines to list the titles of the SharePoint sites in a site collection, you used a number of cmdlets as well as some conditional logic. These multiple lines can all be encapsulated in a function as shown in the following example:

```
Function BlogUsers($SiteCollection) {
Get-SPWeb -Site $SiteCollection | ForEach-Object {
Write-Host "Site Title: " $_.Title
if ( $_.Title -eq "Company Blog" ) {
Write-Host "`t Blog Users:" $_.Users
}}}
```

Figure 14-14 shows creating the BlogUsers function, telling it to list the titles of all sites in a site collection and then print the names of all Company Blog site users — and then running the whole shebang in PowerShell.

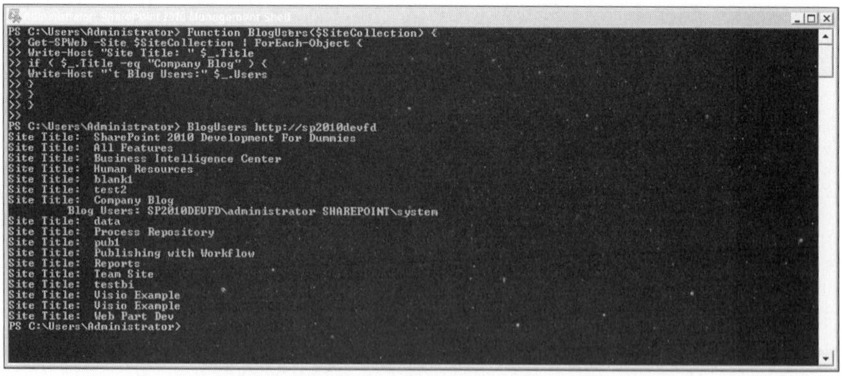

Figure 14-14:
Creating and running the BlogUsers function in PowerShell.

Writing PowerShell Scripts

Up to this point (if you've been following along), you've been working with PowerShell from the command line — one command at a time. The command line is great but can quickly become unwieldy (as you may have found if you tried to type in the BlogUsers function in Figure 14-14). An easier way to work with complex PowerShell commands is to save the code in a text file known as a PowerShell *script*. Then you can run the script on its own without having to type excessive lines at the command prompt every time you want to run a chunk of code.

A PowerShell script is nothing more than a text file that contains commands and code and has a `.ps1` file extension. To run a PowerShell script, you simply type the name of the script at a command prompt. For example, to create and run a PowerShell script that contains the `Get-Date` cmdlet and which is located at `c:\MyScripts\FirstScript.ps1` follow these steps:

1. **Open Notepad by choosing Start⇨All Programs⇨Accessories⇨ Notepad.**

2. **Type the single cmdlet in Notepad `Get-Date`.**

3. **Save the Notepad document as `FirstScript.ps1` in `c:\MyScripts`.**

   Make sure to save the text file with the `.ps1` extension and not the `.txt` extension which is the default for a text file.

4. **Run the PowerShell script by either typing the full path `c:\ MyScripts\FirstScript.ps1` at the PowerShell command prompt or by navigating to the `c:\MyScripts` directory and then typing `.\ FirstScript.ps1`.**

   The `.\` notation tells the PowerShell command to look in the current directory for the script. The result of running the cmdlet script is shown in Figure 14-15.

Figure 14-15:
Running a
PowerShell
script
named
FirstScript.
ps1 from
the c:\
MyScripts
directory.

Part V
The Part of Tens

The 5th Wave By Rich Tennant

"It appears a server in Atlanta is about to go down, there's printer backup in Baltimore and an accountant in Chicago is about to make level 3 of the game 'Tomb Pirate.'"

In this part . . .

This part walks you confidently through some stellar (even if miscellaneous) aspects of SharePoint development. You start with a list of the top ten tools that you should become familiar with — along with ten places to go for more information on SharePoint development. You also get pointers on ten ways to reduce your business costs by using a SharePoint solution (which can come in very handy farther down the road).

Chapter 15

Top Ten Tools for SharePoint Development

In This Chapter

▶ Understanding the tools that you will use when developing a SharePoint solution

▶ Learning why each tool is valuable and how it fits into the SharePoint development process

▶ Discovering which tools to use when you need to solve a particular problem

When the facts change, I change my opinion. What do you do?

— John Maynard Keynes

The tools used for SharePoint development run a wide range. They include everything from the Web browser to standalone tools to components of the SharePoint platform itself.

This chapter walks you through the tools available for SharePoint development; along the way you can expect to see how they fit together and how they're used. More detailed information on some of the tools is found throughout the book, but this chapter provides a simple and cohesive view that you can use to quickly get a feel for a particular tool and its purpose.

Web Browser

When you think of your Web browser, you probably think of going to Web sites and viewing information, and that's fine — for openers. But SharePoint is a Web application born and bred — and it brings a whole new range of uses to your Web browser: You can do a large portion of SharePoint development and management right from the browser.

Microsoft has developed SharePoint Web applications and features to perform all kinds of tasks, so you can create and develop various parts of your SharePoint system in the browser, from large sites and pages to the lists and libraries that appear on those pages. If you're a SharePoint administrator, you even get a Web Application designed for administrators — namely, Central Administration — but you still use your browser to interact with that application and use it. For more about using your Web browser for SharePoint development, check out Chapter 4.

SharePoint Designer

SharePoint Designer is a standalone application created for developing and configuring solutions that run on the SharePoint platform. Because SharePoint stores all its content and configuration information in SQL Server databases, SharePoint Designer acts as a window into those databases, whether you're looking for content or configuration data. The result is a fairly intuitive and straightforward development environment.

SharePoint Designer is tailored specifically to SharePoint Web development. If you're developing Web applications on other Web platforms, then your best choice is a sister tool of SharePoint Designer called Expression Web.

For more information about SharePoint Designer, check out Chapter 8.

Visual Studio

When you're developing solutions that involve writing .NET code, then your application of choice is Visual Studio — a standalone application that serves as an Integrated Development Environment (IDE) for SharePoint.

Using Visual Studio, you can develop everything from custom event handlers to Web Parts. Then you can bundle up the finished code in a solution file and deploy it to SharePoint. (If only the rest of life where like that.)

Chapters 11, 12, and 13 take you farther into Visual Studio and developing .NET code for SharePoint.

Visual Studio wears many hats besides the one that says "SharePoint development tool." In fact, most general development of Microsoft solutions involves Visual Studio in some form or another.

Report Builder

To begin at the beginning, the component of SQL Server that takes care of reporting is Reporting Services. No less than SharePoint, Reporting Services can be configured to provide seamless integration for end users. Under that arrangement, when actual reports are integrated, they live in the SharePoint environment, and are subject to SharePoint content management — versioning, check-in/check-out, security, workflow, the whole nine yards — just like any other content. Reporting Services gives users a fairly friendly, Office-like tool they can use to build their own reports. Result: self service reporting. The tool that gives end users that power has a name that's as clear as it is obvious: Report Builder.

Report Builder uses a feature called ClickOnce to simplify installation, launch, and management of Report Builder on each user's local computer; ClickOnce makes each of these tasks happen automatically when (yes) the user clicks a button — once — on the SharePoint site. Gotta love those no-nonsense feature names.)

The first time you use Report Builder, the tool downloads automatically and installs itself on the local computer; if a Report Builder update becomes available, the update downloads automatically the very next time you launch the tool (all of which might seem a little creepy if it weren't so convenient).

A Reporting Services report, which you build using Report Builder (hey, obvious things need love too), can connect to many different types of data sources in its quest for data to pull into the report. When the data is nicely tucked into the report, you can display the data in handy components such as tables, graphs, and gauges. Using SharePoint, the people who need to see the finished report can call it up and view it in their browsers without undue fuss. You can also embed a report directly into a SharePoint page; the Reporting Services Web Part handles that job. (For a closer look at Report Builder, check out Chapter 9.)

Dashboard Designer

PerformancePoint Services is a component of SharePoint designed to provide the information needed for business intelligence (BI). This information is usually displayed on a Web page called a *dashboard*, which packages scorecards and Key Performance Indicators (KPIs) of business data so they're easily comprehensible at a glance. And the tool used to develop PerformancePoint dashboards has another gloriously obvious name: Dashboard Designer.

Dashboard Designer is a ClickOnce application just like Report Builder. When you create a new PerformancePoint item in SharePoint, ClickOnce launches Dashboard Designer for you. If it's the first time you've opened Dashboard Designer, ClickOnce takes care of downloading and installing the application on your local machine. When an updated version comes out, ClickOnce automatically updates Dashboard Designer the next time you launch it. (Relax. Your computer isn't haunted. That's just ClickOnce doing its thing.) Then, wielding Dashboard Designer, you can create mighty BI dashboard pages for your SharePoint farm.

A Dashboard Designer dashboard is, in essence, a logical container that holds other items such as scorecards, KPIs, reports, and charts. Each item can pull information from a different data source and display a different type of information, but all of them form the same cohesive view of how your business is operating. If a decision-maker is viewing the dashboard, it has fulfilled its purpose in life; when you've put together a dashboard that can do that job with efficiency and (why not?) panache, you publish it to a SharePoint site and watch the kudos (or at least the usable information) roll in. For more about Dashboard Designer, cast a glance at Chapter 10.

Dashboard Designer comes with the PerformancePoint Services feature of SharePoint. In order to get PerformancePoint Services you need the Enterprise edition of SharePoint Server.

Excel

In my experience, one of the most popular and widely used data-analysis programs is Microsoft Excel. Excel has found its way into everything from tracking lemonade-stand profits to crunching numbers at multibillion-dollar multinationals.

Recognizing the importance and pervasiveness of Excel, Microsoft has integrated it tightly with SharePoint, where a feature known as Excel Services endows the humble spreadsheet application with networked superpowers.

Excel Services allows you to continue using Excel spreadsheets to crunch numbers and perform analysis; no traumatic changes there. Then you can embed a finished spreadsheet in a SharePoint page, where users can find, view, and interact with the spreadsheet — without needing (or tweaking) their own copies of the file. They use a browser to navigate to the SharePoint page containing the one true, approved version of the spreadsheet. Gone are the idiosyncratic spreadsheet versions that used to crop up here and there and wander all over the organization via e-mail. The net reduction in confusion boosts morale. Productivity soars. Everybody gets a nice holiday bonus. (Hey, it could happen.)

For more about Excel and Excel Services, check out Chapter 5.

Visio

A wise (or at least visually oriented) person once said that a picture is worth a thousand words. The Microsoft product that takes this principle to heart is called Visio. You can use Visio to create everything from business-process flows to architectural drawings — anything that requires drawings and diagrams. The service application that integrates Visio into SharePoint is called Visio Services.

Visio Services allows you to create interactive drawings and embed them in SharePoint pages; then the users can access and manipulate the images right from their browsers.

Nobody's fool (but we knew that), Microsoft has set up Visio so business analysts can use it to create SharePoint workflow diagrams, export them, and then import them into SharePoint Designer. Once the workflow that was built using Visio has been imported into SharePoint Designer it is only a matter of connecting the conditions and actions of the workflow with the actual lists and libraries in SharePoint. This is often called wiring up the SharePoint workflow that was created by a business user. (Pretty slick.) The opposite is also true: Workflows developed in SharePoint Designer are easy to export to Visio, where you can translate all those words and numbers into a visual diagram that will clobber business users with immediate insight. (Well, we can hope.)

Visio Services also allows for the visualization of a workflow already in progress. For example, if you have an approval workflow going, you can see exactly who has approved the document and who hasn't. Visio Services shows you the status of the workflow as a picture. (Also very slick.) For more information about Visio and Visio Services check out Chapter 7.

Word

Microsoft Office Word has to be one of the most heavily used software applications of all time. Everyone from schoolchildren to company executives have the need for a word-processing application. A persistent problem with documents, however, is that they lack an overall management system. In the business world, where documents proliferate daily, an Enterprise Content Management (ECM) system is critical. One reason SharePoint has taken off so rapidly is that it's a world-class ECM platform. SharePoint integration with Microsoft Office Word allows for much more than simple word processing and content management.

SharePoint integrates with Word in a number ways:

✔ Managing *metadata* (data that describes the other data that makes up each document).

✔ Providing essential ECM features such as

- *Check-in/check-out* — treating documents like library books (remember those?) to keep track of who has them and for how long.

- *Versioning* — business-speak for limiting the number of versions a document can have, thus reducing confusion.

- *Security* — controlling access to documents.

- *Workflow* — fitting the creation and routing of documents into a sequence of tasks established as a file in SharePoint.

Best of all, users can take advantage of these features without leaving the Word client application.

In addition, the Business Connectivity Services (BCS) component of SharePoint enables Word to interact with line-of-business (LOB) systems that are specific to the work of the organization — and with Enterprise Resource Planning (ERP) systems that allocate people and materials to specific jobs.

The result is a seamless and intuitive user experience for front-line workers who are comfortable using Word. (For more about working with Word to develop a SharePoint solution, see Chapter 7.)

Developer Dashboard

The Developer Dashboard in SharePoint provides you with a way to monitor the performance of your development efforts on a page-by-page basis. When the Developer Dashboard is enabled, it shows up at the bottom of every page, (as shown in Figure 15-1).

The Developer Dashboard provides information about the Web server and page such as the database query statistics for loading the page, events that were executed, and the order and timing of controls that loaded on the page. In addition you can also define your own sections of code to monitor and display on the Developer Dashboard.

The Developer Dashboard can be activated in the following ways:

✔ Using the STSADM command (which is being shown the door thanks to PowerShell).

✔ Using a PowerShell script (I explain this method in the upcoming steps).

✔ Using .NET code and the SharePoint object model (see Chapter 12 for more about the SharePoint object model).

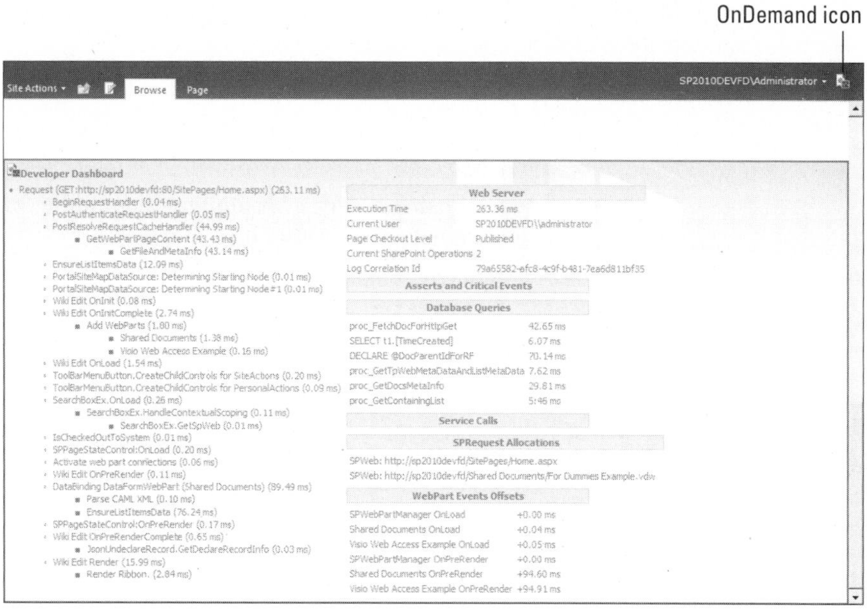

OnDemand icon

Figure 15-1:
The
Developer
Dashboard
displays
information
about a
page that
helps
manage
development
efforts.

When you activate the Developer Dashboard using PowerShell, you can put Developer Dashboard into any of three different modes. You choose the mode by changing a property of SharePoint, which I explain in a moment. The Developer Dashboard modes are

- **Off:** This is the default setting, which disables the Developer Dashboard.

- **On:** This setting turns on the Developer Dashboard for all pages. The result is that all pages that load contain the Developer Dashboard at the bottom of the page.

- **OnDemand:** This mode turns on the Developer Dashboard — but instead of rendering the page statistics automatically, it puts an icon in the top-right corner of the page next to the user's sign-in name. When the user clicks the icon, the Developer Dashboard renders the page statistics and puts them on-screen.

You can activate the Developer Dashboard using the PowerShell command-line utility (for a refresher, see Chapter 14); just follow these steps:

1. **Choose Start⇨All Programs⇨Microsoft SharePoint 2010 Products⇨ SharePoint 2010 Management Shell.**

   The SharePoint PowerShell Management Console opens.

2. **Set a variable to the** `DeveloperDashboardSettings` **object.**

3. **Set the** `DisplayLevel` **property to either** `On` **or** `OnDemand`.

4. **Check to make sure the property was set correctly and then update the** `DeveloperDashboardSettings` **object.**

Listing 15-1 shows an example.

Listing 15-1:   Activating Developer Dashboard in PowerShell

```
PS C:\Users\Administrator>
PS C:\Users\Administrator> $devDashboardSettings = [Microsoft.
        SharePoint.Administration.SPWebService]::ContentService.
        DeveloperDashboardSettings
PS C:\Users\Administrator> $devDashboardSettings.DisplayLevel
Off
PS C:\Users\Administrator> $devDashboardSettings.DisplayLevel = "On"
PS C:\Users\Administrator> $devDashboardSettings.DisplayLevel
On
PS C:\Users\Administrator> $devDashboardSettings.Update()
PS C:\Users\Administrator>
```

Note: When code is indented code in Listing 15-1, the indentation indicates that you should type the code at the prompt on a single line.

If you want to see a list of all the properties of the `DeveloperDashboard Settings` object, just pipe the result of the previous steps (that is, use the | symbol) to the `Get-Member` (gm) command. Here's an example that uses the SharePoint Management Shell to set the `DeveloperDashboardSettings` object to the variable named $devDashboardSettings and then prints out all the members it contains:

```
PS C:\Users\Administrator> $devDashboardSettings = [Microsoft.
        SharePoint.Administration.SPWebService]::ContentService.
        DeveloperDashboardSettings

PS C:\Users\Administrator> $devDashboardSettings | Get-Member
```

For more information about PowerShell and SharePoint, check out Chapter 14.

SharePoint on Windows 7

One of the biggest complaints with previous versions of SharePoint has been the lack of a proper development environment on developers' workstations. Hey, give 'em a break — previous versions of SharePoint had to run on server operating systems such as Windows Server, even though many developers preferred to use a workstation operating system — which these days would be Windows 7. Well, the good news is that SharePoint 2010 can now be installed on the Windows 7 operating system. Just keep the bit width in mind. . . .

SharePoint 2010 requires a 64-bit operating system. Before you try to run SharePoint on Windows 7, make sure the operating system is 64-bit. Trust me, starting with a 64-bit version of Windows will save you gnashing of teeth later.

In addition, Microsoft has streamlined the process for installing a SharePoint 2010 development environment — now you can do it with only the SharePoint media.

If you haven't yet installed Microsoft SQL Server — the part of the system that will house all those lovely SharePoint content and configuration databases — you can do that installation at the same time you're installing SharePoint. If you already have SQL Server installed, you'll need to point SharePoint at your installation during configuration.

For more information and pointers on building a SharePoint 2010 development environment in a Windows 7 system, I've got you covered: Check out Chapter 16.

Chapter 16

Ten Places to Go for SharePoint Development Information

In This Chapter

▶ Finding where to go for more information about SharePoint development

▶ Getting a grip on the resources available for SharePoint development

▶ Listing some of the most valuable SharePoint development resources

> *Information technology and business are becoming inextricably interwoven. I don't think anybody can talk meaningfully about one without talking about the other.*
>
> — Bill Gates

As you continue on your SharePoint development path, you can be sure of one thing: You'll always require additional information. Luckily you can find a wealth of information about SharePoint development — if you know where to look.

This chapter you points you to useful online destinations when you need more information about SharePoint development. As with any technology, SharePoint is constantly changing; keeping up to date is critical. Whether you need to find a complete planning and deployment guide or search a forum for the latest workaround, this chapter will point you in the right direction.

SharePoint Developer Center

The SharePoint Developer Center is a one-stop shop for "everything SharePoint development." The site includes community forums, videos, whitepapers, and other indispensable developer resources.

The SharePoint Developer Center is a great place to explore if you are just getting started. There are a number of videos that walk through some of the basic issues you will encounter as you begin developing on the SharePoint platform. Whenever you find yourself stuck, be sure to visit the forums, where a very active bunch of passionate SharePointers will go above and beyond to answer your questions and get you pointed in the right direction. To access the SharePoint Developer Center, point your browser to this URL:

```
msdn.microsoft.com/sharepoint
```

Office Developer Center

The Office Developer Center is designed especially for developers who work with Microsoft Office products. The site includes resources for all types of Office development — but especially worth checking out is its information on the tight integration between Office products and SharePoint. For example, you might need to get additional information on building those InfoPath forms that you will use in SharePoint (see Chapter 6) or when you start putting together Excel analytical reports (see Chapter 5).

To access the Office Developer Center, point your browser to

```
msdn.microsoft.com/office
```

Developing Applications Guide

The Developing Applications for SharePoint 2010 guide is produced by the Patterns and Practices team at Microsoft. The Patterns and Practices group is tasked with defining best practices and "patterns" that should be used when working with Microsoft products. The guide contains resources for developing SharePoint code along with code samples and a reusable class library.

To find the most recent version of the guide, follow these steps:

1. **Open your favorite Web browser and navigate to**

```
www.microsoft.com/downloads
```

2. **In the Search Downloads text box, type in** Developing Applications for SharePoint 2010.

3. **Look for the title with the most recent release date.**

Channel 9 Developer Course

The Channel 9 site is a production unit at Microsoft that conducts interviews and creates videos. These videos include everything from interviews with products' team members to training courses for particular Microsoft software products. The Channel 9 team has created a series of SharePoint 2010 developer videos that you can find at the following URL:

```
channel9.msdn.com/learn/courses/SharePoint2010Developer/
```

Software Development Kit

The SharePoint 2010 Reference: Software Development Kit includes documentation and code samples, along with information for programming with the SharePoint Foundation and SharePoint Server object models in mind. In addition, the kit includes a set of best practices and guidance on getting started with SharePoint 2010 programming.

To find the most recent version of the kit, follow these steps:

1. **Open your favorite Web browser and navigate to**

   ```
   www.microsoft.com/downloads
   ```

2. **In the Search Downloads text box, type in** SharePoint 2010 Reference: Software Development Kit.

3. **Look for the title with the most recent release date.**

SharePoint 2010 Guides

Microsoft has created a number of guides to assist in your SharePoint planning and deployment process. These guides are more like books; they're extensive and contain a treasure trove of SharePoint information. You can download the planning and deployment guides by using the processes outlined in the next subsections.

Planning Guide

The Planning Guide For SharePoint is a detailed paper (more of a book if you print it out) that walks you through all aspects of planning for SharePoint. The guide includes such useful resources as technical diagrams, project templates, planning worksheets, and checklists. To find the most recent version of the Planning Guide, follow these steps:

1. **Open your favorite Web browser and navigate to**

   `www.microsoft.com/download`

2. **In the Search Downloads text box, type in** Planning Guide For SharePoint.

   Note that guides are available for both SharePoint Server and SharePoint Foundation.

3. **Look for the title with the most recent release date.**

Deployment Guide

The Deployment Guide is designed to provide detailed information about deploying SharePoint. It covers everything from hardware and software requirements to installing and configuring the product. The guide comes in two flavors. The first is designed for SharePoint Foundation and the second is designed for SharePoint Server.

To find the most recent version of the Deployment Guide, follow these steps:

1. **Open your favorite Web browser and navigate to**

   `www.microsoft.com/downloads`

2. **In the Search Downloads text box, type in** Deployment Guide For SharePoint.

   Note that guides exist for SharePoint Server and SharePoint Foundation. Choose the one that applies to your version of SharePoint.

3. **Look for the title with the most recent release date.**

Setting up a SharePoint development environment

Past versions of SharePoint would only install and run on a server operating system — a problem for developers, who often prefer to work in a workstation environment instead of a server environment. SharePoint 2010 solved this dilemma by supporting installation on Windows 7. Finally a developer could install a local version of SharePoint that included the database and all the necessary dependencies. With SharePoint running locally you're free to tweak and play and really get to know the product — in particular, how other users will experience it on their workstations — without leaving the comfort of your own desktop computer.

Keep in mind that SharePoint requires a 64-bit operating system. If you're planning to install SharePoint on Windows 7, make sure it's the 64-bit edition.

If you want more information about installing a SharePoint development environment, you can find it at the following URL:

```
msdn.microsoft.com/en-us/library/ee554869.aspx
```

Deployment Planning Services

Microsoft has a program in place that uses certified partners to assist in your SharePoint planning and deployment efforts. The program is called SharePoint Deployment Planning Services (SDPS); essentially it's a series of information sessions that representatives of those Microsoft-certified partners conduct, making use of planning material created by Microsoft. The sessions offer different materials based on the depth and complexity of the information required; they come in 1-, 3-, 5-, 10-, and 15-day engagements.

If your organization subscribes to the Microsoft Software Assurance program, then the SDPS program may be available to you already at no cost.

For more information about SharePoint Deployment Planning Services check out the following URL:

```
iwsolve.partners.extranet.microsoft.com/sdps/
```

Microsoft Hosted Information

Microsoft maintains a couple of extensive online libraries of information. Although the sites are geared to specific professional groups, the information on both sites is useful regardless of how you interact with SharePoint — and getting familiar with both sites will help you as a developer.

- The Microsoft TechNet site is designed for general IT professionals, and is available at

  ```
  technet.microsoft.com
  ```

- Microsoft Developer Network (MSDN) site is designed especially for developers, and hangs out at

  ```
  msdn.microsoft.com
  ```

SharePoint 2010 Developer Training Kit

Although the SharePoint 2010 Developer Training Kit may not be a whole new development-oriented brain, it does provide a rich set of training materials for the good ol' brain you already have. The kit includes video tutorials, hands-on labs, source-code examples, PowerPoint decks, whitepapers, and articles. Downloading and browsing through the kit is a great way to get started with SharePoint development.

The training kit is updated often — so you'll want to find the most recent version. Fortunately, finding that latest version is a breeze — just follow these steps:

1. **Open your favorite Web browser and navigate to**

   `www.microsoft.com/downloads`

2. **In the Search Downloads text box, type in** SharePoint 2010 Developer Training Kit.

3. **Look for the title with the most recent release date.**

If these steps look hauntingly familiar, that's by design; Microsoft makes all this handy info available with maximum consistency and minimum fuss.

Magazines and Blogs

As SharePoint has gained popularity, a number of online magazines have cropped up that provide a wealth of published SharePoint information. The following magazines — which are either specific to SharePoint or regularly include SharePoint content — offer some good starting points:

- ✔ SharePointPro Connections (`www.sharepointproconnections.com`)
- ✔ SharePoint Magazine (`sharepointmagazine.net`)
- ✔ MSDN Magazine (`msdn.microsoft.com/magazine`)
- ✔ Visual Studio Magazine (`visualstudiomagazine.com`)
- ✔ The Architecture Journal (`msdn.microsoft.com/en-us/architecture/bb410935.aspx`)

   No, you won't find photo spreads of pricey bungalows here; the "architecture" under discussion is strictly the structure-of-your-software variety.

- ✔ Windows IT Pro (`www.windowsitpro.com`)

In addition to the published magazines you can find online, a number of blogs are maintained by SharePoint professionals. The relevance of blogs is constantly shifting — but to find some of the best, visit the SharePoint Developer Center site and look for the blogs written by SharePoint MVPs — the folks even Microsoft recognizes as gurus in the field.

Chapter 17

Ten Ways to Reduce Business Costs through SharePoint Development

In This Chapter

▶ Understanding how to save costs by developing SharePoint solutions

▶ Figuring out what can be consolidated into a company portal

▶ Discovering the power of a SharePoint portal as a one-stop shop for your organization

The new information technologies have practically eliminated the physical costs of communications.

— Peter Drucker

As you read through this chapter on saving money with SharePoint, you'll begin to notice a recurring theme. I've seen it crop up time and again during the years I've been implementing SharePoint — and though I haven't kept score, I'd estimate that I've seen well over a hundred implementations — from billion-dollar multinational conglomerates to local cheese producers. What I've found is that integrating processes and procedures into a portal to create a single point of entry drastically increases efficiency and boosts productivity. When I decided to start my own company with a focus on this premise, I named the company (aptly enough, I thought) Portal Integrators — emphasizing that an integrated portal is essential to an organization that wants to compete in the modern age.

One of the biggest problems with that much-touted "Information Age" is the lack of a homogenous computing environment. As hardware makers and software vendors scramble to dominate the market, the result is a mishmash in the marketplace. No surprise that as companies grow, they adopt assorted technologies and processes to deal with their current needs. Over time, this approach results in a hodgepodge of different systems, bickering technology, and isolated processes.

As a technology consultant, I'm always surprised at what I find when I dig into the computing environments of some top global companies. When I present my findings to executive leadership, *they're surprised too.* The executives are great folks, but they have a lot on their minds — and most of it is about their business per se and not about technology. The IT people on the ground (not to mention the users) feel the pain of the technological hodgepodge but often lack the overall perspective of how other companies do things — and what does and doesn't work in various industries.

Imagine, for example, that you're an administrator in charge of making sure that a particular software system is up and running without issues. Your entire world (or at least a huge swath of it) focuses on that software system; you don't have time to start speculating about how users throughout the organization feel when they have to wrestle with all those systems — especially if the systems don't play nice together as a coherent whole. You need *your* system up, running, and always available. If you can accomplish that task, then you're feeling good.

The executive, on the other hand wants to see the organization meeting its goals. For example, if your outfit is a corporate business, you're trying to make a profit for your shareholders. You don't necessarily care what technology is being used where (SQL? rubber bands? okay, fine, just make it work . . .) or what processes make things happen. If a senior manager comes to you as the executive and insists she needs a particular software system in place, then chances are you're going to give the green light. That may address a short-term problem, but what's missing is a holistic understanding of how all the pieces work together.

The Human Resources department might really want a particular system because it's what the senior manager is accustomed to using. The leaders in manufacturing might have come away from a trade show amazed by the latest technology, and now they're lobbying to install the latest and greatest. The sales folks may be comfortable with an established system for keeping track of their leads and prospects. Individually these systems work great — but unfortunately, the success of the organization rarely depends on a single department or unit. If the organization as a whole is to get where it's going, it needs its parts to work together, in much the same way the pistons in a car engine have to work together.

If a single piston in an engine behaves badly, the entire car is disabled. If the pistons work in a synchronized fashion, they help each other generate power — and produce more power as a whole. In the same manner an errant department can bring down an entire organization; if the departments communicate and cooperate, the "engine" runs more smoothly.

In order to remedy the issues of disparate systems, companies have adopted various versions of a centralized internal Web site called a *portal:* Essentially intended as an easy-to-use gateway to the company intranet, the company portal is supposed to be a one-stop shop for whatever company information the employees need to find.

Sounds great. In theory.

In practice, portals that actually talk to all the other systems in the organization have been difficult and time-consuming to develop. If you want an employee to access his or her company information (say, benefits) through the portal, then somehow you have to integrate the portal with the Human Resources system. If you want the manufacturing managers to be able to post their reports to the portal for executives and others to view, same problem: You have to integrate the manufacturing systems with the portal. And so on till IT has to order an extra-large bottle of aspirin. The end result is a lot of work and money expended in a valiant attempt to link up the company portal with other systems — with very rare success.

To be sure, SharePoint didn't start out as a platform for linking systems into a one-stop portal shop. Initially it was developed as a collaborative environment, in response to a related problem: When employees have to run (virtually) all over the place with different systems and different processes just to get their work done, it takes a huge toll on (you guessed it) efficiency and productivity. When a new person joins the team, the learning curve is steep and the chance of error is large — after all, every system has its own quirks and behaviors that need to be figured out (not to say beaten into submission with a blunt object) over time.

Because collaboration was only part of the solution that a portal solves, SharePoint grew into a full-fledged system for centralizing information, people, and processes in a single portal — cost-effectively. Consolidating processes and systems into a single portal alleviates that former disparity and allows people to focus on the business processes without having to worry so much about the technology. The technological concerns should melt into the background and make the business processes easier instead of causing confusion and wasted brain cycles.

Okay, let's bring that flight of the imagination in for a landing: Here are the top ten ways you can integrate business processes into your company portal using SharePoint.

Organize Digital Content

The Information Age — all 10 to 25 years of it (depending on who you ask and when they went to school) — has unleashed a bigger and bigger deluge of digital content. If you think about your typical day, nearly all *content* — that is, information with a recognized value — is in digital form. Organizations have to slog through, and somehow organize, all that digital content — with more coming in all the time. In pre-computer days, vast rooms of file cabinets would be used to organize content. It amazes me to think of people wading through the swamps of hard copy among walls of file cabinets, searching for a particular piece of paper. (Imagine what happened when someone filed an entire batch of paperwork in the wrong spot. The horror.)

Nowadays most organizations work with digital content — Word documents, PDF documents, Excel spreadsheets, electronic forms, you name it — more of it, generated faster, than would ever fit on all that paper. Every day. The problem is still familiar: organizing all that content. Many organizations still use shared drives and folders. And the same scenario haunts modern organizations: What if *someone* (an intern?) puts an entire directory in the wrong location? And then there's the matter of digital content spawning duplicates. It's as easy as the click of a mouse to make a copy of a document, and then drag it off to a different folder to reside who-knows-where — until it escapes and stirs up confusion. Even in the old paper days, folks probably longed for only a *single* hard copy! A single version of the truth! (What a concept.)

Enter SharePoint, offering you the tools to develop a *content repository* to manage all your digital content. At last you can alleviate the problems associated with shared drives. A SharePoint document library helps control the versions of a document, helps control the use of documents by having users check them in and out, controls access to make the documents more secure, and provides workflows as a way to give the documents a clear place in the sequence of tasks. In addition, having a single portal gives everyone one place to go to find all types of content — ranging from company policies to product documentation — the company portal.

It's often hard to associate a cost to inefficiencies but when you start thinking about how much time people spend searching for past documents or recreating them from scratch the figure becomes enormous. Now take into account how many people across an organization are creating documents with the same purpose at the same time. Using SharePoint to organize documents, called an Enterprise Content Management (ECM) system greatly improves efficiencies and greatly improves cost.

Developing document libraries with nothing up your sleeve but your Web browser is covered in Chapter 4.

Collaborate across a Portal

These days a fundamental aspect of the modern workforce is a need for communication and collaboration — sometimes across international distances. An engineer in the Philippines might have the solution to a problem that an engineer in San Francisco is facing, and vice versa. The Internet has become a mechanism for instant and autonomous communication — but the problem is often lack of a cohesive communication strategy. Some engineers might create their own discussion boards using a third-party hosting software. That works okay for those who are aware of the issues, happen to have the software installed, and are invited to the discussion board — but what about the folks who don't fit that description and still need the information?

Consolidating collaboration into a single portal environment is a vital first step in mobilizing the knowledge that lives all over the place in your organization. With the portal in place, everyone knows that it's the place to go when they have information to communicate within the company. The company portal integrates everyone from the CEO to the cleaning crew. The cost savings that can be achieved by introducing an effective collaboration and communication platform are astonishing. For instant return, the CEO might send out a blog requesting feedback on cutting costs, with an award to those who come up with a great solution. As the crowd begins debating and discussing cost-cutting measures, the best ideas will bubble up to the top. Maybe the executive team didn't realize that by "going green" with some of the manufacturing buildings, the energy costs would be reduced by 30%— but a passionate person in human resources did.

The SharePoint platform is an ideal tool for creating an integrated collaborative environment — because everyone can help develop solutions, using its built-in tools. No computer science degree required. Typical SharePoint users can do the development required to create a collaborative solution, as described throughout this book. SharePoint features designed especially for communication and collaboration include wikis, discussion boards, blogs, publishing portals, comments, and page ratings. Flip to Chapter 4 to find out more.

Consolidate Reports

Reports come in all sizes, shapes, and formats. In the past, report development required getting the business analysts (who understood the data) to speak coherently to the report developers (who understood the technology) and vice versa, even before they got to thrashing out the details. Well, when you put together a couple of SharePoint system components, the whole undertaking gets easier:

- ✔ SQL Server Reporting Services (SSRS) provides a platform for reporting that's tightly integrated with the SharePoint platform.

- ✔ SharePoint itself provides end users with a report-development tool — Report Builder — that they can launch right from the SharePoint portal.

- ✔ Reports can be stored and viewed at the appropriate time from the SharePoint portal — in the browser.

Consolidating the reporting function to SharePoint provides one central place that all users can go to access, read, develop, or deposit reports. It's a self-service approach, and probably the wave of the future: No longer does a report have to morph into a little project with its own complex development cycles; business analysts and technically adept report developers need no longer strain to translate each other's jargon. Empowering the users who have the knowledge saves money by reducing project expense. If the tools aren't available, then the business users have to rely on the IT department. The IT department gets overwhelmed and projects grind to a halt. The IT team feels they need more people (which they do if they are being over-whelmed with project requests), and the businesspeople feel they're not get-ting what they need — so they hire their own "ghost" IT "mini-department" made up of consultants. The chain of events drives up costs by creating a perpetually destructive process. The answer is not in throwing more money at the problem but in approaching the problem in a different way — using the proper tools. When the business users are empowered with tools that the IT department can govern, it's win-win for both teams and a cost reduction for the company.

SharePoint provides self-serve reporting not only through Report Builder but also through content-management features: Users can check reports in and out; rest assured that there's only one version they have to deal with; see the report as an expected task in a workflow; and restrict access to the report to keep it secure. The whole process is more coherent from stem to stern. For more information about Report Builder check out Chapter 9. If you need a refresher on using SharePoint libraries check out *SharePoint 2010 For Dummies.*

Reap the Benefits of Analytics

Data is the lifeblood of an organization; analyzing it to glean useful business insights can be as crucial as a blood test for your annual checkup at the doc-tor's office. Data analysis takes many forms, but one of the most popular is our old friend, the ubiquitous Microsoft Excel spreadsheet. Unfortunately, Excel spreadsheets are self-contained files. Easily copied, e-mailed, stored, modified, sliced, diced, and mutated, they can bring about costly duplication errors and foment the spread of incorrect information. Say you create an Excel spreadsheet and e-mail it to another analyst, who tweaks some num-bers and sends it on to someone else who reviews it, adds to it, and deletes a column or two. After a number of these hops through e-mail and all that miscellaneous doctoring, the spreadsheet starts to look a little monstrous. Maybe it's spawned a brood of mutant offspring. You can only hope that nobody made a mistake along the way.

SharePoint includes a feature called Excel Services that integrates Excel documents with the SharePoint platform. It brings an end to the horror of spreadsheet mutation; one coherent version can be made available for viewing right on the company portal — or embedded within a Web page. Flip to Chapter 5 for details on integrating Excel into a SharePoint site.

In addition, the SharePoint platform includes a feature designed to help decision-makers do up-to-the-minute business analysis with little more than a quick glance at an array of on-screen indicators of how the business is doing — PerformancePoint Services. PerformancePoint's end-user development tool — Dashboard Designer — can be launched right from the SharePoint portal. And again, in true self-service fashion, end users can create their own advanced dashboards — without the need of a programmer. You find details about using Dashboard Designer with PerformancePoint in Chapter 10.

As you have probably figured out by now, SharePoint is able to cut costs by providing powerful tools that can be used to effectively create a one-stop-shop for information. When an analyst can build a report and share it with the entire organization without having to talk to an IT person, everyone wins. The organization gets the right information right away — and the IT team can focus on managing the platform (SharePoint) without having to build one iteration after another of reports they care little about.

Centralize Company Information

The best place to store the company information that serves as its "operator's manual" — such as policies, procedures, and process documentation — is in a single location that all relevant parties can access. Using SharePoint as the portal platform allows you to take advantage of *collaborative* information management. For example, if all your company policies are written using article pages, you can include comments and content rating just by adding the appropriate Web Parts. Presto — users can provide feedback, get involved, and contribute some ideas that everyone can benefit from. Chapter 13 helps you add this functionality to a site.

Using Visio Services, you can document your business processes and develop visual diagrams to illustrate how they work, as you discover in Chapter 7. With all sorts of information under the portal roof the efficiency of getting a new employee up to speed is drastically improved. If you talk to human-resources experts, they'll tell you that a huge cost is employee turnover. Getting a new employee familiar with the systems and up to speed not only costs money (after all, the new employee isn't fully productive *yet*) but also puts a strain on the productivity of the employees who have to take the time to train the new person.

Store Product Documentation

Product documentation comes in many forms, shapes, and sizes. Some of it is helpful; some . . . well . . . not so much. But you might be surprised at how often company representatives don't know what's in it. I can't tell you how many times I've received some new gadget, called for support, and told the customer-service rep exactly which part of the documentation I'm looking at — only to be told (in effect) that this person has absolutely no idea what I'm talking about. Don't let this happen to you. Or to your company.

SharePoint can store and manage nearly any type of digital content — even "manuals" (as in, "Go read the fabled manual"). Wouldn't it be nice if everyone in the organization knew they could go to `http://CompanyPortal/products` and see everything they needed to know about every product — and could comment on how reality compares to the manual, discuss the products, and improve product documentation? Developing a product-documentation solution on the SharePoint platform can make that dream happen.

To implement this collaboration in SharePoint, you could start by developing a site specifically for product documentation. You could start from scratch or pick a site template geared to this task — such as the Document Management Center. (For more about the magic of developing a site using your Web browser, check out Chapter 4.)

The cost benefit by having a one-stop-shop might not seem immediately obvious. But I cannot tell you how many times I've called a support desk as a consumer, only to wait for what seems like hours as the person on the far end of the line tries to figure out the issue with my product. Not only am I wasting my own time but I'm consuming resources from the company (company time, company dime, yikes). If the person is new, then it takes much longer to figure out the problem, especially if someone has to go drag a more experienced representative into the fray.

By removing the issue of where to go to find the information, you let your people focus on solving a problem and not figuring out *where to go to solve a problem*. It doesn't matter if the product is a service (such as your mortgage) or a physical product (such as your DVD player); the essential information needed to answer issues that crop up frequently should be readily available to the people in the hot seat who are trying to help customers with their problems.

Streamline Customer Data Maintenance

I recently had to change my address at a very large bank (which I will refrain from naming). The problems I ran into were amazing. First, our apartment number was included on the checks the bank sent us — but not on our statement. Then the name of our street was incorrect on our statement but correct on our credit card. Each time I called to talk to the customer-service agents, they would have to go on safari through multiple systems to hunt down the offending incorrect portion of our address. It was like whack-a-mole, one rep told me: They'd think they had all our information correct and *another* error would pop up in yet another system. I'm sure that the reason had something to do with the many mergers and acquisitions the bank had made over the years. Apparently the systems were never fully integrated. The result was a Rube Goldberg kludge of different systems; customer information (such as my address) wound up stored in many different locations.

Developing a portal for customer service representatives to use will result in a one-stop shop for customer data. The data might actually be contained in multiple backend systems, but if the customer rep simply has to go to the customer-data portion of the portal (and, of course, it's well designed and up to date), mistakes are much less likely to go unresolved (or even happen).

Okay, I'm not saying that integrating a site with backend systems is as easy as pie — it's not. You have to work with some of the fairly complicated features of SharePoint — such as Business Connectivity Services (BCS) — as well as write a certain amount of .NET code using Visual Studio (Chapter 11) and the SharePoint Object Model (Chapter 12). But take heart: The investment it takes to integrate backend systems with a one-stop portal will save you money — yea, verily, it will bring you closer to those ideals that make the business heart leap up: increasing efficiency and boosting productivity.

Well, I finally got hold of an old-timer customer rep who knew all the systems and managed to finish my address change. Moral: Imagine the training it takes to familiarize new customer reps with all those different systems. (Do I hear gnashing of teeth?) If *only* they had a SharePoint company portal. Then the beleaguered customer reps could simply be familiarized with the customer-service information gathered (and carefully updated — that's a hint) there. The company would save on its training budget, increase the efficiency and effectiveness of its reps, and the customers would be happy. Imagine if the person you're talking to were actually empowered to solve your problem without having to disappear into the tangled jungle of miscellaneous computer systems. Set up a SharePoint portal. Help your customers live the dream.

Help Employees Help Themselves

Where do you go to manage your employee information (such as your address, phone number, and emergency contact)? How do you change your tax information if you have a child or get married? Unfortunately, the answer is often, "To the HR department" — often a land of mystery. You have to e-mail, call, or walk into the Human Resources department itself; find a human being to talk to; and gather the forms, phone numbers, URLs, and other nuggets of information you need to make the changes you have in mind. As an organization gets larger, this situation puts an excessive burden on the resources of the HR team. To cope with the added workload, the department needs to grow and hire more people. But if its systems are (in effect) duct-taped together and out of touch with the rest of the company, those new warm bodies won't help much.

When you develop a solution for employee self-service based on SharePoint, you're shifting the burden of the work to the people who require the change. And it makes sense: Who better to put in a change of address than the person who's moving? The one who knows the new address. The one you've empowered to handle this matter from anywhere he or she can access the company portal. By shifting a small burden to those that are updating their information instead of bloating the HR team, you are saving money on two fronts. The first is the direct cost reduction of less human HR capital and the second is the increase in efficiency of those requesting the change. Imagine the cost of a person spending a few hours to a day finding the right place and person — and then filling out the manual forms. Folks who have to endure complex struggles with the updating of an address are not doing their normal jobs; the inefficiency cascades out to those who rely on the person as well.

Allow for Personal Portal Space

A centralized portal that provides consistent access to the company intranet is potentially a great boon to everyone in the organization — but what do you do when people want to create their own little spaces on the portal? Hey, they're human beings; it'll happen. They might want to store the documents they're currently working on, create a discussion with just their friends to talk about day care, post the score from the company softball team's latest outing, develop procedure documents for a particular department, you name it. SharePoint includes a feature called My Sites that provides a personalized SharePoint site for every single user of the system. The users are free to modify and develop the sites as they want. An individual user can add other users to his or her site as well — and all those folks can collaborate on topics specific to their site. The end result is that SharePoint again shifts the burden of developing a personalized site away from a group or department administrator and toward a self-serve model.

I often hear IT people complain that if *everyone* has a site on the portal, it will create chaos. Everyone will be doing his or her own thing. Civilization will fall. The fact is that all those folks *are* doing their own things anyway — but only on their local computers. People have documents, e-mail, and all types of other content on their local computers but it's off the radar of IT. The problem has been that when a person loses or deletes a document — or (in the scarier scenarios) the hapless user's computer crashes — all that local content vanishes. In order to mitigate this possibility, IT usually takes the step of setting up a file share that they back up. Note, however, that a typical file share has none of the collaborative content-management features of SharePoint. A personal My Site does. So it's a natural step toward further empowering people but also maintaining IT governance and control of information within the company. This shift saves money by empowering users with the power of SharePoint. After all, the IT department doesn't want to set up personal Web sites for every person in the organization. The amount of effort it would take without using SharePoint would be cost-prohibitive. Using SharePoint, however, your organization gains the efficiencies of a self-serve environment without the administrative overhead.

Keep in mind that a personal My Site is nothing different from any other SharePoint site. It is just specific to every person. As you read through the book, you might be doing most of your development on your own personal My Site, depending on how your administrators have set up access. Configuring My Sites is beyond the scope of this book—but once they are configured and you access your My Site, you are free to develop it just as you would any other site.

Move Infrastructure to the Cloud

One of the biggest pain points that technology leans on (sometimes pretty hard) is the physical infrastructure — and not just when you try to move it across the office. The amount of hardware and software it takes to get SharePoint going can be daunting, even for a large company with extensive Microsoft expertise. When hosting SharePoint, you have to think about data centers, servers, operating systems, installation plans, upgrade plans, backup plans, disaster recovery, redundancy, availability, and scalability . . . for openers. The list goes on.

When you start putting the dollars behind an implementation, the costs can be staggering. One way around the infrastructure hurdle is to let Microsoft deal with it. Microsoft SharePoint Online is a "cloud solution" available for a monthly fee: You simply use, configure, and develop SharePoint to fit your business — in a secure online environment that Microsoft maintains for you. The immediate cost savings in pushing off the infrastructure management can be staggering. In addition, you can focus your funding on solving business problems and not on solving technical infrastructure problems. It might be hard to quantify but the result is that a dollar spent solving a business problem is more valuable than a dollar spent solving a technical problem. After all, who wants to spend money on infrastructure when they could spend money on their core business? (For more about SharePoint Online and the "cloud" as an Internet metaphor, float on over to Chapter 2.)

Glossary of SharePoint Development Terms

ad-hoc analysis: A technique of business analysis that seeks to answer questions as they arise. For example, you might start with a canned report but then have questions about a particular region. Ad-hoc analysis, as a feature, would let you drill into that region and categorize the data that the region contains, manipulating the data in real time.

Balanced Scorecard: A visual representation of a business strategy, designed to help an organization balance its progress toward a specific goal from four perspectives: business processes, financial health, customer management, and learning and growth. You can use any of several Microsoft products to build the visualizations needed for a Balanced Scorecard — not only services in SharePoint (such as PerformancePoint Services and SQL Server Reporting Services), but also client applications such as Excel. The visualizations serve as at-a-glance indicators. Compared to managing and monitoring an organization from the four perspectives, these indicators show only the tip of a very large iceberg.

business intelligence (BI): In general, the systematic, enterprise-wide use of networked computer software to get a handle on the mountains of data that flow into, through, and from a modern business. The raw data becomes information that's used to run a business intelligently — in particular, to plan strategies (a use similar to that of military intelligence).

command-line interface (CLI): A simple user interface as opposed to the much more common, and newer, graphical user interfaces (GUIs): All that appears onscreen is a prompt that marks the start of the *command line* where the user types in specific commands and then presses Enter. (The GUI equivalent is to put the mouse pointer on an onscreen control and then click to activate.) Microsoft PowerShell, included with SharePoint, is a CLI still used extensively in developing SharePoint scripts and solutions.

cube: The configuration of data in — and often a synonym for — an OLAP database.

dashboard: A collection of onscreen visual indicators linked to business processes. In PerformancePoint, a dashboard is a Web Part page (developed using the Dashboard Designer) that pulls together various Web Part components into a cohesive view of a SharePoint system. More generally, a dashboard works like the gauges in a car's dashboard: Its output is usually a real-time snapshot of how an operational task is performing. For example, you might have a dashboard for manufacturing that outlines the current status of all machines. If the dashboard is designed to show a red flashing icon when a machine is down or a solid green icon when a machine is up, then anyone in the organization can view the dashboard and quickly understand the current health of the manufacturing process. The scorecard, on the other hand, would show a collection of graphic images, called Key Performance Indicators (KPIs, an example of which might be a progress bar filling in) to represent getting closer to a goal at the end of the current fiscal year.

Dashboard Designer: An application included with SharePoint Server 2010 that you can use to build PerformancePoint dashboards, scorecards, and Key Performance Indicators (KPIs).

data mining: A SQL Server component that provides computer algorithms designed to sift through a large amount of data in search of patterns. For more about data mining, check out *Microsoft Business Intelligence For Dummies.*

development: The process of building a system to solve a particular problem, frequently associated with computer programming. SharePoint 2010 has changed the game by providing powerful tools for developing SharePoint solutions without writing code.

dimension: One of many ways to divide the data contained in an OLAP database; each dimension represents one aspect of an item — whether as a quantitative value (such as length, weight, or price) or as a quality (such as color).

Excel Services: A service of SharePoint that makes Excel documents accessible through a SharePoint site (thus through a Web browser).

Expression Blend: A Microsoft software application for building Silverlight applications.

Extract, Transform, and Load (ETL): The process of extracting raw data from a source system, transforming it into information in a useful form such as an aggregation, and then loading it into a data warehouse for storage.

fact: In database usage, an item of numeric (or aggregated non-numeric) data contained in an OLAP cube. When a database fact is numeric, it's also known as a *measure* or *metric.*

IntelliSense: The Visual Studio auto-completion feature for keywords: The developer types the beginning of a keyword; the Visual Studio editor responds by showing a list of available words. The list of available words narrows as the developer types in more letters of the word. This aids the developer in finding the correct keyword without always having to type the entire keyword.

JavaScript: A scripting language designed for the Web — specifically, to enable a user to interact with a Web page programmatically. JavaScript runs from the client Web browser. The advantage of using JavaScript to provide interactivity is that the Web browser has no need to communicate with the server (which would otherwise cause the page to flicker and reload with each interaction).

Key Performance Indicator (KPI): A piece of information that corresponds to a business process vital to your organization's performance. Examples of KPIs include sales figures, manufacturing data, and financial-health information. In PerformancePoint, a KPI takes the form of a specific logical component bundled inside a scorecard.

keyword: A word that has a specific meaning to a computer language. For example, in the C# (pronounced C-Sharp) programming language, the word `String` is used to define a text based variable. You cannot use the word `String` in any way other than its intended use while you're programming in C#; otherwise the computer will get very confused.

library: A component of SharePoint that is specifically designed to store electronic files.

list: A component of SharePoint specifically designed to store information. Much like a real life list stores information, a SharePoint list stores information in a digital format.

master page: A template that serves as the basis for the layout of the components present on every content page. For example, you wouldn't want to have to arrange the navigational components on every single new page you create. If you did — and ever had to make a change — then you'd have to go back and change every page, one at a time. Keeping everything in sync would be a nightmare. Using a master page, you need only create the navigational components once; then all other pages refer to the master page to find the common components and duplicate the layout.

Microsoft Business Intelligence: A range of software tools and products — specifically SQL Server, SharePoint, and Office — that Microsoft markets as integrated capabilities to be used for business intelligence.

Microsoft .NET: A set of programming languages and canned blocks of reusable programming code known as libraries designed to increase developer productivity and ensure compatibility with Microsoft client and server computers.

multi-dimensional: Data described by many different aspects (each designated a separate *dimension*) in an OLAP database.

object model: A collection of program components (objects) organized in relationship to each other and contained in a software product. The objects that make up the SharePoint Object Model, for example, represent the lists, libraries, content types, and sites you use in SharePoint.

OnLine Analytical Processing (OLAP): A type of database optimized for analytical activities such as viewing data in various aggregations, slicing and dicing data using different criteria, and pivoting on data to understand different groupings.

PerformancePoint Services: A SharePoint service (formerly a stand-alone application) that provides analytical visualizations such as dashboards, scorecards, KPIs, and reports. The primary tool used to build PerformancePoint content is Dashboard Designer.

platform: A general term used to describe an entire group of hardware and software. For example, the SharePoint platform includes all of the tools, server components, operating systems, and hardware that are required to run SharePoint. You can group all of this together and shorten to just say the SharePoint platform.

PowerPivot: A new feature of Excel 2010 that can pull very large spreadsheets — tens of millions of rows — into Excel to perform ad-hoc analysis.

PowerShell: A development tool that works much like DOS (the old Microsoft command-line interface): To create a script to interact with SharePoint, the developer types in commands (in this case, PowerShell instructions called *cmdlets*) at a prompt. For example, you might develop a series of PowerShell cmdlets that backs up the configuration information of your entire SharePoint site.

report: In BI terms, an organized body of information describing the status of a business process. Because reports can come from various Microsoft products — SharePoint features such as Report Builder and Dashboard Designer (or even Web Parts), or connected client applications such as Excel — reports are sometimes mistaken for dashboards or scorecards. Although all these configurations of business information tell end users and decision-makers about how the business is doing, they are not identical.

In fact, what a report *is* (technically) can vary, depending on the tool used to create it. For example, when you build a report using Report Builder, the result is a file with the .RDL extension. You might also build a report using Excel, with the idea of uploading it to a SharePoint site later via Excel Services. Although both files are called "reports" — and both deliver prepared information to decision-makers — they have nothing to do with each other technically.

Report Builder: An application included with SharePoint that's designed to enable non-developers to build SQL Server Reporting Services (SSRS) reports easily without having to use Visual Studio. Users can tell Report Builder what to do by using a set of controls installed on the Office Ribbon.

scorecard: A collection of information about your organization, gathered into a single onscreen view, that tracks progress toward a specific goal. For example, the CEO might outline a goal for sales-per-store figures throughout the country; the corresponding scorecard would track each store's progress toward that sales goal, providing a visual indicator (such as a red, yellow, or green light) to mark the degree of progress. A PerformancePoint Scorecard is a component that displays an array of KPIs and as part of a PerformancePoint dashboard.

script: A series of commands grouped together to run as a single unit. For example, you might write a PowerShell script to search for a particular site name in your SharePoint environment. If the site name is found you might then have the script email some key information, such as the users of the site, to an email account.

SharePoint: A server application from Microsoft, currently the market leader in enterprise-wide communication, collaboration, and content management. SharePoint is made up of two primary products. The first is a free version that comes with the Windows Server operating system — SharePoint Foundation; the second is a commercial software product — SharePoint Server. SharePoint continues to evolve, enfolding existing functionality such as PerformancePoint Services and developing new features such as Sandboxed Solutions. SharePoint 2010 is the most recent release.

SharePoint Designer: A software application used for SharePoint development. The content contained in a SharePoint application lives in the SQL Server database in a SharePoint system. SharePoint Designer provides a window into that database that allows customization and development.

SharePoint workflow: A set of automated processes linked to sequential tasks and actions, usually associated with a SharePoint list, library, or site. A workflow to request feedback on new documents would operate like this: A new document is submitted to a library; in response, the workflow sends an e-mail to a list of people for feedback; when each person has finished the task of reviewing the document, the workflow sends a notification e-mail back to the original author. SharePoint workflows are developed in a tool called Dashboard Designer.

Silverlight: A Microsoft development application designed to give a Web Application the same look and feel from within a Web browser as a user would get from a client application. SharePoint Web Applications work differently from the Office applications that run on local computers: The server gives the user a Web-browser view of content, and normally an interaction with the server (*postback*) happens whenever the user interacts with the Web Application — which causes the Web page to refresh and flicker. Users often find postbacks disruptive, so Silverlight runs on the Web browser of the client computer, compensating for postback to make the Web application operate more like the client application.

site: A collection of Web pages. A *SharePoint site* is also a collection of Web pages but can also contain other components such as lists and libraries. A SharePoint site can be managed and developed using the Web browser; tools such as SharePoint Designer, Dashboard Designer, and Report Builder; or Visual Studio.

site collection: In SharePoint, a collection of (well, yeah) SharePoint sites. A site collection is a top-level site that contains other sub-sites. A site collection acts as a division point for some basic aspects of SharePoint such as security and other features. In addition, the databases that SharePoint uses for content and configuration are separated at the site-collection level.

solution: In SharePoint development, a solution has two meanings. The first is as a deployment packaged called a SharePoint Web Solution Package (WSP). A WSP is a zipped bundle of files configured in a way that allows SharePoint to install the solution. The second meaning stems from the Visual Studio application. A Visual Studio solution is a container for Visual Studio projects. A Visual Studio project is a container for development components such as code files, folders, and images.

SQL Server: Server software from Microsoft that contains four primary components: Database Engine, Reporting Services, Integration Services, and Analysis Services.

SQL Server Analysis Services (SSAS): A component of SQL Server that contains functionality for OnLine Analytical Processing (OLAP) and data mining.

SQL Server Integration Services (SSIS): A component of SQL Server designed to connect to source databases, transform data into SharePoint-compatible information, and load the transformed data into a destination system. This process is the SharePoint version of Extract, Transform, and Load (ETL).

SQL Server Reporting Services (SSRS): A component of SQL Server designed to provide reporting functionality that makes use of various data sources and platforms.

surface: In BI, to display database data to the user as information that's ready to use and easy to access, edit, distribute, or embed in a report, depending on what's needed. Think of the ready-to-use information as submerged in the complexity of business processes; it comes up for air when it's "surfaced."

Visio Services: A SharePoint service that renders Visio diagrams through the Web browser. Using Visio Services, you can embed diagrams inside a SharePoint page or diagram the SharePoint workflow in real time.

Visual Studio: A software application designed for developing Microsoft-compatible scripts and solutions. Visual Studio is called an Integrated Development Environment (IDE) because it incorporates many development features that work together; for example, the capability to run and test code is integrated with other features such as color-coded keywords and IntelliSense.

Web Part: A component of a Web page that can be added, removed, or edited right from the browser. A Web Part is contained in a Web Part zone. You can drag and drop a Web Part from one Web Part zone to another, using only the browser.

Index

• E •

Notes

Notes

Apple & Macs

iPad For Dummies
978-0-470-58027-1

iPhone For Dummies,
4th Edition
978-0-470-87870-5

MacBook For Dummies, 3rd
Edition
978-0-470-76918-8

Mac OS X Snow Leopard For
Dummies
978-0-470-43543-4

Business

Bookkeeping For Dummies
978-0-7645-9848-7

Job Interviews
For Dummies,
3rd Edition
978-0-470-17748-8

Resumes For Dummies,
5th Edition
978-0-470-08037-5

Starting an
Online Business
For Dummies,
6th Edition
978-0-470-60210-2

Stock Investing
For Dummies,
3rd Edition
978-0-470-40114-9

Successful
Time Management
For Dummies
978-0-470-29034-7

Computer Hardware

BlackBerry
For Dummies,
4th Edition
978-0-470-60700-8

Computers For Seniors
For Dummies,
2nd Edition
978-0-470-53483-0

PCs For Dummies,
Windows
7 Edition
978-0-470-46542-4

Laptops For Dummies,
4th Edition
978-0-470-57829-2

Cooking & Entertaining

Cooking Basics
For Dummies,
3rd Edition
978-0-7645-7206-7

Wine For Dummies,
4th Edition
978-0-470-04579-4

Diet & Nutrition

Dieting For Dummies,
2nd Edition
978-0-7645-4149-0

Nutrition For Dummies,
4th Edition
978-0-471-79868-2

Weight Training
For Dummies,
3rd Edition
978-0-471-76845-6

Digital Photography

Digital SLR Cameras &
Photography For Dummies,
3rd Edition
978-0-470-46606-3

Photoshop Elements 8
For Dummies
978-0-470-52967-6

Gardening

Gardening Basics
For Dummies
978-0-470-03749-2

Organic Gardening
For Dummies,
2nd Edition
978-0-470-43067-5

Green/Sustainable

Raising Chickens
For Dummies
978-0-470-46544-8

Green Cleaning
For Dummies
978-0-470-39106-8

Health

Diabetes For Dummies,
3rd Edition
978-0-470-27086-8

Food Allergies
For Dummies
978-0-470-09584-3

Living Gluten-Free
For Dummies,
2nd Edition
978-0-470-58589-4

Hobbies/General

Chess For Dummies,
2nd Edition
978-0-7645-8404-6

Drawing
Cartoons & Comics
For Dummies
978-0-470-42683-8

Knitting For Dummies,
2nd Edition
978-0-470-28747-7

Organizing
For Dummies
978-0-7645-5300-4

Su Doku For Dummies
978-0-470-01892-7

Home Improvement

Home Maintenance
For Dummies,
2nd Edition
978-0-470-43063-7

Home Theater
For Dummies,
3rd Edition
978-0-470-41189-6

Living the
Country Lifestyle
All-in-One
For Dummies
978-0-470-43061-3

Solar Power Your Home
For Dummies,
2nd Edition
978-0-470-59678-4

Available wherever books are sold. For more information or to order direct: U.S. customers visit www.dummies.com or call 1-877-762-2974. U.K. customers visit www.wileyeurope.com or call (0) 1243 843291. Canadian customers visit www.wiley.ca or call 1-800-567-4797.

Internet

Blogging For Dummies,
3rd Edition
978-0-470-61996-4

eBay For Dummies,
6th Edition
978-0-470-49741-8

Facebook For Dummies,
3rd Edition
978-0-470-87804-0

Web Marketing
For Dummies,
2nd Edition
978-0-470-37181-7

WordPress
For Dummies,
3rd Edition
978-0-470-59274-8

Language & Foreign Language

French For Dummies
978-0-7645-5193-2

Italian Phrases
For Dummies
978-0-7645-7203-6

Spanish For Dummies,
2nd Edition
978-0-470-87855-2

Spanish
For Dummies,
Audio Set
978-0-470-09585-0

Math & Science

Algebra I
For Dummies,
2nd Edition
978-0-470-55964-2

Biology For Dummies,
2nd Edition
978-0-470-59875-7

Calculus For Dummies
978-0-7645-2498-1

Chemistry For Dummies
978-0-7645-5430-8

Microsoft Office

Excel 2010 For Dummies
978-0-470-48953-6

Office 2010 All-in-One
For Dummies
978-0-470-49748-7

Office 2010 For Dummies,
Book + DVD Bundle
978-0-470-62698-6

Word 2010 For Dummies
978-0-470-48772-3

Music

Guitar For Dummies,
2nd Edition
978-0-7645-9904-0

iPod & iTunes For
Dummies, 8th Edition
978-0-470-87871-2

Piano Exercises
For Dummies
978-0-470-38765-8

Parenting & Education

Parenting For Dummies,
2nd Edition
978-0-7645-5418-6

Type 1 Diabetes
For Dummies
978-0-470-17811-9

Pets

Cats For Dummies,
2nd Edition
978-0-7645-5275-5

Dog Training For Dummies,
3rd Edition
978-0-470-60029-0

Puppies For Dummies,
2nd Edition
978-0-470-03717-1

Religion & Inspiration

The Bible For Dummies
978-0-7645-5296-0

Catholicism For Dummies
978-0-7645-5391-2

Women in the Bible
For Dummies
978-0-7645-8475-6

Self-Help & Relationship

Anger Management
For Dummies
978-0-470-03715-7

Overcoming Anxiety
For Dummies,
2nd Edition
978-0-470-57441-6

Sports

Baseball
For Dummies,
3rd Edition
978-0-7645-7537-2

Basketball
For Dummies,
2nd Edition
978-0-7645-5248-9

Golf For Dummies,
3rd Edition
978-0-471-76871-5

Web Development

Web Design
All-in-One
For Dummies
978-0-470-41796-6

Web Sites
Do-It-Yourself
For Dummies,
2nd Edition
978-0-470-56520-9

Windows 7

Windows 7
For Dummies
978-0-470-49743-2

Windows 7
For Dummies,
Book + DVD Bundle
978-0-470-52398-8

Windows 7 All-in-One
For Dummies
978-0-470-48763-1

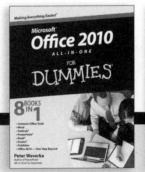

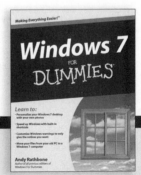

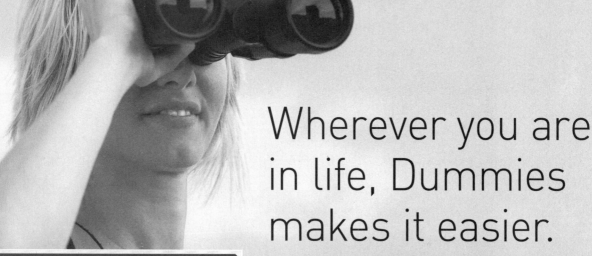

DUMMIES.COM®

Wherever you are in life, Dummies makes it easier.

From fashion to Facebook®, wine to Windows®, and everything in between, Dummies makes it easier.

Visit us at Dummies.com

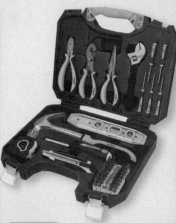